BILL MOYERS

MOYERS ON DEMOCRACY

Bill Moyers was a founding organizer of the Peace Corps, a senior White House assistant (and press secretary) to President Lyndon Johnson from 1963 until 1967, publisher of *Newsday*, senior news analyst for CBS News, and producer of many of public television's groundbreaking series. He is the winner of more than thirty Emmy awards and nine Peabody awards, the Lifetime Achievement Award from the National Academy of Television, the Career Achievement Award from the International Documentary Association, and the Honorary Doctor of Fine Arts by the American Film Institute. Among his bestselling books are *Listening to America*, *A World of Ideas*, *The Power of Myth* (with Joseph Campbell), and *Moyers on America*. He serves as president of the Schumann Center for Media and Democracy.

MOYERS ON DEMOCRACY

MOYERS
ON DEMOCRACY

BILL MOYERS

Anchor Books

A Division of Random House, Inc.

New York

FIRST ANCHOR BOOKS EDITION, MAY 2009

Copyright © 2008 by Bill Moyers

All rights reserved. Published in the United States by Anchor Books,
a division of Random House, Inc., New York, and in Canada by Random House of
Canada Limited, Toronto. Originally published in hardcover in the United States by
Doubleday, a division of Random House, Inc., New York, in 2008.

Anchor Books and colophon are registered trademarks of
Random House, Inc.

"The Low Road," from *The Moon Is Always Female* by Marge Piercy,
copyright © 1980 by Marge Piercy. Used by permission of Alfred A. Knopf,
a division of Random House.

The Library of Congress has cataloged the Doubleday edition as follows:
Moyers, Bill D.
Moyers on democracy / Bill Moyers.
p. cm.
1. United States—Politics and government—1945–1989.
2. United States—Politics and government—1989–
3. Moyers, Bill D.—Political and social views.
4. Mass media—United States. 5. Press—United States.
6. United States—Religion. I. Title.
JK1726.M69 2008
320.973—dc22   2007044910

Anchor ISBN: 978-0-307-38773-8

www.anchorbooks.com

For Lyn and Norman Lear

. . . and Patriots of the Gulley,

who keep fighting the good fight . . .

Contents

Part II. **THE USES OF HISTORY**

Part III. **POLITICS**

Part IV. THE MEDIA

Part V. **RELIGION**

Part VI. **A COMMENCEMENT ADDRESS**

Introduction

Democracy in America is a series of narrow escapes, and we may be running out of luck. The reigning presumption about the American experience, as the historian Lawrence Goodwyn has written, is grounded in the idea of progress, the conviction that the present is "better" than the past and the future will bring even more improvement. For all of its shortcomings, we keep telling ourselves, "The system works."

Now all bets are off. We have fallen under the spell of money, faction, and fear, and the great American experience in creating a different future *together* has been subjugated to individual cunning in the pursuit of wealth and power—and to the claims of empire, with its ravenous demands and stuporous distractions. A sense of political impotence pervades the country—a mass resignation defined by Goodwyn as "believing the dogma of 'democracy' on a superficial public level but not believing it privately." We hold elections, knowing they are unlikely to bring the corporate state under popular control. There is considerable vigor at local levels, but it has not been translated into new vistas of social possibility or the political will to address our most intractable challenges. Hope no longer seems the operative dynamic of America, and without hope we lose the talent and drive to cooperate in the shaping of our destiny.

These are themes that I have addressed in speeches at different times to different audiences. This book contains many of those speeches, slightly revised for print. Such essays are sometimes referred to by librarians as "occasional pieces." As such, their shelf life approximates that of an item in a daily newspaper—"today's headline, tomorrow's fish wrapper," as old-time reporters and editors called it. At first I resisted the publisher's offer to share them with a wide readership on just those grounds.

But reading them again changed my mind. Whatever the immediate context of these talks may have been—an address to environmental journalists, the grateful acceptance of an award from an organization of Chinese Americans, an anniversary celebration of the Peace Corps, a keynote address to educators, a lecture at West Point, a speech to citizens working for more diversity in media—they all revolve around a nucleus of concerns that have preoccupied me in these last few troubled years. If I were to choose a theme song for these concerns, it would be Arlo Guthrie's "Patriot's Dream."

The earth we share as our common gift, to be passed on in good condition to our children's children, is being despoiled. Private wealth is growing as public needs increase apace. Our Constitution is perilously close to being consigned to the valley of the shadow of death, betrayed by a powerful cabal of secrecy-obsessed authoritarians. Terms like "liberty" and "individual freedom" invoked by generations of Americans who battled to widen the 1787 promise to "promote the general welfare" have been perverted to create a government primarily dedicated to the welfare of the state and the political class that runs it. Yes, Virginia, there is a class war and ordinary people are losing it. It isn't necessary to be a Jeremiah crying aloud to a sinful Jerusalem that the Lord is about to afflict them for their sins of idolatry, or Cassandra, making a nuisance of herself as she wanders around King Priam's palace grounds wailing "The Greeks are coming." Or Socrates, the gadfly, stinging the rump of power with jabs of truth. Or even Paul Revere, if horses were still in fashion. You need only be a reporter with your eyes open to see what's happening to our democracy. I have been lucky enough to spend my adult life as a journalist, acquiring a priceless education in the ways of the world, actually getting paid to practice one of my craft's essential imperatives: connect the dots.

The conclusion that we are in trouble is unavoidable. I report the assault on nature evidenced in coal mining that tears the tops off mountains and dumps them into rivers, sacrificing the health and lives of those in the river valleys to short-term profit, and I see a link between that process and the stock-market frenzy which scorns long-term investments—genuine savings—in favor of quick turnovers and speculative bubbles whose inevitable bursting leaves insiders with stuffed pockets and millions of small stockholders, pensioners, and employees out of work, out of luck, and out of hope.

And then I see a connection between those disasters and the repeal of sixty-year-old banking and securities regulations designed during the Great Depression to prevent exactly that kind of human and economic damage. Who pushed for the removal of that firewall? An administration and Congress who are the political marionettes of the speculators, and who are well rewarded for their efforts with indispensable campaign contributions. Even honorable opponents of the practice get trapped in the web of an electoral system that effectively limits competition to those who can afford to spend millions in their run for office. Like it or not, candidates know that the largesse on which their political futures depend will last only as long as their votes are satisfactory to the sleek "bundlers" who turn the spigots of cash on and off.

The property qualifications for federal office that the framers of the Constitution expressly chose to exclude for demonstrating an unseemly "veneration for wealth" are now de facto in force and higher than the Founding Fathers could have imagined. "Money rules . . . Our laws are the output of a system which clothes rascals in robes and honesty in rags. The parties lie to us and the political speakers mislead us." Those words were spoken by Populist orator Mary Elizabeth Lease during the prairie revolt that swept the Great Plains slightly more than 120 years after the Constitution was signed. They are true today, and that too, spells trouble.

Then I draw a line to the statistics that show real wages lagging behind prices, the compensation of corporate barons soaring to heights unequaled anywhere among industrialized democracies, the relentless cheeseparing of federal funds devoted to public schools, to retraining for workers whose jobs have been exported, and to programs of food assistance and health care for poor children, all of which snatch away the ladder by which Americans with scant means but willing hands and hearts could work and save their way upward to middle-class independence. And I connect those numbers to our triumphant reactionaries' campaigns against labor unions and higher minimum wages, and to their success in reframing the tax codes so as to strip them of their progressive character, laying the burdens of Atlas on a shrinking middle class awash in credit card debt as wage earners struggle to keep up with rising costs for health care, for college tuitions, for affordable housing—while huge inheritances go untouched, tax shelters abroad are legalized, rates on capital gains are slashed, and the rich get richer and with each increase in their wealth are able to buy themselves more influence over those who make and those who carry out the laws.

Edward R. Murrow told his generation of journalists: "No one can eliminate prejudices—just recognize them." Here is my bias: extremes of wealth and poverty cannot be reconciled with a genuinely democratic politics. When the state becomes the guardian of power and privilege to the neglect of justice for the people as a whole, it mocks the very concept of government as proclaimed in the preamble to our Constitution; mocks Lincoln's sacred belief in "government of the people, by the people, and for the people"; mocks the democratic notion of government as "a voluntary union for the common good" embodied in the great wave of reform that produced the Progressive Era and the two Roosevelts. In contrast, the philosophy popularized in the last quarter century that "freedom" simply means freedom to choose among competing brands of consumer goods, that taxes are an unfair theft from the pockets of the successful to reward the incompetent, and that the market will meet all human needs while government itself becomes the enabler of privilege— the philosophy of an earlier social Darwinism and laissez-faire capitalism dressed in new togs—is as subversive as Benedict Arnold's betrayal of the Revolution he had once served. Again, Mary Lease: "The great evils which are cursing American society and undermining the foundations of the republic flow not from the legitimate operation of the great human government which our fathers gave us, but they come from tramping its plain provisions underfoot."

Our democracy has prospered most when it was firmly anchored in the idea that "We the People"—not just a favored few—would identify and remedy common distempers and dilemmas and win the gamble our forebears undertook when they espoused the radical idea that people could govern themselves wisely. Whatever and whoever tries to supplant that with notions of a wholly privatized society of competitive consumers undermines a country that, as Gordon S. Wood puts it in his landmark book *The Radicalism of the American Revolution*, discovered its greatness "by creating a prosperous free society belonging to obscure people with their workaday concerns and their pecuniary pursuits of happiness"—a democracy that changed the lives of "hitherto neglected and despised masses of common laboring people."

I wish I could say that journalists in general are showing the same interest in uncovering the dangerous linkages thwarting this democracy. It is not for lack of honest and courageous individuals who would risk their careers to speak truth to power—a modest risk compared to those of some journalists in authoritarian countries who have been jailed or murdered for the identical "crime." But our journalists are not in control of the instruments they play. As conglomerates swallow up newspapers, magazines, publishing houses, and networks, and profit rather than product becomes the focus of corporate effort, news organizations—particularly in television—are folded into entertainment divisions. The "news hole" in the print media shrinks to make room for advertisements, and stories needed by informed citizens working together are pulled in favor of the latest celebrity scandals because the media moguls have decided that uncovering the inner workings of public and private power is boring and will drive viewers and readers away to greener pastures of pabulum. Good reporters and editors confront walls of resistance in trying to place serious and informative reports over which they have long labored. Media owners who should be sounding the trumpets of alarm on the battlements of democracy instead blow popular ditties through tin horns, undercutting the basis for their existence and their First Amendment rights.

These are some of the ideas that run through this collection. They bind the disparate speeches between covers. I am happy to report that the democratic underground is alive and well, putting the lie to the hucksters who insist that they are only giving the public what it wants. When reprinted elsewhere or posted on the Internet, these speeches have drawn deluges of supportive mail, confirming what I have found in my reporting: a widespread recognition that unaccountable authority and cutthroat capitalism will not produce a fair and just society. The sense that so many people believe it is time "to rekindle the patriot's dream"—to make the crooked ways straight—is what I take to justify their transplantation into print.

I regret that in print they will lack something irreplaceable, the living warmth of an auditorium where a speaker is face-to-face with other citizens. For sure, the days when a William Jennings Bryan could stampede a convention with a superlative voice clamoring against crucifying mankind on a cross of gold are gone. The power of radio and television to reach millions simultaneously is awesome and important, as both dictators and democrats with appealing voices have discovered. Print, as a "cool" medium, has a hard time keeping up in spite of its virtue of allowing time to digest and contemplate. I have indeed been fortunate to have made my living in television for almost forty years now, to have enjoyed a long and continuing course in adult education during which my reporting opened doors, enlarged my reading, exposed me to interesting minds and festering problems, and allowed me to draw conclusions from the evidence I had collected—the highest privilege of the First Amendment guarantee of a free press.

Still, I am grateful that from time to time I could steal away from the studio and editing room to stand before live audiences and test my conclusions and their patience. There's nothing quite like the exhilaration of seeing the distance between you and the crowd fast closing, until you are as one in awareness and purpose, conscious that no one—speaker or listener—will ever see the world the same way again because of this experience.

I am grateful to the audiences that heard me out. Every one of them blessed my effort and sent me away believing that the gravediggers of democracy will not have the last word.

Part I

---+---

THE IDEAL OF SERVICE

1. | FOR AMERICA'S SAKE

A New Story for America

DECEMBER 12, 2006

My father dropped out of the fourth grade and never returned to school because his family needed him to pick cotton to help make ends meet. The
Great Depression knocked him down and almost out. When I was born he
was making $2 a day working on the highway to Oklahoma City. He never
took home more than $100 a week in his working life, and he made that only
when he joined the union in the last job he held. He voted for Franklin Roosevelt in four straight elections and would have gone on voting for him until
kingdom come if he'd had the chance. I once asked him why, and he said,
"Because he was my friend." My father of course never met FDR; no politician ever paid him much note. Many years later when I wound up working
in the White House my parents came for a visit and my father asked to see
the Roosevelt Room. I don't quite know how to explain it, except that my father knew who was on his side. When FDR died my father wept; he had lost
his friend. This man with a fourth-grade education understood what the pa-
trician in the White House meant when he talked about "economic royalism"

and how private power no less than public power can bring America to ruin in the absence of democratic controls. When the president said "the malefactors of great wealth" had concentrated into their own hands "an almost complete control over other people's property, other people's money, other people's labor, and other people's lives," my father said amen; he believed the president knew what life was like for people like him. When the president said life was no longer free, liberty no longer real, men could no longer follow the pursuit of happiness against "economic tyranny such as this," my father nodded. He got it when Roosevelt said that a government by money was as much to be feared as a government by mob, and that the political equality we once had was meaningless in the face of economic inequality. Against organized wealth, FDR said that "the American citizen could appeal only to the organized power of government." My father knew the president meant him.

Today my father would be written out of America's story. He would belong to what the sociologist Katherine Newman calls the "missing class"*— the fifty-seven million Americans who occupy an obscure place between the rungs of our social ladder, earning wages above the minimum but below a secure standard of living. They work hard for their $20,000 to $40,000 a year, and they are vital to the functioning of the country, as transit workers, day-care providers, hospital attendants, teachers' aides, clerical assistants. They live one divorce, one pink slip, one illness away from a free fall. Largely forgotten by the press, politicians, and policy makers who fashion government safety nets, they have no nest egg, no income but the next paycheck, no way of paying for their children to go to college. Over the years I have chronicled the lives of some of these people in my documentaries. Now, a few days after the election of 2006, I was asked to speak at a conference sponsored by The Nation, the Brennan Center for Justice, the New Democracy Project,

---

* Katherine S. Newman and Victor Tan Chen, *The Missing Class: Portraits of the Near Poor in America* (Beacon Press, 2007). The authors lay out several promising initiatives that would "sustain the upward movement" of the near poor—from policies to support low-income housing ownership and saving and asset-building strategies, to the government promotion of business ventures in underserved neighborhoods so that predatory establishments, especially banks, car dealers, and grocers, could no longer overcharge their customers. The authors propose the creation of upward employment opportunities within businesses and ways to increase the benefits that go with those better jobs. Perhaps most important of all, as they themselves acknowledge, they outline ways to improve educational opportunities for "missing class" families, from publicly supported day care and after-school programs to legislation—like the GI Bill of an earlier generation—that would make college affordable for everyone, as it was for my brother and me despite the near penury of our parents.

and Demos to discuss the prospects of democracy. Those prospects are dim,
I realized, unless we write a story of America that includes those people who
are living on the edge, with no friend in the White House.

* * *

You could not have chosen a better time to gather. Voters have provided a respite from a right-wing radicalism predicated on the philosophy that extremism in the pursuit of virtue is no vice. It seems only yesterday that the Trojan horse of conservatism was hauled into Washington to disgorge Newt Gingrich, Tom DeLay, Ralph Reed, Grover Norquist, and their band of ravenous predators masquerading as a political party of small government, fiscal restraint, and moral piety and promising "to restore accountability to Congress . . . (and) make us all proud again of the way free people govern themselves."

Well, the long night of the cabal is over, and Democrats are ebullient as they prepare to take charge of the multitrillion-dollar influence racket that we used to call the U.S. Congress. Let them rejoice while they can, as long as they remember that they have arrived at this moment mainly because George W. Bush started a war most people have come to believe should never have been fought in the first place. Let them remember that although they are reveling in the ruins of a Republican reign brought down by stupendous scandals, their own closet is stocked with skeletons from an era when they were routed from office following ABSCAM bribes and savings and loan swindles that plucked the pockets and purses of hardworking Americans. As they rejoice Democrats would be wise to be mindful of Shakespeare's counsel: "Merit doth much, but fortune more." For they were delivered from the wilderness not by their own goodness but by the hubris of the party in power—a recurring phenomenon of American democracy.

Whatever one might say about the 2006 election, the real story is one that our political and media elites are loath to acknowledge or address. I am not speaking of the lengthy list of priorities that progressives and liberals are eager to put on the table now that Democrats hold the cards in Congress. The other day a message popped up on my computer from a progressive advocate who is committed to movement building from the ground up and has results to show for his labors. His request was simple: "With changes in Congress and at our state capitol, we want your input on what top issues our lawmakers should tackle. Click here to submit your top priority."

I clicked. Up came a list of thirty-four issues—an impressive list that began with "African American" and ran alphabetically through "energy" and "guns" to "higher education," "transportation," "women's issues," and "worker's rights." It wasn't a list to be dismissed by any means, for it came from an unrequited thirst for action after a long season of fierce opposition to every aspiration on the agenda. I understand the mind-set. Here's a fellow who values allies and appreciates what it takes to build coalitions; who knows that although our interests as citizens vary, each one is an artery to the heart that pumps life through the body politic, and each is important to the health of democracy. This is an activist who knows political success is the sum of many parts.

But America needs something more right now than a "must-do" list from liberals and progressives. America needs a different story.

The very morning I read the message from the progressive activist, *The New York Times* reported on Carol Ann Reyes. She is sixty-three, lives in Los Angeles, suffers from dementia, and is homeless. Somehow she made her way to a hospital with serious, untreated needs. No details were provided as to what happened to her there, except that the hospital called a cab and sent her back to skid row. True, they phoned ahead to workers at a rescue shelter to let them know she was coming. But some hours later a surveillance camera picked her up "wandering around the streets in a hospital gown and slippers." Dumped in America.

Here is the real political story, the one most politicians won't even acknowledge: the reality of the anonymous, disquieting daily struggle of ordinary people, including not only the most marginalized and vulnerable Americans but also young workers, elders and parents, families and communities, searching for dignity and fairness against long odds in an amoral market world.

Everywhere you turn you'll find people who believe they have been written out of the story. Everywhere you turn there's a sense of insecurity grounded in a gnawing fear that freedom in America has come to mean the freedom of the rich to get richer even as millions of Americans are thrown overboard. So let me say what I think up front: the leaders and thinkers and activists who honestly tell that story and speak passionately of the moral and religious values it puts in play will be the first political generation since the New Deal to win power back for the people.

There's no mistaking America is ready for change. One of our leading analysts of public opinion, Daniel Yankelovich, reports that a majority want social cohesion and common ground based on pragmatism and compromise, patriotism and diversity. But because of the great disparities in wealth the "shining city on the hill" has become a gated community whose privileged occupants, surrounded by moats of money and protected by a political system seduced with cash into subservience, are removed from the common life of the country.

The wreckage of this revolt of elites is all around us. Corporations are shredding the social compact, pensions are disappearing, medium incomes are flattening, and health-care costs are soaring. In many ways, the average household is generally worse off today than it was thirty years ago, and the public sector that improved life for millions of Americans across three generations is in tatters. For a time, stagnating wages were somewhat offset by more work and more personal debt. Both political parties craftily refashioned those major renovations of the average household as the new standard, shielding employers from responsibility for anything Wall Street would not reward. Now, however, the more acute major risks workers have been forced to bear as employers reduce their health and retirement costs have revealed that gains made by people who live paycheck to paycheck are being reversed. Polls show a majority of American workers now believe their children will be worse off than they were. In one recent survey, only 14 percent of workers said that they have obtained the American dream.

It is hard to believe that less than four decades ago a key architect of the antipoverty program, Robert Lampman, could argue that the "recent history of Western nations reveals an increasingly widespread adoption of the idea that substantial equality of social and economic conditions among individuals is a good thing." Economists call that postwar era the "Great Compression." Poverty and inequality had declined dramatically for the first time in our history. Here is how a *Time* magazine report summed up the national outlook in 1953: "Even in the smallest towns and most isolated areas, the U. S. is wearing a very prosperous, middle-class suit of clothes, and an attitude of relaxation and confidence. People are not growing wealthy, but more of them than ever before are getting along . . ."

African Americans were still written out of the story, but that was changing, too, as heroic resistance emerged across the South to awaken our national conscience. Within a decade, thanks to the civil rights movement and President Lyndon Johnson, the racial cast of many federal policies—including some New Deal programs—was aggressively repudiated, and shared prosperity began to breach the color line.

To this day I remember John F. Kennedy's landmark speech at the Yale commencement in 1962. Echoing Daniel Bell's cold war classic *The End of Ideology*, JFK proclaimed the triumph of "practical management of a modern economy" over the "grand warfare of rival ideologies." The problem with this is that the purported ideological cease-fire ended only a few years later. But the Democrats never rearmed. While "practical management of a modern economy" had a kind of surrogate legitimacy as long as it worked, when it no longer worked, the nation faced a paralyzing moral void in deciding how the burdens should be borne. Well-organized conservative forces, firing on all ideological pistons, rushed to fill this void with a story corporate America wanted us to hear. Inspired by bumper-sticker abstractions of Milton Friedman's ideas, propelled by cascades of cash from corporate chieftains like Coors and Koch and "Neutron" Jack Welch, fortified by the pious prescriptions of fundamentalist political preachers, the conservative armies marched on Washington. And they succeeded brilliantly.

When Ronald Reagan addressed the Republican National Convention in 1980, he told a simple political story with great impact. "The major issue of this campaign is the direct political, personal and moral responsibility of Democratic Party leadership—in the White House and in Congress—for this unprecedented calamity which has befallen us." He declared: "I will not stand by and watch this great country destroy itself." It was a speech of bold contrasts, of "good" private interest versus "bad" government, of course. More important, it personified these two forces in a larger narrative of freedom, reaching back across the Great Depression, the Civil War, and the American Revolution, all the way back to the Mayflower Compact. It dazzled his followers and so demoralized Democrats that they could not muster a response to the social costs that came with the Reagan revolution.

But there is another story of freedom to tell, and it, too, reaches back across the Great Depression, the Civil War, and the American Revolution, all the way back to the Mayflower Compact. It's a story with clear and certain foundations, like Reagan's, but also a tumultuous and sometimes violent history of betrayal that he and other conservatives consistently and conveniently ignore.

Reagan's story of freedom superficially alludes to the Founding Fathers, but its substance comes from the Gilded Age, devised by apologists for the robber barons. It is posed abstractly as the freedom of the individual from government control—a Jeffersonian ideal at the root of our Bill of Rights, to be sure. But what it meant in politics a century later, and still means today, is the freedom to accumulate wealth without social or democratic responsibilities and the license to buy the political system right out from under everyone else, so that democracy no longer has the ability to hold capitalism accountable to notions of fairness and justice.

And that is not how freedom was understood when our country was founded. At the heart of our experience as a nation is the proposition that each citizen has a right to "life, liberty, and the pursuit of happiness." As flawed in its reach as it was at the time, that proposition carries an inherent imperative:

> Inasmuch as the members of a liberal society have a right to basic requirements of human development such as education and a minimum standard of security, they have obligations to each other, mutually and through their government, to ensure that conditions exist enabling every person to have the opportunity for success in life.

The quote comes directly from Paul Starr, whose book *Freedom's Power: The True Force of Liberalism* is a call for liberals to reclaim the idea of America's greatness as their own.

Starr's book is one of three that in a just world would be on every desk in the House and Senate when Congress convenes again.

John E. Schwarz, in *Freedom Reclaimed: Rediscovering the American Vision*, rescues the idea of freedom from market cultists whose "particular idea of freedom . . . has taken us down a terribly mistaken road" toward a political order where "government ends up servicing the powerful and taking from everyone else." The free-market view "cannot provide us with a philosophy we find compelling or meaningful," Schwarz writes. Nor does it assure the availability of an economic opportunity "that is truly adequate to each individual and the status of full legal and political equality." Yet since the late nineteenth century it has been used to shield private power from democratic accountability, in no small part because conservative rhetoric has succeeded in denigrating government even as reactionary ideologues plunder it.

But government, Schwarz reminds us, "is not simply the way we express ourselves collectively, but also often the only way we preserve our freedom from private power and its incursions." That is one reason the notion that every person has a right to meaningful opportunity "has assumed the position of a moral bottom line in the nation's popular culture ever since the beginning." Freedom, he says, is "considerably more than a private value." It is essentially a social idea, which explains why the worship of the free market "fails as a compelling idea in terms of the moral reasoning of freedom itself." Let's get back to basics, is Schwarz's message. Let's recapture our story.

Norton Garfinkle picks up on both Schwarz and Starr in *The American Dream vs. the Gospel of Wealth*. He describes how America became the first nation on earth to offer an economic vision of opportunity for even the humblest beginner to advance, and then moved, in fits and starts, to the invocation of positive government as the means to further that vision through politics.

No one understood this more clearly, Garfinkle writes, than Abraham Lincoln, who called on the federal government to save the Union. He turned to large government expenditures for internal improvements—canals, bridges, and railroads. He supported a strong national bank to stabilize the currency. He provided the first major federal funding for education with the creation of land grant colleges. And he kept close to his heart an abiding concern for the fate of ordinary people, especially the ordinary worker but also the widow and orphan. Our greatest president kept his eye on the sparrow. He believed that government should be not just "of the people" and "by the people" but "for the people." Including, we can imagine, a Carol Ann Reyes.

The great leaders of our tradition—Jefferson, Lincoln, and the two Roosevelts—understood the power of our story. In my time it was FDR who exposed the false freedom of the aristocratic narrative. He made the simple but obvious point that where once *political* royalists stalked the land, now *economic* royalists owned everything standing. Mindful of Plutarch's warning that "an imbalance between rich and poor is the oldest and most fatal ailment of all republics," FDR famously told America, in 1936, that "the average man once more confronts the problem faced by the Minute Man." He gathered together the remnants of the great reform movements of the Progressive Era—including those of cousin Teddy—into a singular political cause that would be ratified again and again by people who categorically rejected the laissez-faire anarchy that had produced destructive, unfettered, and ungovernable power. Now came collective bargaining and workplace rules, cash assistance for poor children, Social Security, the GI Bill, home mortgage subsidies, progressive taxation—democratic instruments that checked economic tyranny and helped secure America's great middle class. And these were only the beginning. The Marshall Plan, the civil rights revolution, reaching the moon, a huge leap in life expectancy—every one of these great outward achievements of the last century grew from shared goals and collaboration in the public interest.

So it is that contrary to what we have heard rhetorically for a generation now, the individualist greed-driven free-market ideology is only one current of our history and is at odds with what most Americans really care about. More and more people agree that growing inequality is bad for the country, that corporations have too much power, that money in politics is corrupting democracy, and that working families and poor communities need and deserve help when the market system fails to generate shared prosperity. Indeed, the American public is broadly committed to a set of values that almost perfectly contradicts the right-wing agenda now installed in Washington.

The question, then, is not about changing people; it's about reaching people. I'm not speaking simply of better information, a sharper and clearer factual presentation to disperse the thick fogs generated by today's spin machines. Of course we always need stronger empirical arguments to back up our case. It would certainly help if at least as many people who believe that God sent George W. Bush to the White House also know that the top 1 percent of households now has more wealth than the bottom 90 percent combined. Yes, people need far-different information than they get from media conglomerates. And we need, as we keep hearing, "new ideas." But we are at an extraordinary moment. The conservative movement stands intellectually and morally bankrupt while Democrats talk about a "new direction" without convincing us they know the difference between a weather vane and a compass. The right story will set our course for a generation to come.

The wrong story can doom us. In *Collapse: How Societies Choose Success or Failure*, Jared Diamond tells of the Viking colony that disappeared in the fifteenth century. The settlers had scratched a living on the sparse coast of Greenland for years, until they encountered a series of harsh winters. Their livestock, the staple of their diet, began to die off. Although the nearby waters teemed with haddock and cod, the colony's mythology prohibited the eating of fish. When their supply of hay ran out during a last terrible winter, the colony was finished. They had been doomed by their story.

Here in the first decade of the twenty-first century the story that becomes America's dominant narrative will shape our collective imagination and our politics for a long time to come. In the searching of our souls demanded by this challenge, those of us in this room and kindred spirits across the nation must confront the most fundamental liberal failure of the current era: the failure to embrace a moral vision of America based on the transcendent faith that human beings are more than the sum of their material appetites, our country is more than an economic machine, and freedom is not license but responsibility—the gift we have received and the legacy we must bequeath.

Although our sojourn in life is brief, we are on a great journey. For those who came before us and for those who follow, our moral, political, and religious duty to make sure that this nation, which was conceived in liberty and dedicated to the proposition that all are equal under the law, is in good hands on our watch.

The conservative story would return America to the days of radical laissez-faire, when there was no social contract and all but the privileged and powerful were left to forage on their own. Our story joins the memory of struggles that have been waged with the possibility of victories yet to be won. Like the mustard seed to which Jesus compared the Kingdom of God, this story has been a long time unfolding. It reminds us that the freedoms and rights we treasure were not sent from heaven and did not grow on trees. They were, as John Powers wrote in his July 4, 2003, *LA Weekly* cover story,

> born of centuries of struggle by millions who fought and bled and
> died to assure that government can't just walk into our bedrooms
> or read our mail, to protect ordinary people from being overrun

by massive corporations, to win a safety net against the sometimes cruel workings of the market, to guarantee that businessmen could not compel employees to work more than 40 hours a week without compensation, to make us free to criticize our government without having our patriotism impugned, and to make sure our leaders are answerable to the people when they send our soldiers into war.

Here is the lesson we must never forget: the eight-hour day, the minimum wage, the conservation of natural resources, free trade unions, old-age pensions, clean air and water, safe food—all began with citizens and won the endorsement of the political class only after long struggles and bitter attacks. Democracy works when people claim it as their own.

It is rarely remembered that the notion of democracy immortalized by Abraham Lincoln in the Gettysburg Address had been inspired by Theodore Parker, the abolitionist prophet. Driven from his pulpit, Parker said: "I will go about and preach and lecture in the city and glen, by the roadside and field-side, and wherever men and women may be found." He became the 'Hound of Freedom,' and helped to change America through the power of the word. We have a story of equal power. It is that the promise of America leaves no one out. Go now, and tell it on the mountains. From the rooftops, tell it. From your laptops, tell it. From the street corners and from Starbucks, from delis and from diners, tell it. From the workplace and the bookstore, tell it. On campus and at the mall, tell it. Tell it at the synagogue, sanctuary, and mosque. Tell it where you can, when you can, and while you can—to every candidate for office, to every talk-show host and pundit, to corporate executives and schoolchildren. Tell it—for America's sake.

2. | AT LARGE

Peace Corps Twenty-fifth Anniversary Memorial Service

SEPTEMBER 21, 1986

In 1961 I negotiated my way from the office of the vice president, where I was an assistant to Lyndon B. Johnson, to the far more exhilarating work of helping to organize the Peace Corps. Congress was skeptical of this most visible of John F. Kennedy's New Frontier initiatives, but the man charged by JFK to make it happen, Sargent Shriver, and I called on every member of Congress to make our pitch, coached and prodded by LBJ, who knew his old allies and adversaries on Capitol Hill better than he knew the palm of his hand. We succeeded, and Shriver asked me to become associate director and then deputy director under him. It fell to me one weekend to call the parents of the first Peace Corps volunteer to die abroad, an experience I will never forget. Now, twenty-five years later, many of the original organizers and returned volunteers had gathered at Normandy American Cemetery and Memorial to mark the first quarter century of the Peace Corps and to remember those of our ranks who had died during the intervening years. As I rose to speak I could see the rows upon rows of white crosses that tattooed the sloping hillsides surround-

ing us, reminders of the men and women who served America in times of war. It seemed fitting to be there and to acknowledge the different ways in which love of one's country can be fulfilled.

* * *

The Peace Corps volunteers and staff we honor today would not wish us to be sentimental, to make heroes or martyrs of them. I never met a volunteer who did not wince at the tales of idealism and sacrifice spun at headquarters to impress Congress or the media. They would shun our praise and agree with that good friend of the Peace Corps, journalist Murray Kempton, who said that "the true heroes are those who die for causes they cannot quite take seriously." Despite the stirring rhetoric of the time, our most idealistic volunteers and staff kept their fingers a little bit crossed.

We are here for our sake, not for theirs. The current Peace Corps director, Lorette Ruppe, as dedicated a Republican as Sargent Shriver was a Democrat, has renewed the bipartisan vision of a forward agenda. But she has acknowledged that if new ideas are to move us, new purpose engage us, and new dreams inspire us, they will be summoned by remembrance of the values that connect the past to the present and us to the work yet to be done.

We have, in a sense, come full circle. A cartoon in the 1950s showed Uncle Sam with his arm around a young American. They were looking at students demonstrating in some foreign country as Uncle Sam said, "We want our young people reading history, not writing it."

Once again a generation of Americans is tempted to live undisturbed, buying tranquillity on credit while hearts atrophy, quarantined from any great enthusiasm but private ambition. Some years ago I interviewed the poet laureate of America, Archibald MacLeish. "Every now and then," he said, "the deepest need of a generation appears to be a need not to make sense of our lives but to make nonsense of them." He recalled how in the Dark Ages colonies of frightened folk withdrew from the world to pray for death in filthy cells with their backs turned to the green leaf and blue water. What MacLeish called "the snake-like sin of coldness-at-the-heart" is celebrated today by the politics and commerce of images mass-produced in the media to do our feeling for us.

The century has constantly reminded us that civilization is a thin veneer of civility, stretched across the passions of the human heart. Little did Marshall McLuhan know when he said the world is a global village that its name would be Belfast, Beirut, and Baghdad. The image of Chernobyl dwells in the mind: just as we were finally about to admit that no man is an island, we all woke up one morning to realize we live on Three Mile Island. No wonder so many seek refuge in the modern anchorites' cell, counting their money and getting high while television experiences the world for them. We find it hard to hear the "faint flutter of wings, the gentle stirring of life and hope."

Listening this weekend to news reports of a possible summit between the two superpowers, I was reminded of a proposal made by the scholar Oskar Morgenstern just before his death a few years ago. He said all meetings of the world's statesmen should take place in one very specific setting—a bare, uncomfortable frame building in some unpleasant spot, hot in summer, frigid in winter, furnished with a plain tablecloth and straight wooden chair. The high walls of the conference room would be covered with large photo-murals depicting memorable scenes that would register our leaning toward violent and inhumane behavior. The statesmen would negotiate surrounded by blowups of the wretched trenches of Verdun and the Somme, where 1,100,000 men died in a single battle. There would be pictures of the bodies piled up at Belleau Wood and Château-Thierry; of the deep-eyed children kicked and battered in the Warsaw ghetto before being shipped to the chambers of Auschwitz; of the SS using makeshift nooses of piano wire to hang boys and girls in rural Poland; of the dead at Iwo Jima and Dresden and Hiroshima; of the prisoners bayoneted before cheering crowds in the soccer stadium during the Indian-Pakistani war; of Stalin's gulags and Pol Pot's death squads; of John Kennedy's limousine in Dallas, standing empty except for blood and flowers; of Robert Kennedy lying on a hotel kitchen floor; of Martin

Luther King shot down on a Memphis balcony; of a boy dying on the sidewalk at Kent State University as the blood flowed from his head; of a little Vietnamese girl running naked down the road, seared by napalm; of Armenians simply vanished from life; of civilians slaughtered in Lebanon and the carnage of worshippers in a synagogue; of unmarked and unnumbered graves the world over.

Sometimes I envy the clarity of the soldier's mission. Look at the thousands of crosses surrounding this amphitheater. When Tolstoy compared battle to a vast triangle, with Napoleon at the apex and the soldier at the base, he was saying that the closer a man is to the fighting—the nearer he is to the danger—the more important he is to the outcome of the battle, and if not to the battle then to his buddy. When veterans relive their exploits and swap their stories at reunions, they are celebrating the shared remembrance of emotions and commitments. In war, ordinary people make history together.

Should war be the only trumpet calling us to courage and commitment? Soldiers are patriots and honored for it. But no matter how brave and devoted, the warrior's patriotism serves a nationalist spirit. The Prussian officers who fought for Hitler were patriots. As a patriot General Curtis LeMay urged Vietnam be bombed into the Stone Age. General Westmoreland was a patriot. So was his adversary, General Giap. In uniform patriotism can salute one flag only, embrace but the first circle of life—one's own land and tribe. In war that is necessary, in peace it is not enough.

When the young George Washington spoke of his country, he meant Virginia. Events enlarged his embrace to a wholly new idea of nation— the United States of America. But less than a century later his descendant by marriage could not slip the more parochial tether. In the halls of the family home standing on the hill above us, General Robert E. Lee paced back and forth as he weighed the offer of Abraham Lincoln to take command of the Union Army on the eve of the Civil War. Lee turned the offer down and that evening took the train to Richmond. His country was still Virginia.

We struggle today with the imperative of a new patriotism and citizenship. The Peace Corps has been showing us the way, and the volunteers and staff whom we honor this morning are the vanguard of that journey. The writer William Least Heat-Moon reminds us of those old radio broadcasts that spoke of escaped criminals being "at large." It's a fine phrase, he writes, with its implications of an immensity and awareness of life that can result. America, he said, put that self-absorption behind you and go outward—be at large!

To be a patriot in this sense means to recognize that we are members of a particular culture and society, but so are all others. It is to acknowledge that their kinship and bonds—their sacred places—are as important to them as ours are to us. Love of country, yes. But we carry two passports: one stamped the United States of America, the other as a citizen of the world at large. Human beings belong to the same species but our tents are pitched on different ground, and so we look out on the world from separate angles. This has practical results. You go abroad cautious about the help you can be to others, knowing that the only real change you can accomplish will be within. But you go because the world is your home.

As every volunteer testifies, the Peace Corps is more than a program or mission. It is *a way of being in the world.* This is a conservative notion because it holds dear the ground of one's own being—the culture and customs that give meaning to a particular life. But it is a liberal notion for respecting the ground revered by others. This double helix in America's DNA may yet be the source of a new politics and patriotism that could save us from toxic self-absorption.

We have learned something else from these volunteers. We learned about living intensely whatever our time here is.

When I was his deputy, Sargent Shriver gave me a copy of Chaim Potok's book *The Promise,* with this paragraph highlighted:

> Human beings don't live forever, Reuven. We live less than the
> time it takes to blink an eye, if we measure our lives against eternity. So it may be asked what value there is to human life. There
> is so much pain in the world. What does it mean to have to suffer

so much if our lives are nothing more than a blink of an eye . . . I learned a long time ago, Reuven, that a blink of the eye itself is something. A span of life is nothing. But the man who lives that span, he is something. He can fill that tiny span with memory, so that its quality is immeasurable.

And so they have—the men and women of the Peace Corps whom we honor today.

3. | THE BROAD MARGIN

Peace Corps Commemoration of the Death of John F. Kennedy

NOVEMBER 22, 1988

John F. Kennedy remains an enigma to me. During the successful Kennedy–Johnson campaign of 1960, when I had been a liaison between the traveling entourages of the two candidates, two ambitious politicians who only days earlier had been competing for their party's nomination, JFK's speeches had inspired me. Standing in the bitter cold at his inauguration, my wife, Judith, and I were moved by his summons to "ask not what your country can do for you but what you can do for your country." Then and there I realized that once he launched the Peace Corps, I wanted to be part of it. Only years later, after I had left Washington, did we begin to learn more about this complex man whose personal life had been as driven by common human appetites as his rhetoric had been inspiring. I am fortunate to have lived in Washington when the inner life of a public figure was not the obsession it would later become. When the Peace Corps held a memorial service for JFK at St. Matthew's Cathedral, the site of his funeral, marking the twenty-fifth anniversary of his assassination, I chose to dwell on his ability to requite some-

thing in me—and in my generation—that aspired to excel despite the personal flaws that could have thwarted our dreams.

* * *

I sometimes hear a soundtrack of memories in my head, playing back the incongruities of the 1960s.

I hear the sounds of cheering crowds and burning cities; of laughing children and weeping widows; of night riders, nightmares, and napalm; of falling barriers and new beginnings and animosities as old as Cain and Abel.

I hear the summons that opened the decade—"Let the word go forth"—and the melancholy lament that closed it, composed by a disconsolate young man who had given his heart to three leaders gunned down by assassins: "The stone was at the bottom of the hill, and we were alone."

But something survived those years which bullets could not stop. An idea survived, embodied in the Peace Corps volunteers who are now 125,000 strong and still coming. This idea survived the flawed stewardship of those of us who were its first custodians and it survived the premature death of the man who had asked us to serve it.

Of the private man John Kennedy I knew little. I saw him rarely. Once, when the 1960 campaign was over and he was ending a postelection visit to the LBJ Ranch, he pulled me into a corner and urged me to abandon my plans for graduate work at the University of Texas and join his administration in Washington. I told him that I had already signed up to teach at a Baptist university in Texas while pursuing my doctorate. I said, "You're going to have to call on the whole faculty at Harvard. You don't need a graduate of Southwestern Baptist Theological Seminary." In mock surprise he said, "Didn't you know that the first president of Harvard was a Baptist? You'll be right at home."

And so I was.

JFK of course was flawed; it runs in our presidents. But I remember him not so much for what he was or wasn't but for what he empowered in me. We all edit history to give some form to the puzzle of our lives, and I cherish the late president's memory for awakening me to a different story for myself. The best leaders sign us up for civic duty, knowing, as John Stuart Mill wrote, that "the worth of a state, in the long run, is the worth of the individuals composing it." Rather than encouraging us to exalt in our self-interest they challenge us to act beyond our apparent capacities, offering us the chance to sharpen our skills as citizens.

The theologian Karl Barth was five years old when he first heard the music of Mozart. It would delight him all his life. And in 1955 Barth addressed a letter to the long-deceased Mozart, thanking him for all the pleasure and discovery of the music. "With an ear open to your musical dialectic," he wrote, "one can be young and become old, can work and rest, be content and sad: in short, one can live."

Politics has its music. In many of his speeches John Kennedy challenged my generation to what Henry David Thoreau called "the broad margin" of life. The music said: "signify, serve, and make a difference." Our volunteers were not naïve. They waged hand-to-hand combat with cynicism, and most of the time they won. Because they did, the Peace Corps has earned a reputation hailed by *The Washington Post* as one of the world's most effective grass-roots development organizations.

The idea was around. It was in the air. General James M. Gavin, a wartime hero, had called for a peacetime volunteer force to be started as an alternative to military service. Senator Hubert Humphrey was preparing legislation for it. Congressman Henry Reuss and Senator Richard Neuberger had co-sponsored a Point Four Youth Corps. But it took a president's bully pulpit to sound the trumpet. The Talmud tells us that "in every age there comes a time when leadership suddenly comes forth to meet the needs of the hour. And so, there is no man who does not find his time, and there is no hour that does not have its leader."

Kennedy was right on time with this idea. And we responded: Catholics, Protestants, humanists, Jews, blacks, whites, from every part of the country, from all economic levels, from various and sundry backgrounds— skiers, mountain climbers, teachers, big-game hunters, preachers, journalists, prizefighters, football players, polo players, enough lawyers to staff a firm, and enough PhDs for a liberal-arts college.

What drew them? From my own Peace Corps experience came a gift from Albert Schweitzer, a photograph inscribed "to the affirmation of life." By this Schweitzer meant the spiritual act by which we cease to live unreflectively. Early on some critic said the urge to join the Peace Corps was passion alone. Not so. Thousands of men and women looked their lives over and decided to affirm. They came from a vein in American life as idealistic as the Declaration of Independence and as down-to-earth as a mechanic's manual.

Recently I interviewed the octogenarian dean of American historians, Henry Steele Commager. He talked about how great things were done by the generation that won independence and then formed our government, by the generation that saved the Union and ended slavery, and by the generation that defeated the fascists of Europe and warlords of Japan and then organized the peace that followed. And he said there are still great things to be won here at home and in the world.

We know this to be true. We also know that if we are to reckon with the growing concentration and privilege of power; if from the silos of our separate realities we are to create a new consensus of shared values; if we are to exorcise the toxic remnants of racism, reduce the extremes of poverty and wealth, and overcome our ignorance of our heritage, history, and world, we must reach deep into the vein which gave rise to the Peace Corps and commit ourselves once again to the broad margins of life.

In his "Letters at 3 A.M.," Michael Ventura wrote:

> The dream we must now seek to realize, the new human project,
> is not "security," which is impossible to achieve on the planet
> Earth in the latter half of the 20th century. It is not "happiness,"

by which we generally mean nothing but giddy forgetfulness about the danger of all our lives together. It is not "self-realization," by which people usually mean a separate peace. There is no separate peace . . . The real project is to realize that technology has married us all to each other, has made us one people on one planet, and that until we are more courageous about this new marriage—ourselves all intertwined—there will be no peace and the destination of any of us will be unknown . . . How far can we go together . . . men and women, black, brown, yellow, white, young and old? We will go as far as we can because we must go wherever it is we are going together. There is no such thing as going alone. Given the dreams and doings of our psyches, given the nature of our world, there is no such thing as *being* alone. If you are the only one in the room it is still a crowded room. But we are all together of this planet, you, me, us: inner, outer, together, and we're called to affirm our marriage vows. Our project, the new human task, is to learn how to consummate, how to sustain, how to enjoy this most human marriage—all parts, all of us.

America has a rendezvous it has scarcely imagined with what the late Joseph Campbell called "a mighty multicultural future." It will not be easy to negotiate our way in a world crowded with so many aspirations and appetites. But contrary to the forlorn lament of the disconsolate young man who thought it was all over, the stone is not at the bottom of the hill and we are not alone. More than 125,000 Peace Corps volunteers have scouted the journey ahead of us. They have been to where the future is taking shape—truly the New Frontier.

4. | THE HAPPY WARRIOR

The Hubert H. Humphrey Institute of Public Affairs in
Commemoration of Hubert H. Humphrey's Speech to the
Democratic National Convention in 1948

JUNE 23, 1998

Ask my generation to name the landmarks of the civil rights movement and
you are not likely to be surprised by what you hear: The 1954 Supreme
Court decision to desegregate public schools. The 1961 Freedom Rides. The
March on Washington in 1963 when Martin Luther King proclaimed "I have
a dream." The Civil Rights Act of 1964 and the Voting Rights Act of 1965.
Birmingham. Selma. Little Rock. But I would add to that litany another
place and date: Philadelphia, 1948. There in a sweltering hall the young
mayor of Minneapolis rocked the Democratic National Convention and
roused the conscience of the country. Mercifully short as compared to later
speeches by Hubert H. Humphrey, its impact reverberated far and wide. I
was fourteen at the time. His words penetrated and disturbed the deeply seg-
regated town in East Texas where I was growing up; there were murmurs in
the barbershops and diners and on the courthouse square. The South that had

changed so little over so long had heard the first thunderclap of a coming storm. Humphrey would go on to become one of the most influential senators ever, a frustrated vice president, and an almost-president, losing to Nixon by only 511,944 popular votes. I would get to know and work with him over six intense years in Washington, and we talked on more than one occasion about That Speech, as he called it. I never more eagerly accepted a speaking engagement than when I was asked to make the keynote address at the Fiftieth anniversary of That Speech.

* * *

I have a hard time imagining my life without the impact of Hubert Humphrey. He was the friend who toasted me on my thirtieth birthday and the mentor who nurtured my political sentiments. Some of you will remember that it was Senator Humphrey who first proposed that young Americans be offered the chance to serve their country abroad in peace and not just in war. Newly arrived in Washington, I read his speeches on the subject and liberally borrowed from them for the speech I helped to write for Senator Lyndon B. Johnson during the campaign of 1960 when, at the University of Nebraska, he proposed "a youth corps." Two weeks later, on the eve of the election, Senator John F. Kennedy called for the creation of the Peace Corps. This speech, too, owed its spiritual lineage to Hubert Humphrey.

After the 1960 election I finagled my way onto the Peace Corps Task Force, where I worked with Senator Humphrey on the legislation that turned the idea from rhetoric to reality. President Kennedy then nominated me to be the Peace Corps deputy director. The nomination ran into trouble on the Senate floor when Senator Frank Lausche announced that "a twenty-eight-year-old boy recently out of college" was being given too much responsibility, too fast, at a salary far too high for someone so green behind the ears. Senator Lausche was probably right about that (although I had informed him during the committee hearings that I was not twenty-eight, I was twenty-eight and a half!). But it didn't matter; he was no match for Hubert Humphrey, who rushed to the floor of the Senate not only to defend me but to champion the cause of youth in public service. Some of you who knew Hubert Horatio Humphrey will understand when I say there should have been a fourth "H" in his name—for "hyperbole." But the hyperbole felt good to those on whom it was showered—in this case, me:

> I know this man [Moyers] well. I have spent countless hours with him on the Peace Corps legislation. He was in my office hour after hour working out the details of the legislation. He was at the Foreign Relations Committee Room during the period of the hearings on the legislation and the markup on the legislation. If I know any one member of this government, I know Bill Moyers.

And then, he took off, his words rocketing across the Senate chamber:

> Did not Pitt, the younger, as a rather young man, prove his competence as Prime Minister of Great Britain? He did not have to be fifty, sixty, or sixty-five. He was in his twenties. I invite the attention of my colleagues to the fact that most of the great heroes of the Revolutionary War period . . . were in their twenties and early thirties . . . that many great men in history, from Alexander to Napoleon, achieved greatness when they were in their twenties . . . that the average age of the signers of our Declaration of Independence was thirty-six. I do not wish to use any invidious comparisons, but have seen people who have lived a long time who have not learned a great deal, and I have seen people who have lived only a short time who have learned a very great deal. I think we should judge persons not by the calendar but by their caliber, by the mind and heart and proven capacity . . . My good friend from Ohio [Senator Lausche] said that when this nomination comes to the floor of the Senate he will be here to speak against [it] . . . Just as surely, I say the senator from Minnesota will be here to speak in favor of [it].

He kept his word. And I have been indebted to him ever since. I wish he knew my grandchildren are growing up here in his state, and I wish he could see this throng of old friends and admirers, gathered to commemorate one of the great acts of courage in American politics.

Let's go back to July of 1948—three weeks after the Republicans triumphantly nominated Thomas E. Dewey and began measuring the White House for new drapes. The dispirited Democrats met in Philadelphia resigned to nominating their accidental president, Harry Truman. Truman had surprised many Americans earlier that year when he had demanded that Congress pass a strong civil rights package, but now he and his advisers had changed their tune. A strong civil rights plank in the party platform, they were convinced, would antagonize the South and destroy Truman's chances for election. The specter of a bitter fight dividing the convention was all the more frightening to the Democrats since for the first time television cameras were making their debut on the convention floor and the deliberations would be carried to the country. So the party leaders decided to back away from a strong civil rights stand and offer instead an innocuous plank that would not offend the South.

The mayor of Minneapolis disagreed. Hubert Humphrey was thirty-seven. After graduating magna cum laude from the University of Minnesota he and his young wife, Muriel Buck, had gone to Louisiana for Humphrey to earn his master's degree. What they saw there of the "deplorable daily indignities" visited upon Southern blacks was significantly responsible for his long commitment to the politics of equal opportunity. He came back to Minneapolis to run for mayor, lost, ran a second time, and won. Under his leadership the city council established the country's first enforceable Municipal Fair Employment Practices Commission. He sent six hundred volunteers walking door-to-door, to factories and businesses, schools and churches to expose discrimination previously ignored. Their report, said Mayor Humphrey, was "a mirror that might get Minneapolis to look at itself." He saw to it that doors opened to blacks, Jews, and Indians. He suspended a policeman for calling a traffic viola-

tor "a dirty Jew" and then established a human relations course for police officers at the University of Minnesota. What Hubert Humphrey
preached about civil rights, he practiced. And what he practiced, he
preached.

He arrived at the Democratic Convention in Philadelphia fifty years
ago with convictions born of experience. As a charismatic spokesman for
the liberal wing of the party he was named to the platform committee,
and when after a ferocious debate that very committee voted down a
strong civil rights plank in favor of the weaker one supported by the Truman White House, Humphrey agonized over what to do. Should he defy
the party and carry the fight to a showdown on the convention floor? The
old bulls of his own party said no. "Who does this pip-squeak think he is?"
asked one powerful Democrat. President Truman referred to him as one
of those "crackpots" who couldn't possibly understand what would happen if the South left the party. It was a thorny dilemma. If Humphrey
forced the convention to amend the platform in favor of a stronger civil
rights plank, the delegates might refuse, not only setting back the fledg-
ling civil rights movement but making a laughingstock of Hubert Humphrey and spoiling his own race for the Senate later that same year. On
the other hand, if he took the fight to the floor and won, the Southern
delegates might walk out and cost Harry Truman the presidency.

He wrote in his memoir:

> In retrospect, the decision should have been easy. The plank was
> morally right and politically right . . . [But] clearly, it would have
> grave repercussions on our lives: it could make me an outcast to
> many people; and it could even end my chances for a life of pub-
> lic service. I didn't want to split the party; I didn't want to ruin
> my career, to go from mayor to "pipsqueak" to oblivion. But I did
> want to make the case for a clear-cut commitment to a strong civil
> rights program.

Years later he recalled the dilemma in a conversation with an old
friend, who told him: "That sounds like the politics of a nunnery—you'd

rather have been right than been president." "Not at all," Humphrey shot back. "I'd rather be right *and* be president." Which might explain in part, said the friend, why he never was.

Here's exactly what the plank said: "We call upon Congress to support our President in guaranteeing these basic and fundamental rights: 1) the right of full and equal political participation; 2) the right to equal opportunity of employment; 3) the right of security of person; and 4) the right of equal treatment in the service and defense of our nation."

It sounds so obvious now. All people, no matter what their skin color, had the same right to vote, to work, to live safe from harm, to serve their country. But it's hard to remember, half a century later, how radical those fifty words really were. In 1948 the South was still a different country. Below the Mason-Dixon Line—or, as some blacks called it, the Smith & Wesson Line—segregation of the races was rigorously upheld by law and custom, vigorously protected by violence if necessary. To most whites, this system was their "traditional way of life," and they defended it with a holy fervor. To most blacks, "tradition" meant terror, oppression, humiliation, even death.

Revisit with me what life was like for black Americans in the late 1940s, when Hubert Humphrey was facing the choice between dishonoring his conscience and becoming a pip-squeak. Every day, black people were living lives of quiet desperation. The evidence was everywhere.

You see it in the numbers, the raw measurements of the quality of life for black people. Flip open the Census Bureau's volumes of historical statistics and look under any category for 1948 or thereabouts. Health, for instance. Black people died on average six or seven years earlier than whites. Nearly twice as many black babies as white babies died in their first year. And more than three times as many black mothers as white mothers died in childbirth.

Or take education. Young white adults had completed a median of just over twelve years of school, while blacks had not gotten much past eighth grade. Among black people over seventy-five—those who had been born during or just after slavery times—fewer than half of them had even finished fourth grade.

Recall the standard of living. The median family income for whites was $3,310, for blacks just half that. Sixty percent of white agricultural workers were full owners of their farms and about a quarter were tenants, while for blacks, the numbers were almost exactly opposite: only a quarter of blacks owned their own farms, and more than two-thirds were tenants.

You see the ethos of the time in popular culture, full of cartoon creatures like Stepin Fetchit, Amos 'n' Andy, and Buckwheat; you could look till your eyes ached for a single strong, admirable, human black character in a mainstream book or movie. There's a scene in one of the most beloved movies ever made, *Casablanca,* in which Humphrey Bogart's lost love, the beautiful Ingrid Bergman, walks into Rick's Café and says to Claude Rains, "The boy who's playing the piano—somewhere I've seen him . . ." She's referring, of course, to Dooley Wilson, who at nearly fifty was almost twice Bergman's age, but in those days, to whites, it was okay to call a black man a "boy."

You see it in a slim book written by Ray Sprigle, an adventurous reporter for the Pittsburgh *Post-Gazette.* With a shaved head and a deep Florida suntan he traveled through the South in 1948 posing as a black man to see what life was really like on the other side of the color line. Throughout his trip his black hosts told him horrific stories of indignities, humiliations, lynchings, and murders. While nothing untoward happened to Sprigle himself, it was because, as he put it,

> I gave nobody a chance. That was part of my briefing: "Don't jostle a white man. Don't, if you value your safety, brush a white woman on the sidewalk." So I saw to it that I never got in the way of one of the master race. I almost wore out my cap, dragging it off my shaven poll whenever I addressed a white man. I "sired" everybody, right and left, black, white and in between. I took no chances. I was more than careful to be a "good nigger."

You see it in the recollections of Willie Morris, who in his celebrated memoir of growing up in Mississippi during the '40s recalls his complicated and mysterious relationship with the black people of his town, a relationship that warped and scarred both black and white. As a small child, he says, he had learned the special vocabulary of racism: " 'keeping house like a nigger' was to keep it dirty and unswept. 'Behaving like a nigger' was to stay out at all hours and to have several wives or husbands. A 'nigger street' was unpaved and littered with garbage." Morris writes of casual cruelties like the time he hid in the bushes until a tiny black child walked by, then leaped out to kick and cuff the child. "My heart was beating furiously, in terror and a curious pleasure," Morris wrote. "For a while I was happy with this act, and my head was strangely light and giddy. Then later, the more I thought about it coldly, I could hardly bear my secret shame."

In the small town where I grew up in East Texas, there were highschool kids—classmates of mine—who made a sport out of "niggerknocking." Driving along a country road they would extend a broom handle out of the rear window at just the right moment and angle to deliver a stunning blow to an unsuspecting black pedestrian. Then they would go celebrate over a few beers. While I never participated, it was my secret shame that I never tried to stop them.

There was a study in 1946 by the Social Sciences Institute at Fisk University, the black college in Nashville, about white attitudes toward black people. In interview after interview, average citizens throughout the South never talked of overt violence or flaming hatred, but their detached and imperturbable calm was in some ways even more grotesque than physical violence. Listen to their voices:

A female teacher in Kentucky: "We have no problem of equality because they are in their native environment. If we permitted them to be equal they wouldn't respect us. We never have any riots because their interests are looked after by the white people."

A housewife in North Carolina: "They are as lovable as anyone in a lower order of life could be . . . I had to go see an old sick woman yesterday. We feel toward them like we do about our pets. I have no horror of a black man. Why, some of them are the nicest old black niggers. They are better than a barrel of monkeys for amusement."

A businessman in North Carolina: "I have a feeling of aversion toward a rat or snake. They are harmless but I don't like them. I feel the same toward a nigger. I wouldn't kill one but there it is."

Or a mechanic in Georgia: "During the war I was stationed at a northern naval yard. The southern Negro was given the same privileges as white men. He was not used to it, and it ruined a good Negro. In the south he is treated as a nigger and is at home here. He knows this treatment is the best for him . . . We have a good group around here. It's years and years since we've had a lynching. It's not necessary to lynch them. The sheriffs in this county take more care of the darky than the white man."

By now these words are making you twist and cringe in your seats. I have trouble forcing them out of my mouth. But these words were the coin of the realm in 1948. After more than two centuries of slavery and nearly another of Jim Crow segregation, black people were still struggling to realize their most basic rights as human beings, let alone as citizens. The framers of the Constitution made their notorious decision in 1787 that for census purposes each slave would count as three-fifths of a person. In the minds of many white Southerners in 1948, that fraction still seemed about right.

Yet something was beginning to change. The steadfast but quiet resistance long practiced by many Southern blacks was now being strengthened by a new development: thousands of black veterans were coming home from Europe and the Pacific.

These men had fought for their country. Some had even fought for the right to fight for their country, not just to dig ditches and drive trucks and peel potatoes for their country. They had served in a segregated army that had accepted their labor and their sacrifice without accepting their humanity. Some of them had come home heroes, others had come home embittered, and many had also come home determined that things would be different now. They had earned the respect of their fellow Americans and it was time they got it. That meant starting at the ballot box—a tool both practical and symbolic in the struggle to ensure their status as full citizens.

All over the South, where for decades blacks had been systematically harassed, intimidated, or overtaxed to keep them from voting, intense registration drives for the 1946 campaigns swelled the rolls with first-time black voters. And the white supremacists were fighting back. Sometimes it was brute and random violence. In Mississippi a group of black veterans was dumped off a truck and beaten up. In Georgia two black men, one a veteran, were out driving with their wives when they were ambushed and shot by a mob of whites. The mob then turned on the women who had witnessed the crime. In South Carolina, a black veteran returning home by bus after fifteen months in the South Pacific angered the driver with some minor act that struck the white man as uppity. At the next stop the soldier was taken off the bus by the local chief of police and beaten so badly he went blind. Permanently. Under pressure from the NAACP, something unusual happened: the chief was put on trial. Then normalcy returned. The chief was acquitted, to the cheers of the courtroom.

But the demagogues also made deliberate efforts to stop the black vote by whatever means necessary. In Georgia, Gene Talmadge ran for governor and won on a frankly, even joyfully, racist platform. "If I get a Negro vote it will be an accident," he declared, and his machine figured out ways to challenge and purge the rolls of most of them. The brave black voters who went to the polls anyway often paid dearly for their rights. Another veteran, the only black to vote in Taylor County, was shot and killed as he sat on his porch three days after the primary and a sign posted on a nearby black church boasted that THE FIRST NIGGER TO VOTE WILL NEVER VOTE AGAIN.

In Mississippi, the racist Theodore Bilbo was reelected to the Senate with the help of a campaign of threats and violence that kept most black people home on Election Day. "The way to keep the nigger from the polls is to see him the night before," Bilbo was fond of saying. But this time black voters fought back and filed a complaint with the Senate. Nearly two hundred black Mississippians trekked to Jackson—and its segregated courtroom—to testify about the myriad pressures, both subtle and brutal, that had kept them from voting. Their eloquent testimony failed to convince the honorable members. Bilbo was exonerated by the majority of the committee members—despite (or perhaps because of) having used the word "nigger" seventy-nine times during his own testimony. It was a toxic word, a poisonous and deadly word. And it was still prevalent as a term of derision in the early 1960s. In August 1964, following the death of his father, the writer James Baldwin said on television: "My father is dead. And he had a terrible life. Because, at the bottom of his heart, he believed what people said of him. He believed he was a nigger."

When Hubert Humphrey stood up at the Democratic National Convention in Philadelphia and urged the delegates to support his civil rights plank, he could have had no doubt how ferociously most Southern delegates would oppose his words—and how desperately all Southern citizens, white and black, really needed to hear them. It was a short speech and it took less than ten minutes to deliver—doubtless some kind of record for the man whose own wife reportedly once told him, "Hubert, you don't have to be interminable to be immortal." Most of the time he couldn't help being interminable. Someone said that when God passed out the glands, Hubert took two helpings. He set records for the number of subjects he could approach simultaneously with an open mouth. At a press conference in California, his first three answers to questions lasted, respectively, fourteen, eighteen, and sixteen minutes. No one dared ask him a fourth question for fear of missing dinner!

But in Philadelphia in 1948, Hubert Humphrey spoke briefly. And these not interminable words became immortal because they were right. He had agonized, he had weighed the odds as any politician must; he was a politician, and this was a time when the way to get ahead was not to go back on your party. But now he was listening to his conscience, not his party, and he was appealing to the best, instead of the basest, instincts of his country, and his words rolled through the convention hall like "a swelling wave."

> To those who say that we are rushing this issue of civil rights, I say to them we are 172 years late . . . To those who say that this civil-

rights program is an infringement on states' rights, I say this: The time has arrived in America for the Democratic party to get out of the shadow of states' rights and to walk forthrightly into the bright sunshine of human rights.

When he finished a mighty roar went up from the crowd. Delegates stood and whooped and shouted and whistled; a forty-piece band played in the aisles, and the tumult subsided only when Chairman Sam Rayburn ordered the lights dimmed throughout the hall. The platform committee was then overruled and Humphrey's plank voted in by a wide margin. Mississippi's entire delegation and half of Alabama's stalked out in protest. The renegades later formed the Dixiecrat Party on a platform calling for "the segregation of the races and the racial integrity of each race," and nominated Strom Thurmond for president. "There's not enough troops in the army to break down segregation and admit the Negro into our homes, our eating places, our swimming pools, and our theaters," Thurmond declared on the campaign trail. A majority of the voters in South Carolina, Mississippi, Alabama, and Louisiana agreed with him.

But Harry Truman didn't lose. The *Minneapolis Star* got it right the morning after the convention when it said Humphrey's speech "had lifted the Truman campaign out of the rut of just another political drive to a crusade." Harry Truman won—and the Southern walkout to protest civil rights actually ended up helping the civil rights agenda. If a Democrat could go on to win the presidency anyway, even without the solid South behind him, then the segregationist stranglehold on the party was clearly weaker than advertised, and even the most timid politician could see that supporting civil rights might not be a political death sentence after all. The late Murray Kempton once wrote that "a political convention is just not a place from which you can come away with any trace of faith in human nature." This one was different, because Hubert Humphrey kept the faith.

There were other forces at work of course. As a *Star-Tribune* editorial put it recently, it would be misleading to suggest the Democratic ship turned on a few eloquent phrases from a young upstart, or that the party had experienced a moral epiphany. Politics is rarely that simple. There were other forces at work. During the cold war America needed to put its best face forward. Democrats needed to consolidate their hold on the northern industrial states. America needed to respond affirmatively to those returning black veterans. But it would be equally wrong to underestimate what Hubert Humphrey did. An idea whose time has come can pass like the wind on the sea, rippling the surface without disturbing the depths, if there is no voice to incarnate and proclaim it. In a democracy a moral movement must have its political moment to crystallize and enter the bloodstream of the nation. This was such a moment, and Humphrey embodied it.

But 1948 wasn't the end of the struggle. It turned out to be just the beginning. Sixteen years later, in 1964, Lyndon Johnson staked his reputation on getting a comprehensive civil rights bill passed into law. And Hubert Humphrey, now Senator Humphrey, was the man assigned the gargantuan challenge of shepherding the bill through Congress in the face of a resolute Southern filibuster. Once again I was privileged to work with him. By now I was an assistant to the president, and the Civil Rights Act of 1964 was our chief imperative.

The face of the segregated South had changed—somewhat. The landmark Supreme Court decision *Brown vs. Board of Education* had given legal aid and comfort to the long moral crusade to open the public schools to all races, while courageous activists were putting their own bodies on the line in determined efforts to desegregate the buses, the lunch counters, the beaches, the restrooms, the swimming pools, and the universities of the South.

But all the court decisions and sit-ins in the world had not changed the determination of the die-hard segregationists to defend their vision of the South "by any means necessary," and the few federal laws on the books were too weak to stop them. A lot of this story, while awful, is familiar. We may think we have a pretty good idea what was at stake when Hubert Humphrey made his second great stand for civil rights. We've seen the photographs and the television images; we know about the ugly mobs taunting the quiet black teenagers outside the schools and inside the Woolworth, we know about the beatings and attack dogs and fire hoses, we know about the murders. During Freedom Summer—the very same summer that the Senate completed work on the civil rights bill—Mississippi endured thirty-five shootings, the bombing or burning of sixty-five homes and churches, the arrest of one thousand activists and the beating of eighty, and the killing of three volunteers with the active connivance of the Neshoba County sheriff's department, their bodies bulldozed into an earthen dam.

But we don't know as much about another, more silent tactic of white resistance that was just as oppressive, and in some ways maybe even more effective than the violence. I mean the spying, the smearing, the sabotage, and the subversion ordered by the highest officials in states across the South.

We were reminded of the twisted depths of official segregation just this spring, when after decades of court battles Mississippi was ordered to open the secret files of the State Sovereignty Commission. This was an official government agency, bountifully funded with taxpayer money, lavished with almost unlimited police and investigative powers, and charged with upholding the separation of the races. Most of the Southern states had similar agencies, but Mississippi had a well-deserved reputation as the worst.

I have read some of those Sovereignty Commission files. And I understand how a longtime activist in Jackson could recently tell a reporter: "These files betray the absolute paranoia and craziness of the government in those times. This was a police state."

The commission devoted astonishing amounts of effort, time, and money to snooping into the private lives of any citizen who supported civil rights, who *might* be supporting civil rights, or whom they suspected of stepping over the color line in any way. It tracked down rumors that this northern volunteer had VD and that one was gay. Its staff combed through letters to the editor in local and national newspapers, and wrote indignant personal replies to anyone who held a contrary opinion. It sent agents to a Joan Baez concert at a black college to count how many white people came, and posted people at NAACP meetings to write down the license numbers of every car in the parking lot. It stole lists of names from Freedom Summer activists and asked the House Un-American Activities Committee to check on them. It went through the trash at the Freedom Houses and paid undercover informants to report on leadership squabbles and whether the white women were fornicating with the black men.

The most incriminating documents were purged long ago, but buried deep in those files is still ample evidence of the violence and brutality. I am haunted by the case of a black veteran named Clyde Kennard. When he insisted on applying to the local college, one for whites only, he was framed on trumped-up charges of stealing chicken feed and sent to Parchman, the infamous prison farm, for seven years. While there he developed colon cancer and for months was denied treatment. Eventually, after prominent activists brought public pressure to bear on the governor, Kennard was released, but it was too late. In July 1963, a year before the passage of the Civil Rights Act, Clyde Kennard died following surgery. He was thirty-six years old.

Reading these files you are struck by the brutality and banality of evil. You find in them the story of a divorced mother of two who was investigated after the commission heard a rumor that her third child was fathered by a black man. An agent arrived to interview witnesses, confront the man, and look at the child. "I had a weak feeling in the pit of my stomach," he reported; he and the sheriff "were not qualified to say it was a part Negro child, but we could say it was not 100 percent Caucasian." After that visit, the woman's two older boys were removed from her custody.

You can read in these files about how a local legislator reported to the commission that a married white woman had given birth to a baby girl with "a mulatto complexion, dark hair that has a tendency to 'kink,' dark hands, and light palms." A doctor and an investigator were immediately dispatched to examine the child, then shelled out $62 for blood tests to determine its paternity. The tests came back inconclusive but a couple of months later shots were fired at night into the family's home and a threatening letter signed by the KKK, referring to "your wife and Negro child," was left on their doorstep. They moved out immediately.

It was insane and it was official. This was the rampant and unchecked abuse of state power turned against citizens of the United States of America. And this was the Southern background music to Lyndon Johnson's 1964 civil rights bill, which called for the integration of public accommodations, authorized the attorney general to sue school districts and other segregated facilities, outlawed discrimination in employment, and further protected voting rights. When Senator Humphrey accepted the assignment as floor manager for this bill, he knew how crucial as well as how difficult it would be to gather enough votes to end the Southern filibuster. He also knew his own career was again on the line, as LBJ was using the assignment to test Humphrey's worth as his potential vice presidential candidate.

The filibuster began on March 9 and went on, it seemed, forever. But Humphrey was prepared and organized. A couple of times during those long months of debate I slipped into the gallery of the Senate to watch him lead the fight. The same deep fire of justice that burned in him at the 1948 convention burned within him still. He was utterly determined. He held regular strategy meetings. He issued a daily newsletter. He enlisted a different colleague to focus on each title of the bill. He schmoozed and coaxed and charmed the key men whose support he needed. He persuaded the Republican leader, Everett Dirksen, to retreat from at least forty amendments that would have gutted the bill. He orchestrated the support of religious organizations until it seemed the corridors and galleries of Congress were overflowing with ministers, priests, and rabbis. "The secret of passing the bill," he said, "is the prayer groups."

But the open secret was Hubert Humphrey. As Robert Mann reminds us in *The Walls of Jericho*, his good humor and boundless optimism prevented the debates from dissolving into personal recrimination. Once again he kept the faith. As he told his longtime supporters at the Americans for Democratic Action after more than two months of frustration and delay,

Not too many Americans walked with us in 1948, but year after year the marching throng has grown. In the next few weeks the strongest civil rights bill ever enacted in our history will become the law of the land. It is not saying too much, I believe, to say that it will amount to a second Emancipation Proclamation. As it is enforced, it will free our Negro fellow-citizens of the shackles that have bound them for generations. As it is enforced, it will free us, of the white majority, of shackles of our own—for no man can be fully free while his fellow man lies in chains.

His skills and commitment paid off. Seventy-five days later, on June 10, the Senate finally voted for cloture with four votes to spare. A California senator, ravaged with cancer, was wheeled in to vote, which he could only do by pointing to his eye. After cloture ended the filibuster, the bill passed by a wide margin. On July 2, President Johnson signed it.

During all that time Hubert Humphrey broke only once—on the afternoon of June 17, two days before the historic vote. Summoned from the Senate floor to take an urgent call from Muriel, he learned their son Robert had been diagnosed with a malignant growth in his throat and must have immediate surgery. There in his office, Hubert Humphrey wept. As his son struggled for his life and his own greatest legislative triumph was in sight, Hubert Humphrey realized how intermingled are the triumphs and tragedies of life.

We talked about this the last time I saw him, early in the summer of 1976. He came to our home on Long Island where I interviewed him for public television. We talked about many things: about his father who set such high standards for the boy he named Hubert Horatio; about his granddaughter Cindy (a little pixie, he called her); about waking up on the morning after he had lost to Richard Nixon by only 511,944 votes out of 73 million cast; about the tyrannies of working for Lyndon Johnson (said Humphrey of Johnson: "He often reminded me of my father-in-law and the way he used to treat chilblains. Grandpa Buck would get some chilblains and he said the best way to treat them was put your feet first in cold water, then in hot water. And sometimes [with LBJ] I'd feel myself in hot water, then I'd be over in cold water. I'd be the household hero for a week and then I'd be in the doghouse").

We talked about the necessity of compromise, the obligation to stand firm when necessary against the odds, and the difficulty of making the distinction. We talked about the life-threatening illness he had himself recently endured and what kept him going through the vicissitudes of life. Growing up on the great northern plains had made a difference, he told me:

> I used to think as a boy that in the Milky Way each star was a little place, a sort of light for somebody who had died . . . I used to go pick up the milk—we didn't have milk delivery in those days— I'd go over to Dreyer's Dairy and pick up a gallon of milk. I can remember those cold, wintery nights and blue sky, and I'd look up and see that Milky Way and I'd think every time anybody died they got a star up there. And all the big stars were for the big people. You know, like Caesar or Lincoln. It was a childhood fantasy. But it was a comforting thing.

He was called the "Happy Warrior" because he loved politics and because of his natural ebullience and resiliency. I asked him: "Some people say you're too happy and that this is not a happy world." He answered:

> Well, maybe I can make it a little more happy . . . I realize and sense the realities of the world in which we live. I'm not at all happy about what I see in the nuclear arms race . . . and the machinations of the Soviets or the Chinese . . . the misery that's in our cities. I'm aware of all that. But I do not believe that people will respond to do better if they are constantly approached by a negative attitude. People have to believe that they can do better. They've got to know that there's somebody that's with them that wants to help and work with them, and somebody that hasn't tossed in the towel. I don't believe in defeat, Bill.

He lost some elections in his long career, but Hubert Humphrey was never defeated. More than anyone else in politics, he gave me to believe that in time, justice comes—not because it is inherent in the universe but because somewhere, at some place, someone will make a stand and do the right thing, turning the course of events.

As Hubert Humphrey did.

My own recollections of Hubert Humphrey were rekindled by three books I highly recommend: Carl Solberg's *Hubert Humphrey: A Biography*; Robert Mann's *The Walls of Jericho*; and Humphrey's memoir, *The Education of a Public Man*. I am indebted to them and to my editorial associate Andie Tucher for contributions to this speech.

5. | REMEMBERING BILL COFFIN

Eulogy for William Sloane Coffin, June 1, 1924–April 12, 2006

Two strokes had slurred his speech and robbed his legs of agility and his fingers of their feel for the piano. But the last time I saw William Sloane Coffin, he remained a hopeful man. "Hope," he told me, "arouses as nothing else can arouse, a passion for the possible"—even in the face of death. He was troubled, as always, by the state of America and was angry, as Jesus was angry when he tossed the money changers from the temple. "People in high places make me really angry," he said, "because they are so callous. When you see uncaring people in high places, everybody should be mad as hell." He was, nonetheless, more hopeful than angry—"hope being a state of mind independent of the state of the nation. The opposite of hope is not pessimism but despair, and we can't afford despair; it numbs and paralyzes." He lived a long life in hope, reflection, and public service. A captain in the U.S. Army, three years with the CIA, seventeen years as chaplain at Yale University, a decade serving the historic Riverside Church in New York as senior minister, then years of campaigning for nuclear disarmament. He had been arrested more often than any eighty-one-year-old I knew—as a civil rights Freedom Rider, opponent of the Vietnam War, protester against the arms race. Grief had been so frequent a visitor that he finally accepted sorrow as an old companion; his eulogy to his twenty-four-year-old son, killed in an accident, borrowed from Hemingway to remind us of the one hope that above all helps us negotiate the inescapable: "The world breaks everyone, then some become strong at the broken places." A host of friends and followers gathered in Riverside Church to pay our final respects to this broken but strong man of faith and action, lying now in a plain pine coffin, wearing a red plaid shirt.

* * *

There are so many of you in this vast congregation who should be up here instead of me. You rode with Bill Coffin through the Deep South chasing Jim Crow from barriers long imposed on freedom. You rose with Bill against the Vietnam War, were arrested with him, jailed with him, and at night in your cells joined in singing the Hallelujah Chorus with him. You rallied with him to protest the horrors of the bomb. You sang with him, laughed with him, drank with him, prayed with him, grieved with him, worshipped and wept with him. Even at this moment when your hearts are breaking with loss, you must be comforted by the balm of those memories. I envy your lifelong membership in his beloved community, and I am honored that Randy, his wife, asked me to speak today about the Bill Coffin I knew.

I saw little of him personally until late in his life. We met once in the early '60s when he was an adviser to the Peace Corps, which I had helped to organize and run. He spoke to the staff, inspired us to think of what we were doing as the moral equivalent of war, and told us the story of how as a young captain in the infantry, following military orders at the end of World War II, he had been charged with sending back to the Soviet Union thousands of Russian refugees made prisoners by the Germans. Some of them he had deceived into boarding trains for home that carried them to sure death at the hands of Stalin. That burden of guilt sat heavily on Bill's heart for the rest of his life. He wrote about it in his autobiography, and raised it forty years later when we met in the waiting room of the television studio where I was about to interview him. That's the moment we bonded, two old men by now, sharing our grief that both in different ways had once confused duty with loyalty, and confessing to each other our gratitude that we had lived long enough to atone— somewhat. "Well," said Bill, "we needed a lot of time. We had a lot to atone for."

I had called him for the interview after mutual friends had told me that his doctors had said his time was now running out. When he came down from Vermont to the studio here in New York, I greeted him with the question, "How you doing?" He threw back his head, his eyes flashed, and with that slurred but still-vibrant voice, he answered, "Well, I am praying the prayer of St. Augustine: Give me chastity and self-restraint . . . but not yet."

He taught us how to be a Christian.

His witness taught us—he preached what he practiced. His writings taught us, too—*Once to Every Man, Living the Truth in a World of Illusion, The Heart Is a Little to the Left, Credo, Letters to a Young Doubter,* and of course that unforgettable eulogy to his drowned son, Alex, when he called on us to "improve the quality of our suffering." During my interview with him I asked him how he had summoned the strength for so powerful a message of suffering and love. He said, "Well, we all do what we know how to do. I went right away to the piano. And I played all the hymns. And I wept and I wept, and I read the poems, like A. E. Houseman—'To an Athlete Dying Young.' Then I realized the folks in Riverside Church had to know whether or not they still had a pastor. So I wrote the sermon. I wanted them to know."

They knew, Bill, they knew.

This may surprise some of you. Not too long ago Bill told Terry Gross that he would rather not be known as a social activist. The happiest moments of his life, he said, were less in social activism than in the intimate settings of the pastor's calling—"the moments when you're doing marriage counseling . . . or baptizing a baby . . . or accompanying people who have suffered loss—the moments when people tend to be most human, when they are most vulnerable."

So he had the pastor's heart but heeded the prophet's calling. There burned in his soul a sacred rage—that volatile mix of grief and anger and love that produced what his friend, the artist and writer Robert Shetterly, described as "a holy flame." If you lessen your anger at the structures of power, he said, you lower your love for the victims of power.

I once heard Lyndon Johnson urge Martin Luther King to hold off on his marching in the South to give the president time to neutralize the old guard in Congress and create a consensus for finally ending institutionalized racism in America. Martin Luther King listened, and then he answered (I paraphrase): "Mr. President, the gods of the South will never be appeased. They will never have a change of heart. They will never repent of their sins and come to the altar seeking forgiveness. The time has passed for consensus, the time has come to break the grip of history and change the course of America." When the discussion was over Dr. King had carried the day. The president said, "Dr. King, you go on out there now and make it possible for me to do the right thing." Lyndon Johnson had seen the light. For him to do the right thing someone had to subpoena America's conscience and send it marching from the ground up against the citadels of power and privilege.

Like Martin Luther King, Bill Coffin knew the heart of power is hard, knew it arranged the rules for its own advantage, knew that before justice could roll down like water and righteousness like a flowing river, the dam of oppression, deception, and corruption had first to be broken, cracked open by the moral power of people demanding the right thing be done. "In times of oppression," he said, "if you don't translate choices of faith into political choices, you run the danger of washing your hands, like Pilate."

So he aimed his indignation at root causes. "Many of us are eager to respond to injustice," he said, "without having to confront the causes of it . . . and that's why so many business and governmental leaders today are promoting charity. First these leaders proclaim themselves experts on matters economic, and prove it by taking the most out of the economy. Then they promote charity as if it were the work of the church, finally telling troubled clergy to shut up and bless the economy as once we blessed the battleship."

When he came down from Vermont two years ago for that inter-view, we talked about how democracy had reached a fork in the road. Take one fork and the road leads to an America where military power serves empire rather than freedom; where we lose from within what we are trying to defend from without; where fundamentalism and the state scheme to write the rules and regulations; where true believers in the gods of the market turn the law of the jungle into the law of the land; where in the name of patriotism we keep our hand over our heart pledg-ing allegiance to the flag while our leaders pick our pockets and plunder our trust; where elites insulate themselves from the consequences of their own actions.

Take the other fork and the road leads to the America whose prom-ise of "life, liberty, and the pursuit of happiness" includes everyone. Bill Coffin spent his life pointing us down that road in that direction. There is nothing utopian about it, Bill said; he was an idealist but he was not an ideologue. He said in our interview that we have to keep pressing the socialist questions because they are the questions of justice, but we should be dubious about the socialist answers because while Amos may call for justice to roll down as waters, figuring out the irrigation system is damned hard!

He believed in democracy. There is no simpler way to put it. He be-lieved democracy was the only way to assure that the rewards of a free society would be shared with everyone, and not just the elites in charge. That last time we talked he told me how much he had liked the story he had heard Joseph Campbell tell me in our series *The Power of Myth*—the story of the fellow who turns the corner and sees a brawl in the middle of the block. He runs right for it, shouting: "Is this a private fight, or can anyone get in it?"

For Bill, democracy was everyone's fight. He'd be in the middle of the fork-in-the-road action. And his message would be the same today as then: Sign up, jump in, fight on.

Someone sidled up to me the other night at another gathering where Bill's death was discussed. This person said, "He was no saint, you know." I wanted to answer: "You're kidding?" We knew. Saints flourish in a mythic world. Bill Coffin flourished here, in the cracked common clay of an earthly and earthy life. He liked it here. Even as he was trying to cooperate gracefully with the inevitability of death, he was also coaching Paul Newman to play the preacher in the film version of Marilynne Robinson's novel *Gilead*. He enjoyed nothing more than wine and song at his home with Randy and friends. And he never lost his conviction that a better world is possible if we fight hard enough. At a dinner in his honor in Washington he had reminded us that "the world is too dangerous for anything but truth and too small for anything but love." But as we left he winked at me and said, "Give 'em hell."

Faith, he once said, "is being seized by love." Seized he was, by what he called "everlasting arms." "You know," he told me, "I lost a son. And people will say, 'Well, when you die, Alex will come forth and bring you through the pearly gates.' That's a nice thought, and I welcome it. But I don't need to believe that. All I need to know is, God will be there. And our lives go from God, in God, to God again. Hallelujah, you know? That should be enough."

He's there now—in those everlasting arms. But we are still here. I hear his voice in my heart: "Don't tarry long in mourning. Organize."

6. | THE MEANING OF FREEDOM

Excerpt from the Sol Feinstone Lecture at the
United States Military Academy

NOVEMBER 15, 2006

The invitation was short and simple: "It is with a great deal of pleasure that
I write to inform you that the Superintendent of the United States Military
Academy has approved the recommendation of the selection committee to in-
vite you as our speaker for the Sol Feinstone Lecture." *The details followed,
but I could hardly get beyond the first sentence. The committee had to have
known of my opposition to the invasion of Iraq, in no small part because I
had served in the White House during President Lyndon Johnson's escalation
of the war in Vietnam, and I saw the Bush administration repeating many of
the same mistakes. What would I say to young men and women who within
a year could be dying in another unnecessary war because their civilian leaders misled the country? These cadets had committed themselves to Duty,
Honor, Country and were now being asked to fulfill those obligations in a
war they should never have been asked to fight. As I weighed the decision to
accept or decline, I fastened on the title of the lecture series: The Meaning of*

Freedom. *The annual event dated back to 1971 and included, among others, Herman Wouk, Sidney Hook, Isaac Bashevis Singer, Carl Sagan, George Will, Milton Friedman, Elie Wiesel, A. Bartlett Giamatti, Madeleine Albright, Doris Kearns Goodwin, Stephen Jay Gould, and H. Ross Perot. Just who was Sol Feinstone, to want such an array of speakers in his name? And why "The Meaning of Freedom?" Researching his life proved instructive. He was born to an impoverished family in Lithuania, then part of Poland, the son of a Torah scribe, at a time when the czarist government controlled everything, including permission to leave the country. Without standing or rubles to obtain passports, most impoverished emigrants had to get out illegally. When he was fourteen, Sol Feinstone hid in a peasant's cart under a load of hay to reach a barn where thirty-five other emigrants, mostly young men trying to escape the czar's army, were hiding. They made it across the German border to Antwerp where Sol boarded a ship for America with a $40 ticket paid for by his brother and sister who were already in New York, working in a sweatshop. Young Sol wound up making sleeves for coats, earning $6 a week and taking $2 from each paycheck to pay off the money he owed his siblings. With no elementary or high-school education he attended night school for fifteen months, was accepted at Syracuse University to study forestry, went on to the University of Pennsylvania for chemistry, and then made his fortune in real estate and construction. He so cherished the liberty he found in the new country that he collected original documents of the American Revolution and set up libraries to house them, including the Sol Feinstone Collection at the academy. To the cadets he had given a legacy of history; to me, a reminder that the meaning of freedom is what you make of it.*

* * *

As I prepared for this occasion, I constantly reminded myself that many of you will be heading for Iraq. I have never been a soldier myself, never been tested under fire, never faced hard choices between duty and conscience under deadly circumstances. I will never know if I have the courage to be shot at, or to shoot back, or the discipline to do my duty knowing the people who dispatched me to kill—or be killed—had no idea of the moral abyss into which they were plunging me.

I have tried to learn about war from those who know it best: veterans, the real experts. But they have been such reluctant reporters of the experience. My father-in-law, Joe Davidson, was thirty-seven years old with two young daughters when war came in 1941; he enlisted and served in the Pacific but I never succeeded in getting him to describe what it was like to be in harm's way. My uncle came home from the Pacific after his ship had been sunk, taking many friends down with it, and when I asked him about the experience he would look away and change the subject. One of my dearest friends, who died this year at ninety, returned from combat in Europe as if he had taken a vow of silence about the terrifying things that came home with him, uninvited.

Curious about this, some years ago I produced a documentary called *From D-Day to the Rhine*. With a camera crew I accompanied several veterans of World War II who for the first time were returning together to the path of combat that carried them from the landing at Normandy in 1944 into the heart of Germany. Members of their families were along this time—wives, grown sons and daughters—and they told me that until now, on this trip, forty-five years after D-Day, their husbands and fathers rarely talked about their combat experiences. They had come home, locked their memories in their mind's attic, and hung a NO TRESPASSING sign on it. Even as they retraced their steps almost half a century later, I would find these aging GIs, standing alone and silent on the very spot where a buddy had been killed, or they themselves had killed, or where they had been taken prisoner, a German soldier standing over them with a Mauser pointed right between their eyes, saying, "For you, the war is over." As they tried to tell the story, the words choked in their throats. The stench, the vomit, the blood, the fear: What outsider— journalist or kin—could imagine the demons still at war in their heads?

What I remember most vividly from that trip is the opening scene of the film: Jose Lopez—the father of two, who had lied about his age to get into the army (he was too old)—went ashore at Normandy, fought his way across France and Belgium with a water-cooled machine gun, rose to the rank of sergeant, and received the Congressional Medal of Honor after single-handedly killing one hundred German troops in the

Battle of the Bulge. Jose Lopez, back on Omaha Beach at age seventy-nine, quietly saying to me, "I was really very, very afraid. That I want to scream. I want to cry and we see other people was laying wounded and screaming and everything and it's nothing you could do. We could see them groaning in the water and we keep walking"—and then, moving away from the camera, dropping to his knees, his hands clasped, his eyes wet, as it all came back, memories so excruciating there were no words for them.

Over the years I've turned to the poets for help in understanding the realities of war; it is from the poets we outsiders most often learn what you soldiers experience. I admired your former superintendent General William Lennox, who held a doctorate in literature and taught poetry classes here because, he said, "poetry is a great vehicle to teach cadets as much as anyone can what combat is like." So it is. From the opening lines of the *Iliad*

> *Rage, Goddess, sing the rage of Peleus' Son*
> *Achilles . . . hurling down to the House of Death*
> *so many souls, great fighters' souls, but made*
> *their bodies carrion for the dogs and birds . . .*

to Wilfred Owen's pained cry from the trenches of France

> *I am the enemy you killed, my friend . . .*

to W. D. Ehrhart's staccato recitation of the

> *Barely tolerable conglomeration of mud, heat, sweat,*
> *dirt, rain, pain, fear . . . we march grinding under the*
> *weight of heavy packs, feet dialed to the ground . . . we wonder . . .*

poets with their empathy and evocation open to bystanders what lies buried in the soldier's soul. Those of you soon to be leading others in combat may wish to take a metaphorical detour to the Hindenburg Line of World War I, where the officer and poet Wilfred Owen, a man of extraordinary courage who was killed a week before the armistice, wrote: "I came out in order to help these boys—directly by leading them as well as an officer can; indirectly, by watching their sufferings that I may speak of them as well as a pleader can."

People in power should be required to take classes in the poetry of war. As a White House assistant during the early escalation of the war in Vietnam, I remember how the president blanched when the chairman of the Joint Chiefs of Staff said it would take one million fighting men and ten years to win in Vietnam, but even then the talk of war was about policy, strategy, numbers, and budgets, not severed limbs and eviscerated bodies.

That experience, and the experience forty years later of watching another White House go to war, also relying on inadequate intelligence, exaggerated claims, and premature judgments, keeping Congress in the dark while wooing a gullible press, cheered on by partisans, pundits, and editorial writers safely divorced from realities on the ground, ended any tolerance I might have had for those who advocate war from the loftiness of the pulpit, the safety of a laptop, the comfort of a think tank, or the glamour of a television studio. How often we hear the most vigorous argument for war from those who count on others of valor to fight it. As General William Tecumseh Sherman said after the Civil War: "It is only those who have neither fired a shot nor heard the shrieks and groans of the wounded who cry aloud for blood, more vengeance, more desolation."

Rupert Murdoch comes to mind—only because he was in the news last week talking about Iraq. In the months leading up to the invasion Murdoch turned the dogs of war loose in the corridors of his media empire, and they howled for blood, although not their own. Murdoch himself said, just weeks before the invasion, that the "greatest thing to come of this to the world economy, if you could put it that way [as you can, if you are a media mogul], would be $20 a barrel for oil." Once the war is behind us, Rupert Murdoch said, "The whole world will benefit from cheaper oil, which will be a bigger stimulus than anything else."

Today Murdoch says he has no regrets, that he still believes it was right "to go in there," and that "from a historical perspective" the U.S. death toll in Iraq was "minute."

"Minute."

The word ricocheted in my head. I had just been reading about Emily Perez. Your Emily Perez: Second Lieutenant Perez, the first woman of color to become a command sergeant major in the history of the academy, and the first woman graduate to die in Iraq. I had been in Washington when word of her death made the news, and because she had lived there before coming to West Point, the Washington press told us a lot about her. People remembered her as "a little superwoman"—straight As, choir member, charismatic, optimistic, a friend to so many; she had joined the medical service because she wanted to help people. The obituary in *The Washington Post* said she had been a ball of fire at the Peace Baptist Church, where she helped start an HIV/AIDS ministry after some of her own family members contracted the virus. Accounts of her funeral here at West Point reported that some of you wept as you contemplated the loss of so vibrant an officer.

"Minute?" I don't think so. Historical perspective or no. So when I arrived today I asked the academy's historian, Steve Grove, to take me to where Emily Perez is buried, in Section 36 of your cemetery, below Storm King Mountain, overlooking the Hudson River. Standing there, on sacred American soil hallowed all the more by the likes of Lieutenant Perez. I thought that to describe their loss as "minute"—even from a historical perspective—is to underscore the great divide that has opened in America between those who advocate war while avoiding it and those who have the courage to fight it without ever knowing what it's all about.

We were warned of this by our founders. They had put themselves in jeopardy by signing the Declaration of Independence; if they had lost, that parchment could have been their death warrant, for they were traitors to the Crown and likely to be hanged. In the fight for freedom they had put themselves on the line—not just their fortunes and sacred honor but their very persons, their lives. After the war, forming a government and understanding both the nature of war and human nature, they determined to make it hard to go to war except to defend freedom; war for reasons save preserving the lives and liberty of your citizens should be made difficult to achieve, they argued. Here is John Jay's passage in Federalist No. 4:

> It is too true, however disgraceful it may be to human nature, that nations in general will make war whenever they have a prospect of getting anything by it; nay, absolute monarchs will often make war when their nations are to get nothing by it, but for the purposes and objects merely personal, such as thirst for military glory, revenge for personal affronts, ambition, or private compacts to aggrandize or support their particular families or partisans. These and a variety of other motives, which affect only the mind of the sovereign, often lead him to engage in wars not sanctified by justice or the voice and interests of his people.

And here, a few years later, is James Madison, perhaps the most deliberative mind of that generation in assaying the dangers of an unfettered executive prone to war:

> In war, a physical force is to be created; and it is the executive will, which is to direct it. In war, the public treasures are to be unlocked; and it is the executive hand, which is to dispense them. In war, the honours and emoluments of office are to be multiplied; and it is the executive patronage under which they are to be enjoyed. It is in war, finally, that laurels are to be gathered; and it is the executive brow they are to encircle. The strongest passions and most dangerous weaknesses of the human breast; ambition, avarice, vanity, the honourable or venial love of fame, are all in conspiracy against the desire and duty of peace.

I want to be clear on this: Vietnam did not make me a dove. Nor has Iraq; I am no pacifist. But they have made me study the Constitution more rigorously, both as journalist and citizen. Again, James Madison:

> In no part of the Constitution is more wisdom to be found, than in the clause which confides the question of war and peace to the legislature, and not to the executive department. Beside the objection to such a mixture to heterogeneous powers, the trust and the temptation would be too great for any one man . . .

Twice in forty years we have now gone to war paying only lip service to those warnings; the first war we lost, the second is a bloody debacle, and both rank among the great blunders in our history. It is impossible for soldiers to sustain in the field what cannot be justified in the Constitution; asking them to do so puts America at war with itself. So when the vice president of the United States says it doesn't matter what the people think, he and the president intend to prosecute the war anyway, he is committing heresy against the fundamental tenets of the American political order.

This is a tough subject to address when so many of you may be heading for Iraq. I would prefer to speak of sweeter things. But I also know that twenty or thirty years from now any one of you may be the chief of staff or the national security adviser or even the president—after all, two of your boys, Grant and Eisenhower, did make it from West Point to the White House. And that being the case, it's more important than ever that citizens and soldiers—and citizen-soldiers—honestly discuss and frankly consider the kind of country you are serving and the kind of organization to which you are dedicating your lives. You are, after all, the heirs of an army born in the American Revolution, whose radicalism we consistently underestimate.

————

No one understood this radicalism, no one in uniform did more to help us define freedom in a profoundly American way than the man whose monument here at West Point I also visited today—Thadeusz Kosciuszko. I first became intrigued by him more than forty years ago when I arrived in Washington. Lafayette Park, on Pennsylvania Avenue, across from the White House, hosts several statues of military heroes who came to fight for our independence in the American Revolution. For seven years, either looking down on these figures from my office at the Peace Corps or walking across Lafayette Park to my office in the White House, I was reminded of these men who came voluntarily to fight for American independence from the monarchy. The most compelling, for me, was the depiction of Kosciuszko. On one side of the statue he is directing a soldier back to the battlefield, and on the other side, wearing an American uniform, he is freeing a bound soldier, representing America's revolutionaries.

Kosciuszko had been born in the Polish-Lithuanian Commonwealth, where he was trained as an engineer and artillery officer. Arriving in the thirteen colonies in 1776, he broke down in tears when he read the Declaration of Independence. The next year, he helped engineer the Battle of Saratoga, organizing the river and land fortifications that put Americans in the stronger position. George Washington then commissioned him to build the original fortifications for West Point. Since his monument dominates the point here at the academy, this part of the story you must know well.

But what many don't realize about Kosciuszko is the depth of his commitment to republican ideals and human equality. One historian called him "a mystical visionary of human rights." Thomas Jefferson wrote that Kosciuszko was "as pure a son of liberty as I have ever known." That phrase of Jefferson's is often quoted, but if you read the actual letter, Jefferson goes on to say: "And of that liberty which is to go to all, and not to the few and the rich alone."

There is the clue to the meaning of freedom as Thadeusz Kosciuszko saw it.

After the American Revolution, he returned to his homeland, what was then the Polish-Lithuanian Commonwealth. In 1791 the Poles adopted their celebrated May Constitution—Europe's first codified national constitution (and the second oldest in the world, after our own). The May Constitution established political equality between the middle class and the nobility and also partially abolished serfdom by giving civil rights to the peasants, including the right to state protection from landlord abuses. The autocrats and nobles of Russia feared such reforms, and in 1794, when the Russians sought to prevent their spread by partitioning the Commonwealth, Kosciuszko led an insurrection. His untrained peasant forces were armed mostly with single-blade sickles, but they won several early battles in fierce hand-to-hand fighting, until they were finally overwhelmed. Badly injured, Kosciuszko was taken prisoner and held for two years in St. Petersburg, and that was the end of the Polish-Lithuanian Commonwealth, which had stood, by the way, as one of Europe's leading centers of religious liberty.

Upon his release from prison, Kosciuszko came back to the United States and began a lasting friendship with Jefferson, who called him his "most intimate and beloved friend." In 1798, he wrote a will leaving his American estate to Jefferson, urging him to use it to purchase the freedom and education of Jefferson's own slaves, or, as Jefferson interpreted it, of "as many of the children of bondage in this country as it should be adequate to." For this émigré, as for so many who would come later, the meaning of freedom included a passion for universal justice. In his "Act of Insurrection" at the outset of the 1794 uprising, Kosciuszko wrote of the people's "sacred rights to liberty, personal security, and property." Note the term "property" here. For Jefferson's "pursuit of happiness" Kosciuszko substituted Locke's notion of property rights. But it's not what you think: the goal was not simply to protect "private property" from public interference (as it is taught today), but rather to secure *productive* property for all as a right to citizenship. It's easy to forget the difference when huge agglomerations of personal wealth are defended as a sacred right of liberty, as they are today with the gap between the rich and poor in America greater than it's been in almost one hundred years.

Kosciuszko—*General* Kosciuszko, from tip to toe a military man—was talking about investing the people with productive resources. Yes, freedom had to be won on the battlefield, but if freedom did not lead to political, social, and economic opportunity for all citizens, freedom's meaning could not be truly realized.

Think about it: a Polish general from the Old World, infusing the new nation with what would become the marrow of the American dream. Small wonder that Kosciuszko was often called a "hero of two worlds" or that just twenty-five years ago, in 1981, when Polish farmers, supported by the Roman Catholic Church, won the right to form an independent union, sending shock waves across the Communist empire, Kosciuszko's name was heard in the victory speeches—his egalitarian soul present at yet another revolution for human freedom and equal rights.

After Jefferson won the presidency in 1800, Kosciuszko wrote him a touching letter advising him to be true to his principles: "do not forget in your post be always a virtuous Republican with justice and probity, without pomp and ambition—in a word be Jefferson and my friend." Two years later, Jefferson signed into being this professional officers school, on the site first laid out as a fortress by his friend, the general from Poland.

Every turn in American history confronts us with paradox, and this one is no exception. Here was Jefferson, known for his vigorous and eloquent opposition to professional armies, presiding over the establishment of West Point. It's a paradox that you will understand, because you yourselves represent a paradox of liberty. You are free men and women who of your own free choice have joined an institution dedicated to protecting a free nation, but in the process you have voluntarily agreed to give up, for a specific time, a part of your own liberty. An army is not a debating society and neither in the field nor in headquarters does it ask for a show of hands on whether orders should be obeyed. That is undoubtedly a necessary idea, but for you it complicates the already tricky question of "the meaning of freedom."

I said earlier that our founders did not want the power of war to reside in a single man. Many were also dubious about having any kind of regular, or as they called it "standing," army at all. Standing armies were hired supporters of absolute monarchs and imperial tyrants. The men drafting the Constitution were steeped in classical and historical learning. They recalled how Caesar in ancient times and Oliver Cromwell later had used the conquering armies they had led to make themselves dictators. They knew how the Roman legions had made and unmade emperors, and how Ottoman rulers of the Turkish Empire had supported their tyrannies on the shoulders of formidable elite warriors. Wherever they looked in history, they saw an alliance between enemies of freedom in palaces and in officer corps drawn from the ranks of nobility, bound by a warrior code that stressed honor and bravery—but also dedication to the sovereign and the sovereign's god, and distrust amounting to contempt for the ordinary run of the sovereign's subjects.

The colonial experience with British regulars—first as allies in the French and Indian Wars, and then as enemies—did not increase American respect for the old system of military leadership. Officers were chosen and promoted on the basis of aristocratic connections, commissions were bought, and ineptitude was too often tolerated. The lower ranks were often rootless alumni of jails and workhouses, lured or coerced into service by the paltry pay and chance of adventure—brutally hard types, kept in line by brutally harsh discipline.

Not exactly your model for the army of a republic of free citizens.

What the framers came up with was another novelty. The first battles of the Revolution were fought mainly by volunteer militia from the states, such as Vermont's Green Mountain Boys, the most famous militia of the time. They were gung ho for revolution and flushed with a fighting spirit. But in the end they were no substitute for the better-trained regiments of the Continental line and the French regulars sent over by France's king after the alliance of 1778. The view nonetheless persisted that in times of peace, only a small permanent army would be needed to repel invasions—unlikely except from Canada—and deal with the frontier Indians. When and if a real crisis came, it was believed, volunteers would flock to the colors like the armed men of Greek mythology who sprang from dragon's teeth planted in the ground by a divinely approved hero. The real safety of the nation in any hour of crisis would rest with men who spent most of their working lives behind the plow or in the workshop. And this was long before the huge conscript armies of the nineteenth and twentieth centuries made that a commonplace fact.

Who would be in the top command of both that regular force and of volunteer forces when actually called into federal service? None other than the top elected *civil* official of the government, the president. Think about that for a moment. The professional army fought hard and long to create a system of selecting and keeping officers on the basis of proven competence, not popularity. But the highest commander of all served strictly at the pleasure of the people and had to submit his contract for renewal every four years.

And what of the need for trained and expert leadership at all the levels of command which quickly became apparent as the tools and tactics of warfare grew more sophisticated in a modernizing world? That's where West Point came in, filling a need that could no longer be ignored. But what a special military academy it was! We tend to forget that the West Point curriculum was heavily tilted toward engineering; in fact, it was one of the nation's first engineering colleges and was publicly supported and free. That's what made it attractive to young men like Hiram Ulysses Grant, familiarly known as "Sam," who wasn't anxious to be a soldier but wanted to get somewhere more promising than his father's Ohio farm. Hundreds like Grant came to West Point and left to use their civil engineering skills in a country badly needing them, some in civil life after serving out an enlistment but many right there in uniform. It was the army that explored, mapped, and surveyed the wagon and railroad routes to the west, starting with the Corps of Exploration under Lewis and Clark sent out by the protean Mr. Jefferson. It was the army that had a hand in clearing rivers of snags and brush and building dams that allowed steamboats to avoid rapids. It was the army that put up lighthouses in the harbors and whose exhaustive geologic and topographic surveys were important contributions to publicly supported scientific research—*and* to economic development—in the young republic.

All of this would surely have pleased General Kosciuszko, who believed in a society of broad equality. Indeed, add all these facts together and what you come up with is a portrait of something new under the sun—a *peacetime* army working directly with and for the civil society in improving the nation so as to guarantee the greater opportunities for individual success inherent in the promise of democracy. And a *wartime* army in which temporary citizen-soldiers were and still are led by long-term professional citizen-soldiers who were molded out of the same clay as those they command. And all of them led from the top by the one political figure chosen by the entire national electorate. This arrangement—this bargain between the men with the guns and the citizens who provide the guns—is the heritage passed on to you by the revolutionaries who fought and won America's independence and then swore fidelity to a civil compact that survives today, despite tumultuous moments and perilous passages.

Once again we encounter a paradox: not all our wars were on the side of freedom. The first that seriously engaged the alumni of West Point was the Mexican War, which was not a war to protect our freedoms but to grab land—facts are facts—and was not only bitterly criticized by part of the civilian population but even looked on with skepticism by some graduates like Grant himself. Still, he not only fought well in it but it was for him, as well as for most of the generals on both sides in the impending Civil War, an unequaled training school and rehearsal stage.

When the Civil War came, it offered an illustration of how the meaning of freedom isn't always easy to pin down. From the point of view of the North, the hundreds of Southern West Pointers who resigned to fight for the Confederacy—Robert E. Lee included—were turning against the people's government that had educated and supported them. They were traitors. But from the Southern point of view, they were fighting for the freedom of their local governments to leave the Union when, as they saw it, it threatened their way of life. Their way of life tragically included the right to hold other men in slavery.

The Civil War, nonetheless, confirmed the importance of West Point training. European military observers were amazed at the skill with which the better generals on both sides, meaning for the most part West Pointers and not political appointees, maneuvered huge armies of men over vast areas of difficult terrain, used modern technologies like the railroad and the telegraph to coordinate movements and accumulate supplies, and made the best use of newly developed weapons. The North had more of these advantages, and when the final victory came, adulation and admiration were showered on Grant and Sherman, who had come to a realistic and unromantic understanding of modern war, precisely because they had not been steeped in the mythologies of a warrior caste. Their triumph was seen as vindication of how well the army of a democracy could work. Just as Lincoln, the self-educated rail-splitter, had provided a civilian leadership that also proved him the equal of any potentate on the globe.

After 1865 the army shrank as its chief engagement was now in wiping out the last vestiges of Indian resistance to their dispossession and subjugation: one people's advance became another's annihilation and one of the most shameful episodes of our history. In 1898 the army was briefly used for the first effort in exporting democracy—an idea that does not travel well in military transports—when it warred with Spain to help the Cubans complete a war for independence that had been in progress for three years. The Cubans found their liberation somewhat illusory, however, when the United States made the island a virtual protectorate and allowed it to be ruled by a corrupt dictator.

Americans also lifted the yoke of Spain from the Filipinos, only to learn that they did not want to exchange it for one stamped MADE IN THE

USA. It took a three-year war, during which the army killed several thousand so-called insurgents, before their leader was captured and the Filipinos were cured of the illusion that independence meant . . . well, independence. I bring up these reminders not to defame the troops. Their actions were supported by a majority of the American people even in a progressive phase of our political history (though there was some principled and stiff opposition). Nonetheless, we have to remind ourselves that the armed forces can't be expected to be morally much better than the people who send them into action, and that when honorable behavior comes into conflict with racism, honor is usually the loser unless people such as yourself fight to maintain it.

Our brief participation in the First World War temporarily expanded the army, helped by a draft that had also proven necessary in the Civil War. But rapid demobilization was followed by a long period of ever-shrinking military budgets, especially for the land forces.

Not until World War II did the army again take part in such a long, bloody, and fateful conflict as the Civil War had been, and like the Civil War it opened an entirely new period in American history. The incredibly gigantic mobilization of the entire nation, the victory it produced, and the ensuing sixty years of wars, quasi-wars, mini-wars, secret wars, and a virtually permanent crisis created a superpower and forever changed the nation's relationship to its armed forces, confronting us with problems we have to address, no matter how unsettling it may be to do so in the midst of yet another war.

The armed services are no longer stepchildren in budgetary terms. Appropriations for defense and defense-related activities (like veterans' care, pensions, and debt service) remind us that the costs of war continue long after the fighting ends. Objections to ever-swelling defensive expenditures are, except in rare cases, a greased slide to political suicide. It should be troublesome to you as professional soldiers that elevation to the pantheon of untouchable icons—right there alongside motherhood, apple pie, and the flag—permits a great deal of political lip service to replace genuine efforts to improve the lives and working conditions, in combat and out, of those who serve.

Let me cut closer to the bone. The cheerleaders for war in Washington, who at this very moment are busily defending you against supposed "insults" or betrayals by the opponents of the war in Iraq, are likewise those who have cut budgets for medical and psychiatric care; who have been so skimpy and late with pay and with provision of necessities that military families in the United States have had to apply for food stamps; who sent the men and women whom you may soon be commanding into Iraq understrength, under-equipped, and unprepared for dealing with a kind of war fought in streets and homes full of civilians against enemies undistinguishable from noncombatants; who have time and again broken promises to the civilian National Guardsmen bearing much of the burden by canceling their redeployment orders and extending their tours.

You may or may not agree on the justice and necessity of the war itself, but I hope that you will agree that flattery and adulation are no substitute for genuine support.

Much of the money that could be directed to that support has gone into high-tech weapons systems that were supposed to produce a new, mobile, compact "professional" army that could easily defeat the armies of any other two nations combined, but is useless in a war against nationalist or religious guerrilla uprisings that, like it or not, have some support, coerced or otherwise, among the local population. We learned this lesson in Vietnam, only to see it forgotten or ignored by the time this administration invaded Iraq, creating the conditions for a savage sectarian and civil war with our soldiers trapped in the middle, unable to discern civilian from combatant, where it is impossible to kill your enemy faster than rage makes new ones.

And who has been the real beneficiary of creating this high-tech army called to fight a war conceived and commissioned and cheered on by politicians and pundits not one of whom ever entered a combat zone? One of your boys answered that: Dwight Eisenhower, class of 1915, who told us that the real winners of the anything-at-any-price philosophy would be the "military-industrial complex."

I contend that the American military systems that evolved in the early days of this republic rested on a bargain between the civilian authorities and the armed services, and that the army has, for the most part, kept its part of the bargain and that, at this moment, the civilian authorities whom you loyally obey are shirking theirs. And before you assume that I am calling for an insurrection against the civilian deciders of your destinies, hear me out, for that is the last thing on my mind.

You have kept your end of the bargain by fighting well when called upon, by refusing to become a praetorian guard for a reigning administration at any time, and by respecting civil control at all times. For the most part, our military leaders have made no serious efforts to meddle in politics. The two most notable cases were General George McClellan, who endorsed a pro-Southern and pro-slavery policy in the first year of the Civil War and was openly contemptuous of Lincoln. But Lincoln fired him in 1862, and when McClellan ran for president two years later, the voting public handed him his hat. Douglas MacArthur's attempt to dictate his own China policy in 1951 ran head-on into the resolve of Harry Truman, who, surviving a firestorm of hostility, happily watched a MacArthur boomlet for the Republican nomination for the presidency fizzle out in 1952.

On the other side of the ledger, however, the bargain has not been kept. The last time Congress declared war was in 1941. Since then presidents of the United States, including the one I served, have gotten Congress, occasionally under demonstrably false pretenses, to suspend constitutional provisions that required them to get the consent of the people's representatives in order to conduct a war. They were handed a blank check to send the armed forces into action at their personal discretion and on dubious constitutional grounds.

Furthermore, the current president has made extra-constitutional claims of authority by repeatedly acting as if he were commander in chief of the entire nation and not merely of the armed forces. Most dangerously to our moral honor and to your own welfare in the event of capture, he has likewise ordered the armed forces to violate clear mandates of the Uniform Code of Military Justice and the Geneva conventions by claiming a right to interpret them at his pleasure, so as to allow indefinite and secret detentions and torture. These claims contravene a basic principle usually made clear to recruits from their first day in service—that they may not obey an unlawful order. The president is attempting to have them violate that longstanding rule by personal definitions of what the law says and means.

There is yet another way the armchair warriors are failing you. In the October issue of the magazine of the California Nurses Association, you can read a long report entitled "The Battle at Home." In veterans' hospitals across the country—and in a growing number of ill-prepared, underfunded psych and primary-care clinics as well—the report says that nurses "have witnessed the guilt, rage, emotional numbness, and tormented flashbacks of GIs just back from Iraq." Yet "a returning vet must wait an average of 165 days for a VA decision on initial disability benefits," and an appeal can take up to three years. Just in the first quarter of this year, the VA treated 20,638 Iraq veterans for post-traumatic stress disorder, and faces a backlog of 400,000 cases. This is reprehensible.

I repeat: these are not palatable topics for soldiers about to go to war; I would like to speak of sweeter things. But freedom means we must face reality: "You shall know the truth and the truth shall set you free." Free enough, surely, to think for yourselves about these breaches of contract that crudely undercut the traditions of an army of free men and women who have bound themselves voluntarily to serve the nation even unto death.

What, then, can you do about it if disobedience to the chain of command is ruled out?

For one, you didn't give up your freedom to vote nor did you totally quit your membership in civil society when you put on the uniform, even though, as Eisenhower said, you did accept "certain inhibitions" at the time. He said that when questioned about MacArthur's dismissal, and he made sure his own uniform was back in the trunk before his campaign in 1952. It has been most encouraging, by the way, to see veterans of Iraq on the campaign trail in our recent elections.

Second, remember that there are limitations to what military power can do. Despite the valor and skills of our fighting forces, some objectives are not obtainable at a human, diplomatic, and financial cost that is acceptable. Our casualties in Iraq are not "minute" and the cost of the war has been projected by some sources to reach $2 trillion dollars. Sometimes, in the real world, a truce is the most honorable solution to conflict. Dwight Eisenhower—who is a candidate for my favorite West Point graduate of the twentieth century—knew that when, in 1953, he went to Korea and accepted a stalemate rather than carrying out his bluff of using nuclear weapons. That was the best that could be done and it saved more years of stalemate and casualties. Douglas MacArthur announced in 1951 that "there was no substitute for victory." But in the wars of the twenty-first century there are alternative meanings to victory and alternative ways to achieve them. Especially in tracking down and eliminating terrorists, we need to change our metaphor from a "war on terror"—exactly what, pray tell, is that?—to the mind-set of Interpol tracking down master criminals through intense global cooperation among nations, or the FBI stalking the Mafia, or local police determined to quell street gangs without leveling the entire neighborhood in the process. Help us to think beyond a "war on terror"—which politicians could wage without end, with no measurable way to judge its effectiveness, against stateless enemies who hope we will destroy the neighborhood, creating recruits for their side—to counterterrorism modeled on extraordinary police work.

Third, don't let your natural and commendable loyalty to comrades-in-arms lead you into thinking that criticism of the mission you are on spells lack of patriotism. Not every politician who flatters you is your ally. Not everyone who believes that war is the wrong choice to some problems is your enemy. Blind faith in bad leadership is not patriotism. In the words of G. K. Chesterton: "To say my country right or wrong is something no patriot would utter except in dire circumstance; it is like saying my mother drunk or sober." Patriotism means insisting on our political leaders being sober, strong, and certain about what they are doing when they put you in harm's way.

Fourth, be more prepared to accept the credibility and integrity of those who disagree about the war even if you do not agree with their positions. I say this as a journalist, knowing it is tempting in the field to denounce or despise reporters who ask nosy questions or file critical reports. But their first duty as reporters is to get as close as possible to the verifiable truth and report it to the American people—for your sake. If there is mismanagement and incompetence, exposing it is more helpful to you than paeans to candy given to the locals. I trust you are familiar with the study done for the army in 1989 by the historian William Hammond. He examined press coverage on Korea and Vietnam and found that it was not the cause of disaffection at home; what disturbed people at home was the death toll; when casualties jumped, public support dropped. Over time, he said, the reporting was vindicated. In fact, "the press reports were often more accurate than the public statements of the administration in portraying the situation in Vietnam." Take note: the American people want the truth about how their sons and daughters are doing in Iraq and what they're up against, and that is a good thing.

Finally, and this above all—a lesson I wish I had learned earlier. If you rise in the ranks to important positions—or even if you don't—speak the truth as you see it, even if the questioner is a higher authority with a clear preference for one and only one answer. It may not be the way to promote your career; it can in fact harm it. Among my military heroes of this war are the generals who frankly told the president and his advisers that their information and their plans were both incomplete and misleading—and who paid the price of being ignored and bypassed and possibly frozen forever in their existing ranks: men like General Eric K. Shinseki, another son of West Point. It is not easy to be honest—and fair—in a bureaucratic system. But it is what free men and women have to do. *Be true to your principles*, General Kosciuszko reminded Thomas

Jefferson. If doing so exposes the ignorance and arrogance of power, you may be doing more to save the nation than exploits in combat can achieve.

I know the final rule of the military Code of Conduct is already written in your hearts: "I am an American, fighting for freedom, responsible for my actions, and dedicated to the principles which made my country free . . ." The meaning of freedom begins with the still, small voice of conscience, when each of us decides what we will live, or die, for.

I salute your dedication to America and I wish all of you good luck.

7. | THE POWER OF DEMOCRACY

*Woodrow Wilson National Fellowship Foundation Presented
Judith and Bill Moyers with the First Frank E. Taplin Jr.
Public Intellectual Award*

FEBRUARY 7, 2007

*Arthur Levine was on the phone. The former president of Teachers College at
Columbia University now heads the Woodrow Wilson National Fellowship
Foundation named in honor of the political scientist who became our twenty-
eighth president. The foundation's mission is to encourage excellence in teaching, citizenship, and educational innovation. Arthur was calling to say his
colleagues wanted to present Judith—my wife of more than half a century and
my creative partner in all our productions—and me the first ever Frank E.
Taplin Jr. Public Intellectual Award for using television "to bridge formal
learning and the broader public sphere." Although we had never met Taplin,
he had been a figure familiar for his leadership in the arts, environment, and
education; his imprimatur alone was reason enough to be flattered by Arthur's
invitation. But there was another reason: Woodrow Wilson. I had just finished reading two biographies of him for a PBS series about America's progres-*

sive traditions, and I had come to think it was time for a fresh look at his legacy. One moment Wilson was "the supreme figure in world history," as The New York Times said at the time, and the next he was "the embittered hermit of the White House," brought down "on the altar of his own obstinacy" by his inability to "sacrifice one iota of a noble theory for its practical consummation." That of course is the recurring dilemma of democratic politics: how to translate Big Ideas into practical policies. Wilson is our only president to have earned a PhD, and before he was thrust into politics he was a noted scholar, a popular teacher, and, as president of Princeton University, an education reformer. Critics said his mind was clogged with "too much thinking to have common thought," and common thought, they said, is the great essential in a leader of democracy. I believe that criticism wrong. In no small part because of his understanding of the dynamics of government and politics, he called "for the emancipation of the generous energies of a people"—the subtitle of a stirring compilation of his speeches in the campaign of 1912 published as The New Freedom. When in doubt about democracy, I pull the book from my shelf to be reminded of one man's faith in liberty as "a fundamental demand of the human spirit, a fundamental necessity for the life of the soul." His diagnosis of the deepening crisis in democracy's struggle to check and balance the ravenous demands of industrial capitalism proved prophetic:

> We have come upon an age when we do not do business in the way in which we used to do business,—when we do not carry on any of the operations of manufacturing, sales, transportation, or communication as men used to carry them on. There is a sense in which in our day the individual has been submerged. In most parts of our country men work, not for themselves, not as partners in the old way in which they used to work, but generally as employees,—in a higher or lower grade,—of great corporations. There was a time when corporations played a very minor part in our business affairs, but now they play the chief part, and most men are the servants of corporations.
>
> You know what happens when you are the servant of a corporation. You have no instant access to the men who are really determining the policy of the corporation. If the corporation is doing the things that it ought not to do, you really have no voice in the matter and must obey the orders, and you have oftentimes with deep mortification to cooperate in the doing of things which you know are against the public interest. Your individuality is swallowed up in the individuality and purpose of a great organization.

America, he said, had "lifted to the admiration of the world its ideals of absolutely free opportunity . . . where there is supposed to be no distinction of class, no distinction of blood, no distinction of social status, but where men may win or lose on their merits." Now, said Wilson, America was changing "because the laws of this country do not prevent the strong from crushing the weak." After Arthur Levine called, I took The New Freedom from the shelf and read those words again. Almost a century later, with our two political parties both in thrall to huge corporate and financial conglomerates, and two family dynasties dominating those parties, Wilson's words are more urgent than ever.

* * *

Judith and I thank you for recognizing that our work, like our lives, has been a shared project. We have been fortunate to make this journey together and to have made so many friends like you on the way.

I wish we had known Frank Taplin. He was clearly a kindred spirit whose life expressed so many of the passions that have informed our journalism.

As a friend of the environment he inspired people to see the art in an unspoiled mountain meadow or to hear the music in its songbirds. As a trustee of the Environmental Defense Fund he devoted himself to educating the public about global warming—a prophet before his time.

As a supporter of the Third Street Music Settlement he saw it as "a giant sprinkler watering the soils of raw talent and enabling seeds to sprout into blossoms of many varieties, shapes, and colors." As a trustee of Sarah Lawrence he helped preserve the creative environment that had made the college so hospitable to remarkable teachers like Joseph Campbell. As a patron of the arts—including the presidency of the Metropolitan Opera—he found love and joy in music and good company.

Here was a man at home in the world of ideas which Judith and I have made a primary beat as journalists and producers. No honor given us has been more compatible with the life of its benefactor, and we are grateful to you for making the connection.

We are often asked why as journalists we have given so much time over the years to humanists: novelists, playwrights, artists, historians, philosophers, composers, scholars, teachers. I tried to answer this question some years ago when I was invited to testify before a House of Representatives committee on funding of the arts and humanities. Opponents were making their skepticism felt toward the Public Broadcasting Service, the National Endowment for the Arts, and the National Endowment for the Humanities. I had been present at the creation of all three during my time in the White House with Lyndon Johnson, and now all three were once again in the crosshairs of conservatives who were asking: Why should we subsidize intellectual curiosity? Reading Shakespeare, it was said, does not erase the budget deficit. Plunging into the history of the fifteenth century does not ease traffic jams. Listening to Mozart or reading the ancient Greeks does not repair the ozone layer.

At the time of my testimony, we had recently produced two series on poetry called *The Language of Life* and *Power of the Word*. Our series *Joseph Campbell and the Power of Myth* was resonating far and wide, much to the displeasure of sectarian dogmatists. We had created a documentary special called *The Power of the Past*, about how Florence valued art for public, and not merely private, consumption. Our series *World of Ideas* offered conversations from a wide spectrum of voices: Chinua Achebe, Carlos Fuentes, Northrop Frye, Joseph Heller, Thomas Wolfe, Richard Rodriguez, Bharati Mukherjee, Jonas Salk, William L. Shirer, Tu Wei-ming, Toni Morrison, Barbara Tuchman, Ernesto Cortes, M. F. K. Fisher, Mary Ann Glendon, E. L. Doctorow, Leon Kass, and so many others who opened our viewers to what my late friend and colleague Eric Sevareid called "news of the mind."

We had taken note of David Denby's lament in *The Atlantic Monthly* that "Americans have ceased talking to one another. Instead, they entertain one another, and do so in all sorts of places where entertainment is beside the point or corrupting. Under the tyranny of affability and simplicity, public discourse—in politics, religion, and education—has collapsed into smiling drivel." We were also influenced by the educator Herbert Kohl, who wrote:

If we do not provide time for the consideration of people and events in depth, we may end up training another generation of television adults who know what kind of toilet paper to buy, who know how to argue and humiliate others, but who are thoroughly incapable of discussing, much less dealing with, the major social and economic problems that are tearing America apart.

Critics reminded us that these programs taught no one how to bake bread or build bridges. And they were right: despite public television—despite symphony orchestras, municipal libraries, art museums, and public theaters—crime was still rampant, the divorce rate was soaring, corruption flourished in politics, legislatures remained stubbornly profligate, corporations cooked their books, liberals were loose in the world doing the work of the devil, and you still couldn't get a good meal on the Metro to Washington. Why persist, some members of Congress wanted to know, when there are so many more urgent needs to be met, so many more practical problems to be solved?

Not that we hadn't wrestled with these questions ourselves. Judith knows of the angst I experience in choosing between producing a series on faith and reason, as we did last summer, and taking on an investigative documentary on mountaintop mining, skulduggery in the boardroom, or the manipulation of intelligence to justify a war. Life is short and funding scarce, and how to commit one's time and resources is a dilemma not for journalists and producers alone but for anyone struggling to make the best choice when two roads diverge in the yellow wood.

So I went down to Washington without a tried-and-true answer for the representatives. I could not hand them a ledger showing that ideas have consequences. I chose instead to tell them what they could have learned if they had been listening to just a few of the people who appeared in our broadcasts.

They would have heard the novelist Maxine Hong Kingston say: "All human beings have this burden in life to constantly figure out what's true, what's authentic, what's meaningful, what's dross, what's a hallucination, what's a figment, what's madness. We all need to figure out what is valuable, constantly. As a writer, all I am doing is posing the question in a way that people can see very clearly."

They would have heard Peter Sellars, the iconoclastic director of Shakespeare in a swimming pool and Mozart in the Bronx, explain that he wants "to put our society up next to these great masterpieces. Are we thinking big enough? Are we generous of spirit? What does our society look like, next to the greatest things a human being ever uttered?"

They would have heard Vartan Gregorian, president of the New York Public Library, talk about how "in a big library, suddenly you feel humble. The whole of humanity is in front of you. It gives you a sense of cosmic relation, but at the same time a sense of isolation. You feel both pride and insignificance. Here it is the human endeavor, human aspiration, human agony, human ecstasy, human bravura, and human failures—all before you. And you look around and say, 'Oh, my God! I am not going to be able to know it all.'"

They would have heard the philosopher Martha Nussbaum confess that in one sense there is no message or moral in the ancient Greek dramatists—"simply the revelation of life as seen through the sufferer." But there is a value, she went on, "in seeing the complexity in life, and seeing it honestly, without flinching, and without reducing it to some excessively simple theory." You begin "to realize that trying to wrest a good life from the world may lead to tragedy, but you still must try."

They would have heard the filmmaker David Puttnam tell how as a boy he sat through dozens of screenings of *A Man for All Seasons*, the story of Sir Thomas More's fatal defiance of Henry VIII. "It allowed me the enormous conceit of walking out of the cinema thinking, 'Yeah, I think I might have had my head cut off for the sake of a principle.' I know absolutely I wouldn't, and I probably never met anyone who would, but the cinema allowed me that conceit. It allowed me for one moment to feel that everything decent in me had come together."

And they would have heard the educator Mike Rose talk about what it's like teaching disadvantaged older college students in California. He told me of his battle with a streetwise grown-up who was slogging her way through *Macbeth*. She would ask him, "What does Shakespeare have to do with me?" But when she finally got through the play she said to Mike: "You know, people always hold this stuff over you. They make you feel stupid. But now, I've read it. I can say, 'I, Olga, have read Shakespeare.' I won't tell you I like it, because I don't know if I do, or I don't. But I like knowing what it's about." And Mike said: "The point is not that reading Shakespeare gave her overnight some new discriminating vision of good and evil. What she got was something more precious: a sense that she was not powerless and she was not dumb."

I am pleased to report that those members of Congress got it. They realized that we were talking not only about how to improve our lives as individuals but how to nurture a flourishing democracy. Wouldn't we have been likely to deal more effectively and quickly with pollution if we had thought about where we fit into the long sweep of the earth's story? Could we better tackle our spending priorities as a society if we were prepared to acknowledge and confront the pain of conflicting choices, which the ancient poets knew to be the incubus of agony and the crucible of wisdom? Might we better decide how to use our wealth and power if we have measured and tested ourselves against the greatest things a human being ever uttered? Are we not likely to be more wisely led by officials who have learned from history and literature that great nations die of too many lies?

Furthermore, if we nurtured the higher affections of our intuition— what has been called our "inner tutor"—might we be more resolute in sparing our children from the appalling accretion of violent entertainment that permeates American life, what *Newsweek* has described as "the flood of mass-produced and mass-consumed violence that pours upon us, masquerading as amusement and threatening to erode the psychological and moral boundary between real life and make-believe"?

Among the enemies of democracy are what the late Cleanth Brooks identified as the "bastard muses": propaganda, which pleads, sometimes unscrupulously, for a special cause or issue at the expense of the total truth; sentimentality, which works up emotional responses unwarranted by, and in excess of, the occasion; and pornography, which focuses upon one powerful human drive at the expense of the total human personality. To counter the "bastard muses," Cleanth Brooks proposed cultivating the "true muses" of the moral imagination. Not only do these arm us to resist the little lies and fantasies of merchandising, the big lies of power, and the ghoulish products of nightmarish minds, they open us to the lived experience of others. When Lear cried out to Gloucester on the heath, "You see how this world goes," Gloucester, who was blind, answered, "I see it feelingly."

Many years ago we produced a series called *Six Great Ideas* with the didactic, irascible, and provocative philosopher Mortimer Adler—one broadcast each on liberty, equality, justice, truth, beauty, and goodness. From the deluge of mail I kept two letters that summed up the response. One came from Utah.

> Dear Dr. Adler:
>
> I am writing in behalf of a group of construction workers (mostly, believe it or not, plumbers!) who have finally found a teacher worth listening to. While we cannot all agree whether or not we would hire you as an apprentice, we can all agree that we would love to listen to you during our lunch breaks. I am sure that it is just due to our well-known ignorance as tradesmen that not a single one of us had ever heard of you until one Sunday afternoon we were watching public television and Bill Moyers came on with Six Great Ideas. We listened intensely and soon became addicted and have been ever since. We never knew a world of ideas existed. The study of ideas has completely turned around our impression of education . . . We have grown to love the ideas behind our country's composition, and since reading and discussing numerous of your books we have all become devout Constitutionalists. We thank you and we applaud you. We are certain that the praise of a few plumbers could hardly compare with the notoriety that you deserve from distinguished colleagues, but we salute you just the same. We may be plumbers during the day, but at lunch time and at night and on weekend, we are Philosophers at Large. God bless you.

The second letter came from the federal prison in Marion, Ohio. The writer said he had been a faithful viewer of the series. He described the experience as "a truly joyous opportunity . . . for an institutionalized intellectual. After several months in a cell, with nothing but a TV, it was salvation."

Salvation. I had to think about this for a while before I realized what he meant. How is it a man condemned to an institution for the remainder of his years finds salvation in a television program? And then one day I came across a passage from Leo Strauss. The Greek word for "vulgarity," Strauss said, is *apeirokalia,* the lack of experience in things beautiful. Wherever you are and however it arrives, a liberal education can liberate you from the coarseness and crudity of circumstances beyond your control. Even in prison.

Watching and listening to our public discourse today, I realize we are all "institutionalized" in one form or another—locked away in our separate realities, our parochial loyalties, our fixed ways of seeing ourselves and others. For democracy to flourish, we need to escape those bonds and join what John Dewey called "a life of free and enriching communion"—an apt description of the conversation of democracy.

Once upon a time the very concept of "public" could be defined as "a group of strangers who gather to discuss the news." The late scholar James W. Carey wrote that in early America the printing press generated a body of popular knowledge. Towns were small, and taverns, inns, coffeehouses, street corners, and the public greens were places where people gathered to discuss what they were reading. These places of public communication "provided the underlying social fabric of the town and, when the Revolution began, made it possible to quickly gather militia companies, to form effective committees of correspondence and of inspection, and to organize and to manage mass town meetings."

The public was no fiction, Carey said. But without news, the public had no life, no social relationships. The news was what activated conversation between strangers, and strangers were assumed to be capable of conversing about the news. The whole point of the press was not so much to disseminate fact as to assemble people. The press furnished materials for argument—"information" in the narrow sense—"but the value of the press was predicated on the existence of the public, not the reverse." The media's role was to take the public seriously.

It is hard to argue that the mass media takes the public seriously today—except as consumers of advertising. The Internet may prove redemptive for democracy, but so far the results are mixed; but for sure radio and television have combined to transform the public into what J. R. Priestly described as "a vast crowd, a permanent audience, waiting to be amused."

What kind of "public intellectual" thrives in this environment? Turn on the television and you're likely to see one talking about the war in Iraq, which he has cheered on despite having never been there, been shot at, or even worn a uniform. Notice where he sits—in a Times Square studio or on a media stage in Washington, his enthusiasm-for-battle (as long as someone else is fighting it) message beamed uncritically to millions by huge media conglomerates intent on maximizing profit through the delivery to advertisers of mass audiences with short attention spans.

Poor Socrates. The Athenian maverick would be lost in this environment. Arguably the first public intellectual—proclaimed by the oracle of Delphi as the wisest of men—Socrates went about Athens on a divine mandate of self-reflection, some celestial spark glowing in his breast, some voice whispering in his head that only he could hear. He called on the wise men and great poets and master technicians of the city to cross-examine them, casting doubt on their knowledge, especially the received opinions and unexamined assumptions that produced the deep-seated corruption of thought which exposed the city to grave moral danger. He made a nuisance of himself by simply pointing to the common failing of so many experts who mistake their expertise in one subject or practice for universal wisdom about the human condition.

Exposing the ignorance of the leaders was Socrates' way of helping the "cause of God," as he explained when he was put on trial. As he reasoned, the wisest of men is the one who is most conscious of his own ignorance, most aware of the limits of knowledge which are introduced by our limited methods of obtaining knowledge. Meletus, the main accuser featured in the *Apology* (as told by Plato), was a young religious fanatic who charged Socrates with believing in deities of his own invention rather than the gods recognized by the state. Some scholars now believe Meletus to have been simply a front man for political interests, put forward to stir the public against the philosopher—a forerunner of modern punditry.

I think sadly of Colin Powell addressing the United Nations in February 2003, with his artist's renderings of those trailers that were supposed to be mobile biological warfare factories; and I think of all the rest of the cooked intelligence that sold so many of our public intellectuals on advocating the invasion of Iraq. Relying on the knowledge of self-interested experts and deluded leaders proved disastrous. When his peers sentenced Socrates to death, he reminded them that they were proving how groundless knowledge made it impossible to escape from doing wrong. Succumbing to wishful thinking that leads to disastrous self-delusion, he pointed out, is the only real death. "When I leave this court," he said of his jurors, "I will go away condemned by you to death." But his accusers "will go away convicted by truth herself . . ." Not so today. A stockbroker who makes bad picks doesn't last too long. A baseball player in an extended slump gets traded. A worker made redundant by cheaper labor abroad or by a new machine—she's done for, too. But four years after the invasion of Iraq—the greatest blunder in foreign policy since Vietnam—the public apologists and advocates of the war flourish in the media, while the costs of their delusions accrue in body counts and lost treasure. A public that detests the war is relegated to the bleachers, fated to watch from afar the playing out by political and media elites of a game that has been rigged against the truth.

The Hebrew prophet was another kind of public intellectual, also condemned and persecuted by political elites. A century before Socrates, one of those prophets—Jeremiah—came from a small village into Jerusalem to preach repentance to a faithless Israel, with its houses full of treachery, and its rich kings and princes who gave no justice to the poor widow and the fatherless child.

Near the end of his own life, Jesus of Nazareth went to Jerusalem, too, to preach the same message in an even more dangerous public way, confronting the ruling elites before great crowds on the Temple grounds. When he predicted their imminent destruction, in his parable about the wicked tenants who hoarded the fruits of creation, his fate was sealed.

Jesus would not be crucified today. The prophets would not be stoned. Socrates would not drink the hemlock. They would instead be banned from the Sunday talk shows and op-ed pages by the sentries of establishment thinking who guard against dissent with the one weapon of mass destruction most cleverly designed to obliterate democracy: the rubber stamp.

Yet democracy requires a public aroused by the knowledge of what is being done to their country in their name. And here is the crisis of the times as I see it: We talk about problems, issues, policies, but we don't talk about what democracy means—what it bestows on us—the revolutionary idea that it isn't just about the means of governance but the means of dignifying people so they become fully free to claim their moral and political agency. "I believe in Democracy because it releases the energies of every human being." These are the words of Woodrow Wilson, the namesake of your foundation and still your guiding spirit.

The only PhD ever to reach the White House was a public intellectual and genuine reformer who understood that higher education was a major battleground of ideas. He learned what the political struggle was about while a professor and later the president of Princeton, where he lost his share of institutional battles with wealthy alumni who largely controlled the university's development and the nation beyond.

In his political testament *The New Freedom*, Wilson took up something of the ancient, critical task of the public intellectual, a fact all the more remarkable in that he had recently been elected president of the United States. "Don't deceive yourselves for a moment as to the power of the great interests which now dominate our development," he wrote from the center of power. "No matter that there are men in this country big enough to own the government of the United States. They are going to own it if they can. [But] there is no salvation in the pitiful condescensions of industrial masters. Guardians have no place in a land of freemen. Prosperity guaranteed by trustees has no prospect of endurance." From his stand came progressive income taxation, the federal estate tax, tariff reform, and a resolute spirit "to deal with the new and subtle tyrannies according to their deserts."

Wilson described his vision in plain English that no one could fail to understand: "The laws of this country do not prevent the strong from crushing the weak." And those laws must be resisted, as they could be only through releasing the energies of every citizen. That was true in 1800, 1860, 1892, 1912, and 1932, and it is true today, as money holds our politics in a hammerlock, accelerating our divisions of race, class, and power, and frustrating the egalitarian spirit of the American Revolution. Never has it been more imperative to remember that every time we have been pressed to the limit and those energies were released, there came a great wave of reform. I believe one is coming again.

Toward the end of her career, Helen Keller was speaking at a small midwestern college. A student asked her, "Miss Keller, is there anything that could have been worse than losing your sight?" Helen Keller replied, "Yes, I could have lost my vision."

The American vision of life, liberty, and the pursuit of happiness, nurtured in a framework of government of, by, and for the people, has not been lost. What we must determine now, in the words of Woodrow Wilson, your namesake, "is whether we are big enough . . . whether we are free enough, to take possession again of the government which is our own."

8. | HELP

*American Association of Collegiate Registrars
and Admissions Officers*

MARCH 3, 2007

Walking into the library at the University of Texas my first week on campus more than half a century ago, I was overwhelmed at what was there for the asking—stacks upon stacks of books—everything in place because of the labors and generosity of legions of people whom I would never know. Ever since, my heroes have been people who make institutions work for others— especially for poor kids like me who would never have made it by ourselves. The term "future generations" passes our lips so often and so easily it has become a cliché. But it wasn't a cliché for the men who intended our Constitution to "secure the Blessings of Liberty to ourselves and our Posterity." Philosophers debate "the moral status of future persons"—just how much claim they have upon us, how can we have duties to nonexistent beings whom we will never know as individuals, how do we even tell with any confidence just what might benefit "them." Fortunately for me, these abstractions did not deter the framers of the Constitution or the president of the new Repub-

lic of Texas, Mirabeau B. Lamar, who went on a buffalo hunt to the small town of Waterloo on the Colorado River in Central Texas and liked what he saw so much that he moved the capital there in 1839, renamed it Austin, and preached so eloquently the virtues of public education that he became "the father of Texas education." In 1881 Austin became the site of the new university that I would one day attend for tuition fees of $40 a semester. The low-cost but first-class education that I received there was a life-changing gift to me from state legislators, faculty, administrators, maintenance crews, and taxpayers whom I would never know but can never forget. As the cost of a college education today soars beyond the reach of working families like mine in the mid-1950s, I think of a fellow named Dave, whom I met by chance the evening I traveled to Boston to speak to the gatekeepers of higher education. Who is thinking about the Daves of our future?

* * *

When I accepted your invitation to speak I promised your officers and staff that I wouldn't talk about the issues you wrestle with every day on your jobs. You know far more about those subjects than I do. With that promise I ruled out topics such as whether national testing can be done on computers and trusted, and the tug-of-war between those of you who would like to see the tests more oriented to the classroom and those who believe they should assess "aptitude." My promise meant I didn't have to raise with you what the "wasted year" of high-school seniors means for the freshman year at college. Or how state funding growth for higher education is the lowest in two decades, or how tuition at public universities is up 42 percent over five years, resulting in the silent privatization of those institutions as the costs are passed on to parents and students. Or such unpleasant realities as the fact that in 1993 one-third of your students graduated with debt, and in 2004 two-thirds did; or the fact that the total volume of private student loans has grown at an average rate of 27 percent since 2001. Or that private loans now carry interest rates as high as 19 percent even as banks have mobilized against direct lending by the government that is far cheaper and could save students money. I even told myself that I wouldn't go near the scandal waiting to break in how universities are being offered kickbacks by organizations maneuvering to be their preferred lender on campus.

All of these subjects interest me as a journalist, but I thought you deserved a morning off from business as usual. Why bring to Boston the unpleasant issues you tackle every day on your campuses?

Then I met Dave.

Dave is 100 percent Boston. Born and raised here. And he'll die here if he lives that long.

The car service sent Dave to pick me up late last night at the train station. While driving is his livelihood, his joy clearly comes from meeting so many people from faraway places and talking with them while pointing out the oldest church in Boston or the best place to get a great sandwich at midnight.

Dave asked me, "What are you doing in town?" "I'm making a speech," I said. "Who to?" "To college registrars and admissions officers and people like them who run universities all over the country."

He almost drove through a red light as he turned around and in a voice decibels higher said, "You are? You're really talking to those people?" "I am." Then, turning back to the wheel just in time to miss a truck that had stopped abruptly ahead of us, Dave said, more softly now, "Oh, my God. I wish I was talking to them."

"Why?" I asked.

"I got a kid in college here in Boston—good kid, a junior, but it's killing us."

"How's that?"

"Tuition—thirty grand a year plus, and I'm just a working stiff. We don't have any money, but I was determined he would go to college, like I never did."

"How are you managing?" I asked.

"We sat down and looked at our assets. We got $200,000 in equity in the house we saved for but I told him I couldn't risk the house. So I told him I would open my 401(k) and would pay half his college tuition."

"Where's the other half coming from?"

"Loan—7.9 percent. But he won't have to start paying it back for six months after he gets out next year. I just hope he lands in a job where he can pay it back."

"So how are you going to make up in your 401(k) the money you took out to give him?"

"Can't. I won't ever retire. They'll have to lift me out of this car and put me directly in the hearse."

"So what would be your message for those people in my audience to-morrow?" I asked.

He answered, "Help."

As we said goodbye I thanked him. "For what?" he asked. I said, "For inspiring me to throw out the speech I had intended to give and talk about you—and all the people like you."

Educational Testing Service recently concluded that a perfect storm is brewing, with our colleges and universities right at the center of it. Three powerful forces are converging: wide disparities in skill lev-els (reading and math), widening wage gaps of seismic proportions, and sweeping demographic shifts of more people with less education and fewer skills. If we don't confront these changes with new thinking and new policies, we will find it difficult to sustain a vibrant middle class. The American dream of decent jobs and livable wages could vanish in our time.

I heard Lyndon Johnson talk a great deal about that dream back in the 1960s. I was a young assistant to the president. He had been a schoolteacher and often talked about his own experience in a classroom of poor kids. Now he was president, and almost forty-two years ago to this day, I heard him deliver a speech describing America as a land of towering expectations. This was to be a nation, he said, where each cit-izen "could be ruled by the common consent of all—enshrined in law, given life by institutions, guided by men themselves subject to its rule." All people of every station and origin, President Johnson said, "would be touched equally in obligation and in liberty."

It was an eloquent speech. But LBJ was not only eloquent that day, he was adamant. As he spoke America was engaged in a mighty struggle in the streets, in the corridors of Congress, and across the country to consummate the expectations of all Americans for equal treatment under the law. The Civil Rights Act of 1964 had not been law a year, and the resistance was fierce across the South to opening public accommodations to a race that had been forced to sit in the back of the bus, in the balcony of the theaters, and on rough benches in poorly lit, poorly heated, and poorly funded schools. It took some audacity to talk about justice for all people of every station and origin, the "immense thrill of discovery" that should be every American's birthright, and America as a "home for freedom," when in fact we had not come to grips with the profound contradiction at the heart of the American experience.

But when Lyndon Johnson talked about America as a land of towering expectations, he knew that the difference between the promise and the reality was a scar across America's conscience. We had a long way to go, and he intended that day to give us a push. This was the speech the president delivered when he signed the Higher Education Act of 1965. This historic legislation was the first providing college scholarships to high-school graduates as well as support for libraries and faculty development. Those provisions for education were about justice—intended to help fulfill what LBJ called the "fair expectations" inherent in the Declaration of Independence and the Constitution.

Baby boomers were about to stream into higher education far beyond the capacity of the institutions to handle them. Some 50 percent of college libraries didn't meet minimum standards for their collections. Yet this seemed like minor upkeep compared to the social, racial, and class divide in higher education. The rate of college attendance for higher-income households was more than twice that for lower-income households. And many of those at the bottom who got to college didn't make it through the first year because of financial distress. When LBJ signed the bill, nearly half of all high-school graduates were not going to college, hundreds of thousands because of financial need. But now a high-school graduate admitted to college could get up to $1,000 a year in federal grant money, as much as $400 a year in work-study funds, and interest-free loans.

Many of the people I knew in Washington at the time had gone to college on the GI Bill. What's been largely forgotten is that the numerous education programs of the GI Bill were not much less discriminatory than the society soldiers returned to in 1946. After the war, only 4 percent of all college students enrolled through the GI Bill were black veterans. Thirty percent of all veterans in the South at the time were black, but only 8 percent of participants in on-the-job training programs were; 86 percent of the professional jobs filled by the United States Employment Service in Mississippi after the war were held by whites, while 92 percent of the low-wage menial jobs were filled by blacks. The end pattern was clear: for whites, the GI Bill was a powerful motor for upward mobility. By 1955, 41 percent of WWII veterans were professionals, foremen, or skilled workers. But few black veterans found a place in this success story. In those days, affirmative action was for whites only. I might still be working for the grocery store in the small Texas town where I grew up were it not for affirmative action for Southern white boys.

By 1965, America had waged Civil War and survived the Great Depression, but we were still confronting Jim Crow—all in order to fulfill the ideals of freedom and common welfare inscribed in our founding documents. We faced what we thought at the time was the last great hurdle in this struggle. When he signed the Higher Education Act, LBJ pleaded with Americans to heed the destiny it was meant to secure:

> When you look into the faces of your students and your children and your grandchildren, tell them that you were there when it began. Tell them that a promise has been made to them. Tell them that the leadership of your country believes it is the obligation of your Nation to provide and permit and assist every child born in these borders to receive all the education that he can take.

Everywhere we turn today, we hear about education needs and the global economy. There is not an economist or politician—right, left, or center—who does not say that education is critical if America is to compete at the high end of the new global economy. There were already glimmers of such thinking in those education programs we enacted in the 1960s. But Lyndon Johnson was no prophet of the so-called knowledge economy. That sort of technocratic ideal wasn't the real motivation for what he was trying to accomplish back then. And it doesn't explain the rare political courage that Johnson needed to do what he did. He did what he did because he believed in affirmative action for poor children. And he believed it should include higher education.

This is not simply a poignant detail about President Johnson. It is about a president who did more than anyone else to establish federal aid to education, who was himself educated at a small teacher's college—Southwest Texas State in San Marcos. This was hardly the ideal setting or the best credential for launching a political career, but it was the kind of place one could go to get a sense of whether the American dream had a political future. Johnson, a born politician, apparently learned that it did when he was there. A year or two out of college, with some teaching under his belt, he went directly into politics where he remained for the rest of his life. Back then, the American dream was a simple proposition, one widely taught and just as widely denied: from small beginnings you could achieve a secure life and liberty and pursue happiness if you worked hard and had the will to succeed. Johnson called it, simply, justice, and it was as close to a national creed as a free people pledged to religious liberty had ever had.

You can imagine the relish in which Lyndon Johnson traveled back to Texas to sign the Higher Education Act at his old teacher's college. He talked about his first teaching job in the little town of Cotulla, south of San Antonio. Forty years later and through countless political battles those children remained a fixture of his political vision. He repeatedly acknowledged what he had learned from them, and what he felt for them in all the years since. Now he could finally honor them. Now he could give them some portion of the educational opportunities which he first understood to be the most sacred pledge of democracy when he "looked in their eyes," as he often said—there in that segregated "Mexican" school in a backwater of backwaters, rural, impoverished, dark-skinned Cotulla, Texas.

He believed passionately that education was the great overriding power that could throw down the man-made dominions of racial caste and social class. In another speech that same year—this one signing the Voting Rights Act—he talked about how clearing prejudice and material want from the path of each child was a sacred aim of government, and he meant to keep the faith.

LBJ would be delighted today that Americans, in huge majorities, still share this great spirit of assistance and overcoming: a recent survey found 93 percent of Americans agreeing that "we should help people who are working hard to overcome disadvantages and succeed in life." And 72 percent disagreed that "some people are born poor and there's nothing we can do about that." Only a fringe of 16 percent believes that "we shouldn't give special help at all, even to those who started out with more disadvantages than most."

But he would be disturbed at how those attitudes are not shaping public policy. College enrollments are far out of sync with majority public opinion on opportunity and the role of government. For example, African Americans and Hispanics are only about 6 percent of the freshman classes of the 146 most selective four-year colleges today while 74 percent of the students at the most selective colleges come from families in the top quarter of the family income scale. Just 3 percent come from the bottom quarter and only 10 percent from roughly the bottom half.

Since the Reagan revolution almost thirty years ago, the value of federal tuition aid, like the minimum wage and other key forms of public assistance, has plummeted. In the mid-1970s, the maximum Pell Grant for low-income families covered about 40 percent of private college tuition costs. Today it covers only 15 percent. For public schools, the value has dropped from 60 percent of tuition to 40 percent. The composition of student financial aid has changed radically as scholarship aid has declined. Today about 58 percent of student aid is in the form of loans and 41 percent is grant money. That ratio is essentially the reverse of what it was thirty years ago.

I want to make a brief detour here. As a journalist I follow the efforts to deal with legal restrictions on affirmative action and in some states outright bans. When affirmative action was banned in the California public institutions by voter referendum in 1996, African American enrollment in the most selective universities plunged. At UCLA it is now at its lowest point in thirty years, about 2 percent of total enrollment there. Across the whole University of California system, black enrollment is only 3.4 percent today. Michigan now faces the same situation, the state of Washington, too, and ballot efforts in other states are being threatened.

It's no secret that the so-called American Civil Rights Initiative, which has been pushing these ballot efforts, is a darling of right-wing foundations, all catalysts of the white backlash to the civil rights movement. But I bet even they were surprised when one of their leading spokesmen, Ward Connerly, accepted the endorsement of the Ku Klux Klan for his Michigan ballot initiative, saying: "If the Ku Klux Klan thinks that equality is right, God bless them." One of the great injuries to fairness in America is this idea, increasingly commonplace, that banning efforts to create racial diversity in important institutions is a defense of equality. Connerly also reveals a more perverse side to this crusade when he says that if schools and other institutions become less diverse without affirmative action, it's okay because people can mix together in other venues, such as the racetrack. As someone who "frequents the racetrack" himself, he says he enjoys being "thrown in with people from all around the globe."

But nothing trumps the cynicism of John Fund in *The Wall Street Journal*, standing in for a whole generation of reactionaries who have sought to stamp the bleak persisting reality of racial segregation in America with the seal of "constitutional" approval, as newly "color-blind" admissions policies take hold in educational institutions. "Michigan voters struck a blow for equality this month," Fund wrote after the ban on affirmative action passed in that state with 58 percent of the vote last fall. He even compared University of Michigan president Mary Sue

Coleman to George Wallace when she declared, after the vote, that "diversity matters at Michigan. It matters today, and it will matter tomorrow." What Wallace had said was: "Segregation now, segregation tomorrow, and segregation forever."

What kind of degraded discourse permits such distortion of values and intent? Those who try to create more diversity in higher education are likened to white segregationists who denied even basic civil rights to African Americans and others for generations, and when that failed simply used terror. You have to wonder what motivates such desperate revisionism in the minds of so dominant a class.

In *Whitewashing Race*, Angela Harris describes the devastating political logic of such arguments well:

> As the legal structures that continue to disadvantage people of color become increasingly "race-neutral" in a constitutional sense, the moral model of discrimination facilitates both the denunciation of bigotry and the maintenance of existing distributions of wealth and power.

The reactionaries know what they are doing. They embrace the notion of an America ruled by elites served by everyone else. And they know that more than ever, college admissions are a key gatekeeper of wealth and power in America. In 1980, if you obtained a graduate degree you earned about $50,000 a year on average; by 2000 you were earning $70,000 with the same kind of degree; over the same period those with bachelor degrees saw their income rise from about $40,000 to $50,000. In contrast, high-school graduates saw no gain in income, and those without high-school diplomas saw their income drop. The figures from the Census Bureau estimate that college graduates will earn about $2.5 million over their lifetimes in today's dollars, compared with $1.5 million for high-school graduates. Clearly, college education, indeed graduate education, has been critical to upward mobility today. Yet lower-income households remain far less likely to send children to college than upper-income households—precisely the recipe for keeping poor households poor and rich ones rich. And precisely the opposite of Lyndon Johnson's ideal of helping everyone realize "the fair expectations" of a life.

As affirmative action is banned in one place after another, on the grounds of promoting "equality," legacy admissions thrive as the means of achieving the two-tier society—of rich investors served by poor workers—that cause class warriors to salivate. In this worldview the mediocre children of rich alumni are much more deserving of special treatment than the descendants of slaves and sharecroppers struggling to make their way up. George W. Bush is the poster boy of special handling. Our president opposes affirmative action and was appalled at the Michigan undergraduate admissions program that awarded points if a candidate was black or Hispanic or Native American. I wonder what he thought while rehearsing that line in the mirror as he shaved in the morning. I wonder, too, about the person who lost the spot they gave George W. at Yale, solely for his name. What if she were president today?

William Bowen argues that the preference system Bush enjoyed on his way to the White House serves to "reproduce the high-income/high-education/white profile" of leading colleges and universities, providing the offspring of elites like Bush a perpetual trust fund of power, place, and privilege. We can't even kid ourselves about seeking to release the talents of every American from every condition of life until we're honest about the privileges of the rich and the corruption such privileges breed in policy and the law.

You will want to read the book by Isabel Sawhill and Sara McLanahan, *The Future of Children*. They remind us that the American ideal of a classless society was "one in which all children have a roughly equal chance of success regardless of the economic status of the family into which they were born." You'll want to read the work of the economist Jeffrey Madrick, who reminds us that once upon a time only 20 percent of one's future income was determined by the income of one's father. New research suggests that the level of a father's income today determines 60 percent of a son's income. In other words, children no longer have a roughly equal chance of success regardless of the economic status of the family into which they are born. Small wonder that in 2001–2002, according to the research organization Demos, more than 400,000 low-income high-school graduates who were qualified to attend college did not enroll in a four-year college, and 168,000 did not enroll in college at all. Over a decade that trend means millions of qualified students will not go to college. Gaps in enrollment between low-income families and high-income families are as great as they were thirty years ago. Your chances of success are greatly improved if you were born on third base and your father has been tipping the umpire.

In the face of that brewing perfect storm, we are witnessing a slow mortgaging of our future. Our leaders have convinced working Americans that while there may be little we can do to protect them from the loss of good and secure jobs, their children can achieve the American dream, or at least achieve a middle-class life, if they graduate from college. So across every race and class, parents are putting more and more energy into and pressure on their children to insure that they are eligible for advanced education.

Yet the cost of tuition at public universities is soaring—up 42 percent over five years. State governments are slowly reducing the percentage of the cost that they provide to colleges; on a per-pupil basis, state support for public universities is at a twenty-five-year low, and tuition has more than doubled. Between 1994 and 2004, states have shifted financial-aid resources from need-based aid to merit-based aid, seeking to attract high-performing students. Non-need aid has more than doubled, to 27 percent of total state aid.

Yes, we are witnessing the silent privatization of public universities. We are pricing college out of the reach of more and more poor families.

In 2006, the Republican congress took $12 billion out of student loan funds—the largest single cut from discretionary spending—and used it to help pay for the cost of the tax cuts for the wealthiest Americans. Democrats have promised to reverse that and to cut interest rates in half. A bill to achieve that—but only over five years—has passed the House. A Senate bill with more ambitious provisions is now pending.

But neither of these comes close to making college affordable for all who have earned admission. Neither represents the clarion commitment to the next generation that they will have the opportunity to gain the education they deserve. Neither suggests that America is going to ensure that public investment will make advanced training and education accessible to all.

Who knows where it will end? In 1993 one-third of students graduated with debt; in 2004, two-thirds. The average student debt burden is almost 60 percent higher than it was in the mid-1990s. This debt makes public-service jobs less and less affordable, as graduating students can no longer afford to enter community organizing, teaching, nursing, and other helping vocations. According to the College Board, the total volume of private student loans has grown at an average rate of 27 percent per year since 2001, and now totals $17.3 billion, or 20 percent of all student-loan volume. Some private loans carry interest rates as high as 19 percent—compared to 6.8 percent for loans through the government programs. Elizabeth Warren, the Harvard law professor who is an expert on household debt and bankruptcy law, told *The Wall Street Journal* that "student loan collectors have power that would make a mobster envious." Only someone who is "totally, permanently disabled" has a chance of escaping their grip.

Thousands of others who do not meet that standard but have other kinds of real problems struggle to find relief—people like Lori Siler of Westfield, Indiana. She told her story to a columnist at *MSN Money*, and it isn't a happy one. In 1999 she dropped out of Purdue University carrying the maximum amount of federal loans, $46,000. Her unpaid debt exploded to more than $100,000. She has two children and earns $32,000 a year as a secretary, and her lender wants her to pay a quarter of her monthly wages—$650 a month—for the next thirty-five years.

Meanwhile, Sallie Mae, the country's largest student-loan lender, now touts debt management operations (a euphemism for collecting on delinquent and defaulted loans) as a key component of its earnings growth. According to *Fortune* magazine, fee-based revenue accounts for about 30 percent of Sallie Mae's business. As the share price of the company rose precipitously over the last decade, top executives extracted hundreds of millions of dollars in stock options. Between them the chairman and CEO made $367 million between 1999 and 2004. These executives are reaping the benefits of rising tuition costs that force students to assume larger and larger debt burdens. The average student now graduates with about $19,000 worth of debt, more than double the average level in 1993.

Consider what they're up against as they move out into the larger society, where the economic growth has been distributed upward for two decades now. In 1989, CEOs of large American companies earned 71 times more than the average worker. Last year, the average CEO made roughly $10.8 million. The Federal Reserve reports that 10 percent of income earners now own 70 percent of the wealth, and the wealthiest 1 percent own more than the bottom 95 percent. In 2005, the top 700,000 Americans enjoyed about the same share of the national income—218 percent—as the bottom 150 million. Such disparities open wider the advantage of college to heirs of the top, even as working people have to take on great burdens to make it to college, stay in, and pay off the loans.

The economist Paul Krugman illustrates what's been happening by imagining a line of 1,000 people who represent the entire population of America. They are standing in ascending order of income, with the poorest person on the left and the richest person on the right. Their height is proportional to their income—the richer they are, the taller they are.

Start with 1973. If you assume that a height of 6 feet represents the average income in that year, the person on the far left side of the line—representing those Americans living in extreme poverty—is only 16 inches tall. By the time you get to the guy at the extreme right, he towers over the line at more than 113 feet.

Now take 2005. The average height has grown from 6 feet to 8 feet, reflecting the modest growth in average incomes over the past generation. And the poorest people on the left side of the line have grown at about the same rate as those near the middle—the gap between the middle class and the poor, in other words, hasn't changed. But people to the right have been on steroids: the figure at the end of the line is now 560 feet tall—almost 5 times taller than his 1973 counterpart.

We have come to a critical moment in our long self-fashioning as a democratic people. On January 1, 2005, *The Economist* warned:

> A growing body of evidence suggests that the meritocratic ideal is in trouble in America. Income inequality is growing to levels not seen since the Gilded Age, around the 1880s. But social mobility is not increasing at anything like the same pace . . . Everywhere you look in modern America—in the Hollywood Hills or the canyons of Wall Street, in the Nashville recording studios or the clapboard houses of Cambridge, Massachusetts—you see elites mastering the art of perpetuating themselves. America is increasingly looking like imperial Britain, with dynastic ties proliferating, social circles interlocking, mechanisms of social exclusion strengthening and a gap widening between the people who make decisions and shape the culture and the vast majority of ordinary working stiffs.

It is impossible as a reporter to ignore the consequences—towns undone by plant closings, families undone by debt or medical bills or prison. Upward mobility is stalled—a well-hidden fact in the mass media but easy to recognize if you just sit down and talk with people in their living rooms. They will describe a big difference today in how the risks of life are borne. Debt and risk and insecurity flourish in isolated towns and in families, in dark nights of worry and hopeless dawns. We used to pool the risks of life in public systems that bore the brunt of such forces. No more.

The British journalist Godfrey Hodgson has been observing America for forty years. He writes that "great and growing inequality has been the most salient social fact about the America of the conservative ascendancy." And yet our political system and media institutions have done little to challenge such division, while doing much to reward it and simply to deny its existence.

While you are in Boston this weekend, walk the Freedom Trail. Contemplate how long a struggle "We the People" have had to wage to realize the citizen power inherent in democracy—and how far we still have to go. Ever since Americans declared for independence in 1776, the meaning of the word has been contested. "The shepherd drives the wolf from the sheep's throat, for which the sheep thanks the shepherd as a *liberator*, while the wolf denounces him for the same act as the destroyer of liberty." President Lincoln said this in 1864. No one listening made any mistake about who was the wolf. It was the slave power. But the truly disturbing thing was not what slavery did—that was clear—but what it claimed to be, namely, an institution worthy of protection under American principles of freedom. Lincoln said the same conflict of meaning existed in the North, between workers and employers—"all professing to love liberty."

When our forebears declared for independence from the monarchy, they put freedom on a new moral foundation: the assertion that all are created equal. But what of this self-evident truth in a highly stratified, even segregated society, where people can reside in the same city but actually live, breathe, learn, work, and die in two entirely different worlds? You remember George Orwell's sharp rejoinder in *Animal Farm*: ALL ANIMALS ARE CREATED EQUAL, reads a sign in the barnyard. But when some decide they'd rather have power over others than live together in common, the sign is amended: BUT SOME ANIMALS ARE MORE EQUAL THAN OTHERS. *More equal than others.* That must have a familiar ring to college administrators like you who see too many young people turned around at the gateways to a better life.

Unable to deny the obvious facts of growing inequality, conservative elites took to gloating about the public's seeming tolerance for this situation. They boasted that we no longer care about equality or at least no longer think it's a public problem. Godfrey Hodgson writes how the reactionary narrative offered corroborating subplots to bolster it against reality. These were deployed with ruthless efficiency by a well-funded ideological command structure in Washington and a compliant establishment media.

The first subplot, in the 1980s, was the collapse of communism, interpreted not as a triumph of democracy—not even the happiest cold warrior could claim that the result was democratic—but rather as a vindication of American-style free-market capitalism. The second subplot was the growing flood of cheap imported goods in the 1990s, which created a sense of more purchasing power even as skyrocketing health and education and retirement costs made millions increasingly vulnerable to economic ruin. The third subplot was the late-1990s stock bubble and then the housing bubble, which kept the economy afloat even as real wages stagnated and national savings went into the negative. The result was to hide the strategy to perpetuate plutocracy disguised as democracy.

But as you walk the Freedom Trail this weekend, remember that there have been moments like this throughout our history and leaders who seized them to champion our fundamental ideals. Woodrow Wilson, for one—the only professional educator with a PhD to occupy the Oval Office. In his campaign of 1912, with the born-again progressive Teddy Roosevelt breathing fire under his feet, Wilson captured a moment and a spirit quite similar to the changes we feel coming today. He didn't trim his sails on the scale of what was needed, or fail to specify the danger we were in and who was to blame for it. "Why are we in the presence, why are we at the threshold, of a revolution?" he asked. "Because we are profoundly disturbed by the influences which we see reigning in the determination of our public life and our public policy."

Like the guardians of privilege today, the people in power, Wilson said, only care for principles when it benefits them to do so. They are all for declaring equality with Thomas Jefferson, and even equality under law with Martin Luther King. But, in Wilson's words, "they have no consciousness of the war for freedom that is going on to-day."

A century ago Wilson ran for president on a simple moral premise:

the need for fundamental change and the basis for doing so in the values we hold dear. "What form does the contest between tyranny and freedom take to-day?" he asked. "What are to be the items of our new declaration of independence?" Aristocracy was gone. The slave power fell. But a new tyranny loomed:

> By tyranny, as we now fight it, we mean control of the law, of legislation and adjudication, by organizations which do not represent the people, by means which are private and selfish. We mean, specifically, the conduct of our affairs and the shaping of our legislation in the interest of special bodies of capital and those who organize their use. We mean the alliance, for this purpose, of political machines with selfish business. We mean the exploitation of the people by legal and political means.

The great enmity against human dignity and the destiny of democracy that Wilson saw all around him was never so nakedly exposed as it had been in the first Gilded Age whose devastating effects both Theodore Roosevelt and Woodrow Wilson had to answer. A century later, the words of that era once again echo clearly, just as the cry of the sharecropper and the former slave became one in Lyndon Johnson's eyes. The trapped miner, the gang-raped maid, the stooped migrant fruit picker, the unemployed autoworker, the homeless veteran—the very notion of "We the People" makes their struggle one cause, one hope, and one dream. "Injustice anywhere is a threat to justice everywhere," Martin Luther King Jr. wrote from a jail in Birmingham, Alabama. "We are caught in an inescapable web of mutuality, tied in a single garment of destiny. Whatever affects one directly, affects all indirectly." King subpoenaed the nation's conscience. He was killed for it.

Right now America's conscience asks us to consider one basic thing amid a vast array of challenges: the escalating plight of ordinary Americans, searching for dignity and fairness in a world where governments side with the predators of privilege.

You have a role in this fight. I can imagine how hard it is to take responsibility for what you do in an age of new educational "business models" and high-stakes development campaigns. And I imagine it is even harder if you care about equality of opportunity in America. But we can take heart from our knowledge of American history. The egalitarian roots of this country run deep. The time has come to reclaim those roots—to resurrect the revolution that held out "life, liberty, and the pursuit of happiness" for all. The time has come to raise hell until America squares its performance with its promise.

9. | FAREWELL TO LADY BIRD

Eulogy for Lady Bird Johnson,
December 22, 1912–July 11, 2007

JULY 14, 2007

For a long time Lady Bird Johnson and I had seen less of each other than either of us wished. But I had left the White House two years before her husband had thought I should or would, and my relationship with him was strained to the breaking point, for reasons neither he nor I wholly understood. Mrs. Johnson, I learned, grieved over the situation. She and I had bonded many years earlier. We had been born in the same East Texas county (although years apart), attended the same high school, and went to the same university, where we both majored in journalism. We confessed to each other a chronic homesickness for our roots, where intimacies of nature, culture, and friendships forged a nostalgia that was hard to explain given the persistent power of race to divide and conquer. We also shared a deep affection for the man she had married and who would become my mentor. I first met her when I went to work for him. During my White House years we had laughed and labored and plotted together and occasionally cried on each other's shoulder.

But my exit was abrupt and we didn't see each other for years. Then, after his death, our paths began to cross again. After her stroke, which robbed her of speech but not of her acute interest in public affairs, she had been a faithful viewer of my broadcasts, listened to audiotapes of my speeches, and had some of my writings read to her. She asked me to lay the wreath on LBJ's grave at one of the ceremonies she held annually on his birthday. It was on that occasion she let me know that she wanted me to speak at her funeral. I refused to let the thought of that inevitability take hold in my head. Not until three years later, when I received the call that she was just hours from death, did I take out my yellow pad and begin to write. At the service in Austin a few days later, I looked out on the host of mourners—presidents, first ladies, official families, veterans of campaigns and environmental causes, old retainers, scores of Secret Service agents who had been her guardians and then her friends, the nurses and technicians who had attended her final days, friends from across the years, grandchildren and great-grandchildren, and strangers whose admiration had prompted them to drive for hours across long distances to be there—and realized there was one thing above all that I most wanted to say about Lady Bird Johnson.

* * *

It is unthinkable to me that she is gone.

Lady Bird was so much a part of the landscape, so much a part of our lives and our times, so much a part of our country for so long that I began to imagine her with us always. Now, although the fields of purple, orange, and blue will long evoke her gifts to us, that vibrant presence has departed, and we are left to mourn our loss even as we celebrate her life.

Some people arriving earlier today were asked, "Are you sitting with the family?" I looked around at this throng and said to myself, "Everyone here is sitting with the family. That's how she would treat us. All of us."

When I arrived in Washington in 1954, to work in Senator Lyndon Johnson's mailroom between my sophomore and junior years, I didn't know a single person in town—not even the Johnsons, whom I only met that first week. She soon recognized that the weekends were especially lonesome for me, and she called one day to ask me over for Sunday brunch.

I had never even heard of Sunday brunch, much less been to one; for all I knew, it was an Episcopalian sacrament. When I arrived at 30th Place the family was there—the two little girls, Lady Bird, and himself. But so were Richard Russell and Sam Rayburn and J. Edgar Hoover—didn't look like Episcopal priests to me. They were sitting around the smallish room reading the newspaper—except for LBJ, who was on the phone. If this is their idea of a sacrament, I thought, I'll just stay a Baptist. But Mrs. Johnson knew something about the bachelors she had invited there, including the kid fresh up from her native East Texas. On a Sunday morning they needed a family, and she had offered us communion at her table. In a way, it was a sacrament.

It was also very good politics. She told me something that summer that would make a difference in my life. She was shy, and in the presence of powerful men, she usually kept her counsel. Sensing that I was shy, too, and aware that I had no experience to enforce any opinions, she said, "Don't worry. If you are unsure of what to say, just ask questions, and I promise you that when they leave, they will think you were the smartest one in the room, just for listening to them. Word will get around."

She knew the ways of the world, and how they could be made to work for you, even when you didn't fully understand what was going on. She told me once, years later, that she didn't even understand everything about the man she had married—nor did she want to, she said, as long as he needed her.

Oh, he needed her, all right. You know the famous incident. Once, trying to locate her in a crowded room, he growled aloud: "Where's Lady Bird?" And she replied: "Right behind you, darling, where I've always been."

"Whoever loves, believes the impossible," Elizabeth Barrett Browning wrote. Lady Bird truly loved this man she often found impossible. "I'm no more bewildered by Lyndon than he is bewildered by himself," she once told me.

Like everyone he loved, she often found herself in the path of his Vesuvian eruptions. During the campaign of 1960 I slept in the bed in their basement when we returned from the road for sessions of the Senate. She knew I was lonesome for Judith and our six-month-old son who were back in Texas. She would often come down the two flights of stairs to ask if I was doing all right. One night the senator and I got home even later than usual. He brought with him some unresolved dispute from the Senate cloakroom. At midnight I could still hear him upstairs, carrying on as if he were about to purge the entire Democratic caucus. Pretty soon I heard her footsteps on the stairs and I called out: "Mrs. Johnson, you don't need to check up on me. I'm all right." And she called back, "Well, I was coming down to tell you I'm all right, too."

She seemed to grow calmer as the world around her became more furious.

Thunderstorms struck in her life so often, you had to wonder why the gods on Olympus kept testing her. She lost her mother in an accident when she was five. She was two cars behind JFK in Dallas. She was in the White House when Martin Luther King was shot and Washington burned. She grieved for the family of Robert Kennedy, and for the lives lost in Vietnam.

Early in the White House, a well-meaning editor up from Texas said, "You poor thing, having to follow Jackie Kennedy." Mrs. Johnson's mouth dropped open, in amazed disbelief. And she said, "Oh, no, don't pity me. Weep for Mrs. Kennedy. She lost her husband. I still have my Lyndon."

She aimed for the consolation and comfort of others. It was not only her talent at negotiating the civil war raging in his nature. It was not just the way she remained unconscripted by the factions into which family, friends, and advisers inevitably divide around a powerful figure. She did her best to keep open all the roads to reconciliation.

Like her beloved flowers in the field, she was a woman of many hues. A strong manager, a canny investor, a shrewd judge of people, friend and foe—and she never confused the two. Deliberate in coming to judgment, she was sure in conclusion.

But let me speak especially of the one quality that most captured my admiration and affection—her courage.

It is the fall of 1960. A few days before the election we're in Dallas, where neither Kennedy nor Johnson are local heroes. We start across the street from the Adolphus to the Baker Hotel. The reactionary congressman from Dallas has organized a demonstration of women—pretty women, in costumes of red, white, and blue, waving little American flags above their cowboy hats. At first I take them to be cheerleaders having a good time. But suddenly they are an angry mob, snarling, salivating, spitting. A roar, a primal frightening roar, swells around us—my first experience with collective hate roused to a fever pitch. I'm right behind the Johnsons. She's taken his arm and as she turns left and right, nodding to the mob, I can see she is smiling. And I see in the eyes of some of those women a confusion—what I take to be their realization that this is them at their most uncivil, confronting a woman who is the triumph of civility. So help me, her very demeanor created a small zone of grace in the middle of that tumultuous throng. And they move back a little, and again a little, Mrs. Johnson continuing to nod and smile, until we're inside the Baker and upstairs in the suite.

Now LBJ is smiling—he knows that Texas was up for grabs until this moment, and the backlash will decide it for us. But Mrs. Johnson has pulled back the curtains and is looking down that street as the mob disperses. She has seen a dark and disturbing omen. "Things will never be the same again," she says, quietly.

Now it is 1964. The disinherited descendants of slavery, still denied their rights as citizens after a century of segregation, have resolved to claim for themselves the American promise of life, liberty, and the pursuit of happiness. President Johnson has thrown the full power of his office to their side. He has just signed the Civil Rights Act—the greatest single sword of justice raised for equality since the Emancipation Proclamation. A few weeks later, both Johnsons plunge into his campaign for election in his own right. After that historic legislation he has more or less given up on the South, but she will not. These were her people, here were her roots, and she is not ready to sever them. So she sets out on a whistle-stop journey of nearly seventeen hundred miles through the heart of her past. She is on her own now—campaigning independently—across the Mason-Dixon Line past the buckle of the Bible Belt all the way down to the port of New Orleans. I cannot all these years later do justice to what she faced: the boos, the jeers, the hecklers, the crude signs and cruder gestures, the insults, and the threats. This is the land still ruled by Jim Crow and John Birch, who control the law and enforce it with the cross and club. It's 1964, and bathroom signs still read WHITE LADIES and COLORED WOMEN.

In Richmond, she is greeted with signs that read FLY AWAY, LADY BIRD. In Charleston, BLACKBIRD GO HOME. Children planted in the front row hold up signs practically in her face: JOHNSON IS A NIGGER LOVER. In Savannah they curse her daughter. The air has become so menacing that we run a separate engine fifteen minutes ahead of her in case of a bomb. She later said, "People were concerned for me, but I was concerned for the engineer in the train out in front; he was in far greater danger." Rumors spread of snipers, and in the panhandle of Florida the threats are so ominous that the FBI orders a yard-by-yard sweep of a seven-mile bridge that her train would cross.

She never flinches. Up to forty times a day from the platform of the caboose she will speak, sometimes raising a single white-gloved hand to punctuate her words—always the lady. When the insults grew so raucous in South Carolina, she tells the crowd the ugly words were coming "not from the good people of South Carolina but from the state of confusion." In Columbia she answers hecklers with what one observer called "a maternal bark." And she says, "This is a country of many viewpoints. I respect your right to express your own. Now is my turn to express mine."

An advance man called me at the White House from the pay phone at a local train depot. He was choking back the tears. "As long as I live," he said, in a voice breaking with emotion, "I will thank God I was here today, so that I can tell my children that I saw the difference courage makes."

Yes, she planted flowers and worked for highways and parks and vistas that opened us to the Technicolor splendors of our world. Walk this weekend among the paths and trails and flowers and see the beauty she loved. But as you do, remember: she also loved democracy, and saw a beauty in it—rough though the ground may be, hard and stony, as tangled and as threatened with blight as nature itself. And remember that this shy little girl from Karnack, Texas—with eyes as wistful as cypress and manners as soft as the whispering pine—grew up to show us how to cultivate the beauty in democracy: the voice raised against the mob, the courage to overcome fear, convictions as true as steel. Claudia Alta Taylor—Lady Bird Johnson—served the beauty in nature and the beauty in us, and right down to the end of her long and bountiful life, she inspired us to serve them, too.

Part II

─────┼─────

THE USES OF HISTORY

10. | A REFUSAL TO REMEMBER

Honorary Doctorate from the Jewish Theological Seminary

MAY 14, 1987

When the Jewish Theological Seminary invited me to accept an honorary doctorate, I felt as if I were going home. I am of course a Baptist from East Texas with a Master of Divinity from a Baptist Seminary, and the Jewish Theological Seminary, located on the Upper West Side of New York City, is the preeminent center outside of Israel for the academic study of Judaica. The bond I felt, however, had nothing to do with geography or theology and everything to do with a mutual regard for the power of memory. The JTS library houses the most complete collection of Judaica in the western hemisphere, and you can touch there—physically and emotionally—records of a mighty commitment to preserve the past. I had chosen the library as the venue for the premier of the PBS series Heritage Conversations in which I explored what The New York Times called "a perennial, elusive, and possibly unanswerable question: What is a Jew?" In that first episode I mentioned to my guest, the scholar Yosef Yerushalmi, something I had learned years ago in Hebrew class in that Baptist seminary in Texas—that the Hebrew word for remember, zakhor, *occurs in the Bible 169 times. I wanted to know why this is im-portant in Jewish history.* "The biblical command to remember," *Professor Yerushalmi answered,* "is one of the crucial commandments . . . part of the original fabric of Jewish religion from its inception." *But why, say, in the book of Job are Jews commanded to remember minute, concrete genealogies and obscure kings and rulers and others? The professor said I had it wrong—a lot could and should be forgotten;* "if a king did evil in the sight of the Lord, then he doesn't rate." *The Jews, he said, had developed a very special kind of historical writing.* "They remembered that which was vital to remember." *He had given me the text for my speech.*

* * *

This one-hundredth anniversary of your seminary stirs the power of memory, and that is no small feat in a society hypnotically fascinated with the moment.

My own business—broadcast news—helps to make this an anxious age of agitated amnesiacs. Not a disaster happens in the world that we do not instantly hear of it. But rarely is there context for the endless procession of problems, crimes, accusations, and contradictions. We seem to know everything about the last twenty-four hours but very little of the last sixty years or the last sixty centuries. In his speech accepting the Nobel Prize for Literature in 1980, the poet Czeslaw Milosz said, "Our planet that gets smaller every year, with its fantastic proliferation of mass media, is witnessing a process that escapes definition, characterized by a refusal to remember."

One of the documentaries in my recent series, A Walk Through the Twentieth Century, deals with the propaganda battles of World War II. Propaganda is as old as the sorcery and pageantry by which ancient emperors awed their subjects—as old as missionaries and the Declaration of Independence. But in the twentieth-century superstate, propaganda has become a fearful means for a zealous few to manipulate the minds of millions. This documentary explores the black art through the work of Fritz Hippler, the chief of Hitler's film ministry. We found him living in Berchtesgaden—healthy and unrepentant; he thinks the only mistake Hitler made was to lose the war. In a chilling interview Hippler speaks of how he tried to reach the "soul of the masses" through appalling movies like *The Eternal Jew*, which planted the seed for genocide.

The other portrait in the documentary is of the cocky little Sicilian immigrant Frank Capra, famed for his gentle movies like *Mr. Smith Goes to Washington*, in which ordinary folks and apple-pie virtue come out ahead. Frank Capra was drafted by FDR to answer Hitler's propaganda. He was in his nineties when I interviewed him, and he brought a portfolio of pictures with him to our meeting. They were photographs taken by American soldiers entering Dachau and Buchenwald as the war ended. Capra had kept them all to remind him of what had been at stake.

Such horrors help to explain what has happened to history as a concept and discipline in the twentieth century. Bernard Weisberger, the historian who advised us on *A Walk Through the Twentieth Century*, reminded me that around 1900 academic and popular historians alike looked upon history as a current whose force could be measured and whose direction could be charted, and it was taking us to glorious destinations. Writers like John Fiske and Francis Parkman "proved," as it were, that Galileo and Luther and Columbus and Newton had unwittingly been working together, weaving the design of progress. As Bernard Weisberger explained, history as either art or science showed how all the pieces fit nicely together in a pattern of improving civilization. Only skeptics like Mark Twain and Henry Adams doubted that we were getting better all the time. The general buoyancy of the times was expressed by Robert Underwood Johnson, editor of the popular *Century Magazine*, in his poem "In Tesla's Laboratory," written after he had witnessed an experiment in the phenomena of high-tension electricity:

> . . . *Blessed spirits waiting to be born—*
> *Thoughts to unlock the fettering chains of Things;*

> The Better Time, the Universal Good,
>   Their smile is like the joyous break of morn . . .

Then came the grim reaper. After the Somme and Verdun, after Lenin and Stalin, Hitler and the Holocaust, the neatly constructed edifice of optimism lay in shambles. Reinhold Niebuhr said that the Devil was back. We'd seen him in the Berliner Sportpalast and in Red Square, in the death camps and the gulags, in the rubble of cities. The barbarians weren't "out there" in jungle and steppe, waiting to be transformed by the advancing wave of civilization. We'd seen them—in uniform, chanting slogans, pulling down synagogues, burning books, herding people into barbed-wire enclosures and cattle cars and dispatching them to the furnace.

One way or another, they were there right in the center of our amazing new webs of technology, our complex political labyrinths, our sophisticated economic networks. Henry Adams had said that modern men and women were gripped by forces that simply flung them around as if they had grabbed hold of a live wire. The new century's cruelties were as awful as the marvels were awesome. It seemed as if the Dark Ages were back. Now historians wrote of a "post-historic" era. In the 1960s, many young people threw out the whole rational and scientific frame of mind of their parents and grandparents, denounced history as a fraud, and dived into the depths of I Ching and astrology. The world made so little sense to them that one might well believe in character formation by birth date. Not only had optimism perished under dreadful events but now the sheer velocity of change toppled the familiar landmarks as if they were the last dry leaves of autumn, shaken and swept away by the first howling wind of winter.

It was argued that we no longer had a usable past. Don't look to history for guidance, we were told. In his account of Vienna at the turn of the century, Carl Schorske wrote that "the modern mind has been growing indifferent to history because history, conceived as a continuous nourishing tradition, has become useless to it." Nathan Teitel describes as one of the most disquieting features of American life "the lack of historical continuity and communication between the generations. What is happening today, this hour, this very minute, seems to be our sole criterion for judgment and action."

What a sad world it is that exists only in the present, unaware of the long procession behind us.

Sad, and dangerous, too. It is no accident that Big Brother, in the novel *1984*, banishes history to the memory hole where inconvenient facts simply disappear. The power of despotism described by Orwell relies on the police for enforcement, but it rests on an obliteration of the past. O'Brien, the personification of Big Brother, says to Winston Smith, the protagonist: "We shall squeeze you empty, and then we shall fill you with ourselves." And they do. People are made to remember only what they are taught to remember and the content of their memory is changed overnight. The bureaucrats in the Ministry of Truth destroy the records of the past and publish new versions. These in turn are superseded by yet more revisions, until history becomes one long erasure for the convenience of the state.

Why do those in charge go to such lengths to wipe out memory? Because they know the past is indispensable to freedom. People without memory are at the mercy of their rulers because there is nothing against which to measure what they are told today. Winston Smith says, "History has stopped."

It has also been tortured beyond recognition. Hitler composed his own selective version of the past to give emotional force to his vision of the future. Germany had *not* been defeated in 1918, he insisted; it had been stabbed in the back—betrayed by Jews, Marxists, and liberals, who were undermining traditional Germanic values. His twisted account of history became the touchstone for wiping out the shame of 1918, purging the evil in German life, and restoring the German nation to its rightful place in the world. History became the scribe to malice. In his speech in Stockholm, Milosz said, "We are surrounded today by fictions about the past, contrary to common sense and to an elementary perception of good and evil." So it is that the number of books in various languages which deny that the Holocaust ever took place now exceeds one hundred.

It is possible even in a free society for history to perish not by design but by ignorance, until we are reduced to one dimension of being. The refusal to remember becomes a collective national habit—a costly one. Mark Twain noted that a cat, once it had sat on a hot stove, would never do so again, but it would never sit on a cold one, either. We human beings can count and weigh and sort our experiences and the reflections they prompt, and share them with others.

Abraham Lincoln understood the power of memory to shape the continuity and character of people. In his first inaugural address he talked about "the mystic chords of memory stretching from every battlefield and patriot grave to every living heart and hearthstone all over this broad land." Those words define the power of human beings to transmit experience through generations of time. Instead of a row of bare facts to be memorized by schoolchildren or an old picket fence slowly and silently rotting away in our own backyard, history becomes the perpetual conversation between the past and the present. Each of us lends our voice to that conversation, but no one of us has the last word.

As Bertolt Brecht wrote in his poem "New Age":

> New ages don't begin all at once;
> My grandfather lived in the new age.
> My grandson will still live in the old.
> New meat is eaten with old forks,
> From the new antennae come the old stupidities,
> Wisdom is passed from mouth to mouth.

This seminary is a crucial institution to Conservative Judaism. You are the keepers of historic wisdom held up to the light of new experience. Where the past and the future meet, you are witnesses. One of your own said it eloquently: "In remembrance is the secret of redemption."

11. | THE BIG STORY

Texas State Historical Association

MARCH 7, 1997

How is it you can grow up well churched, well taught, and well loved and still be so unaware of what is happening to other people living a few blocks across town? Many Southerners of my generation—coming to majority in the late 1950s and the 1960s—have wrestled with this question. We were nurtured by caring parents, instructed by devoted teachers, and prayed over by compassionate pastors—and yet it took the Freedom Rides, the bombs in Birmingham, the snarling dogs and water hoses of Police Chief Bull O'Connor, and the martyrdom of black resisters against segregation before the scales fell from our eyes. I could not have been happier growing up in Marshall, Texas, as Southern a culture as any below the Mason-Dixon Line. The population was roughly half white, half black; I drank from water fountains marked WHITES ONLY near others marked COLORED ONLY. On Saturday afternoons I went to matinees through the front entrances of the Paramount and Lynn theaters while black kids my age had to enter by a side door leading to the "crow's nest" in the balcony. No place was more segregated than the sanctuary on

Sunday morning, except for classes in our public schools all day, every day, Monday through Friday. I recall not a single black friend from those days. As my life unfolded and my work in government and journalism took me into the conflicts of color and race, I realized how inadequately my conscience had been touched by the experience of black people in the very place where I had lived so comfortably. When I was invited to give the keynote address at the annual convention of the Texas State Historical Association in 1997, I welcomed the opportunity to think out loud about how we had been taught history in those formative years. The association had been organized in 1897 on the principle that "History like that of Texas is rare. In its color, dramatic movement, and its instructiveness when viewed from the standpoint of political and social science, it has few parallels." Its founding president, Oran M. Roberts, asserted in his inaugural address that "any and everything that the people do or think, that tends to form habits of life, or to build up prevailing institutions affecting society, constitutes material for history." Yes, but for many years that material had been so carefully winnowed that what we learned had been half a history.

* * *

Every Texas schoolchild knows the old story about General Philip Sheridan. When he passed through Galveston in 1866 he was quoted as saying that if he owned Texas and all hell, he'd rent out Texas and live in hell. From that day on Sheridan suffered the unremitting fury and disgust of every right-thinking Texan.

But as historians you know the rest of the story. When General Sheridan came back many years later to attend a dinner honoring Ulysses S. Grant, he tried to apologize. He explained that at the time he had been returning from a difficult journey to Mexico; it was August, hot and dusty, and he had traveled for days without a break. His men were sick, and when he arrived in Galveston desperate for a bath and bed, the first person he met was a journalist who rushed up to him and asked him how he liked the city. Sheridan said he replied with something intemperate and ill-considered, but he really didn't mean it; he was just angry at the journalist for asking such a question under the circumstances.

The very next day after the general's apology, a local reporter wandered out to get some man-in-the-street commentary about the incident. The first person he talked to said, "I have never understood that there was any feeling of bitterness toward General Sheridan on account of his having made that remark. The only reason people thought hard of him, at all, was on account of his failing to kill the reporter."

I've often pondered the differences between journalism and history, and there's one thing I know for sure: more people have wanted to kill reporters than historians. So I take heart from the fact that your current president and former president sitting here at the head table are both journalists who not only survived hanging around historians but were chosen by historians to lead this association. Some might call that "defining deviancy upward," but I call it a triumph for both journalism and history.

There's always been a tension between these two ways of figuring the world out—between history and journalism—and when you first think about it, the historians seem to get the better deal. Journalists tackle the here and now, which can rear up and bite you; historians tend to deal with the dead and gone, who are in no position to complain. Journalism encourages the making of snap judgments and the drawing of facile conclusions; history grows out of sustained study and a patient resolve to connect the dots. Journalists who make mistakes get sued for libel; historians who make mistakes get to publish a revised edition.

There's a bigger difference yet. One of my valued colleagues is both a journalist and a historian. Andie Tucher won the Allan Nevins Prize a few years ago for her doctoral dissertation, which was then published as a fine book entitled *Froth and Scum*. As a high-school student Andie was fascinated by my PBS series *A Walk Through the Twentieth Century*, and in time she wrote me to inquire about working in television. For five years she was my editorial researcher, and she made many singular contributions to my productions, as well as to this speech tonight. When we were talking about this event I asked Andie what she thought the difference is between history and journalism. "About a year," she said.

Time can make all the difference in our understanding of the events of our lives. And of course history is never done, once and for all. While journalists must contend with the frustration of feeling that we never finish the story, historians often find themselves going back to the same story over and over again because they have found new information, gained new insights, outgrown old ideas, or discarded old prejudices. Time invites and requires second thoughts. We journalists should visit the past more often.

This impulse to reexamine the old stories is what underlies one of the noisiest and most difficult debates in history today: multiculturalism. It raises the most basic of questions: Who owns history? Who gets to participate in history? Who gets to tell history? Who's been left out of history? And whose history gets told?

Sometimes this debate can get ugly. Recently the historians' ivory tower has been shaken by vociferous voices questioning the accuracy and inclusiveness of one historical reconstruction or another. The Enola Gay exhibition in Washington was simply supposed to commemorate the fiftieth anniversary of the flight that dropped the first atomic bomb on Japan, but it aroused such a passionate battle over big questions of national responsibility and guilt that the curators gave up, took out all the parts that were offending one side or another, and ended up with virtually nothing to show.

If you consider "Enola Gay" to be fighting words, try these: "Thomas Jefferson." What with all the recent books, magazine articles, documentaries, and movies rehashing the question of his relationship with slavery in general—and one female slave in particular—he's been more in the news these past months than the entire congressional delegation from Virginia.

It's easy to ridicule much of this passion as "PC"—shorthand among many critics for history they think is too balkanized, too concerned with inclusiveness, too ethnically oriented. These critics portray a cadre of historians preoccupied with making sure that every book, every newspaper, every magazine, every movie include a proper number of clearly discernible women, children, people of color, old people, working-class people, disabled people, fat people, short people, gay people, people in recovery, and vegetarian people. The subtext is that taking a multicultural approach to history—that parceling out one's attention among the amazing diversity of the people who have lived the nation's story—is bad because it places more emphasis on not hurting people's feelings than on searching out some pure and eternal truth. Sometimes those critics are right.

But sometimes they can be grievously wrong. Sometimes ignoring the stories of those who have been less visible can lead to some pure and nearly eternal lie—even fatal lies. I can give you one example that strikes very close to home. Many of you in this audience recall *Texas History Movies,* those rip-roaring cartoon accounts of the early days of the Lone Star State. They started running in the *Dallas News* in 1926, but within a couple of years the Magnolia Petroleum Company—the forerunner to Mobil Oil—was issuing the comics in booklet form and distributing them to schools all over Texas. In its preface to the books, the company said it was "prompted by a desire to be of service to the pupils of the public schools of Texas and to have some small part in helping impress upon them the remarkable past of their state, its today, and its future, offering unlimited opportunities to every person in Texas."

In many places those cartoons became de facto curriculum; not only in elementary school but in what we then called junior high school, encompassing the seventh, eighth, and ninth grades. They had the cultural status of official history, and they painted in bold relief the swashbuckling drama of Texas heroes. They told of the exploits of Cabeza de Vaca and the wonders of the New World; of men who bravely stepped over the line when Colonel Travis slashed into the dirt with his sword at the Alamo; of exploits bound to stir the imagination of a young white boy walking home from Sam Houston Elementary School, down Crockett or Bowie or Fannin Streets to his home at 801 E. Austin, two blocks from Alamo Boulevard.

In time, though, I took a second look at those booklets, and saw that not only had those simple pictures and breezy captions enshrined our heroes, but they had encapsulated our bigotry and chauvinism. They told the story completely from the winner's circle, where anyone who was not a white Protestant American male was either invisible or ridiculous. In one strip a Texan slams a Mexican soldier in the head with his rifle butt shouting, "Sweet Dreams, Greaser!"—while another yells, "Down with the Tamale Eaters!" A Texan seeing Spaniards bathing remarks, "It must be Saturday." An American prisoner in a Mexican jail boasts of having assaulted a priest. Black people with spiky hair, white eyes, and enormous lips say things like: "Ah sho likes dis place" or "Ah wish Ah wuz way down souf in Africa." Chinese people sporting pigtails mutter, "I no talkee Englesh."

Any youngster reading *Texas History Movies* could have reasonably concluded that black people enjoyed being owned body and soul by a master. Of course it was some of the masters—or some of their children and grandchildren—who were telling those tales. Not until many years later did it occur to me to wonder how these stories would have sounded had they been written by the children and grandchildren of slaves.

As schoolchildren we read: "Any man who inherited slaves was bound to free one-tenth of the number." That was a lie; slaves were legally designated chattel, not flesh and blood, and any man who inherited slaves was no more bound to free a single one of them than he was obligated to liberate a portion of his cotton fields, his pigs, or his grandmother's silver.

"Slaves could change masters at will," we read. Another lie. And we read: "The law provided for the education of Negroes even while they were slaves"—this under a picture of a little barefoot black child in a shabby schoolroom spelling out "K-A-T." In truth, the law provided for the severe punishment of any slaves caught educating themselves.

The comics have been revised since then, most recently in the 1970s. The racism has been eradicated, the propaganda has been diluted, new text has been added. A big eraser has been taken to other scenes, removing what would have been offensive odors to the modern nose. There's less casual violence in them, for one thing—the irate Mexican official who once vented his fury by kicking the cat high across the room now kicks at nothing at all, looking more like a Rockette than a bully. And a bottle of what was clearly an alcoholic beverage has been removed from the governor's desk.

Yes, some of the revisions smack of what might be called political correctness. But the issue with history as cartoon caricature isn't that their casual brutality hurt people's feelings; the issue is that their casual brutality did in fact represent the group mind of the times. Those cartoons were true to life. I don't mean, of course, true to the lives of Indians in the sixteenth century or black people in the nineteenth; they were true to the worldview of these white Texans who thought Mexicans were greasy, Indians stupid, Spaniards dirty, and slaves happy in a state of nature.

I have wrestled with what it meant for generations of Texas school-children to read all this, in books given to us by gentle, intelligent, and caring teachers—given to us by the very same people telling us other truths, like five times five equals twenty-five and Paris is the capital of France. No wonder so many of us who grew up well churched, well loved, and well taught could also remain so ignorant of what life was like for others. Bad history can have consequences as devastating as bad journalism. The whiskey bottle could be erased from the governor's desk and the abused cat eliminated from the reach of the kicker's foot more easily than the mind's eye cleansed of stereotypes and distortions insinuated into it by culture. History may be "one damned thing after another," as the British poet laureate John Masefield once said, but it is not only the thing itself, the event; history is also what people think, and wish, and imagine. What people believe is often the progenitor of history, the sources of those roiling waters of which the journalist sees only the surface.

Macaulay maintained that history is a compound of poetry and philosophy and "impresses general truths on the mind by a vivid representation of particular characters and incidents." What happens if the "vivid representation of particular characters and incidents" impress on the mind not 'general truths' but persistent lies? No wonder it took us so long to do justice. It was not only laws on the books that had to be changed but pernicious images in the mind in which were incubated powerful habits of the heart. When I think back on the impact of bad history, I ask myself: What are we blind to now? What is happening that we cannot see? What are we believing that our children will have to learn to disbelieve?

Texas History Movies illustrate one lesson time has taught us about how history can go wrong: it can denigrate and dehumanize people who have no voice to tell their own stories. But there's another problem with history written only from the winner's circle: the losers can disappear completely. The people without voices are at risk of being erased altogether. Not only historians but journalists have a great power here. Not writing about someone can write them out of existence. Around the same time that I was reading *Texas History Movies*, I was also listening to the radio. My father bought our first console radio so we could listen to the news pouring out of that magic box every night. Even as a boy I knew that I was living in the midst of great events, that giants like Franklin Roosevelt and monsters like Adolf Hitler were shaking the world around me and my world to come. What I didn't know was what life was like for others whose worlds were being upended by those events. Untold numbers of children were going to their deaths in Europe while I was playing marbles in Marshall, Texas.

There I was, growing up poor but pleasantly in a small town in East Texas, playing chase down safe streets, roaming the piney woods that surrounded us, going to movies on Saturday afternoon and family re-unions and church suppers, while on the same planet at the same time boys and girls my age were being shattered and assaulted and buried in pits.

Some of you may have seen our recent PBS series on the stories of Genesis, the first book of the Bible. In the episode on Cain and Abel we spend considerable time on the first murder. Two brothers both seek God's favor. Cain, the farmer, brings the first fruit of the soil. Abel, the shepherd, brings the firstborn of the flock. God, playing favorites, chooses Abel's offering over Cain's, and the elevation of the younger leads to the humiliation of the elder, who then murders his brother when they are alone in the field. Abel is innocent, yet Abel dies. The novelist Mary Gordon goes on to say that the challenge for a moral person "is always to be a witness to Abel. To be an ethical human being is to say, 'I'm in the place of that person unjustly cut down. I am a witness to that.'" Here history, like literature and journalism, finds a moral purpose, connecting us to what the novelist E. L. Doctorow calls the Big Story: Who are we? What are we trying to be? What is our fate? Where will we stand in the moral universe when these things are reckoned?

We need history to make that connect—for a boy shooting marbles in Marshall, Texas, one day to know his contemporary was a little girl named Anne Frank hiding in an Amsterdam attic.

On a cross-country flight recently I read Thomas Cahill's bestselling *How the Irish Saved Civilization*. Cahill writes of the cloistered monks who on their isolated island rescued so much of our Western intellectual heritage from the chaos of the Dark Ages by copying and preserving hundreds of classical manuscripts—Plato, Aristotle, Thucydides, Cicero, Tacitus. It's a lovely book, beautifully written, and has astounded the publishing world by selling almost one million copies with very little publicity or promotion. As I was reading a fellow across the aisle leaned over and asked, "Is that a good book?" And when I said, "Oh yes, it's wonderful," he asked, "Is it hard? I've been wanting to read it, my mother gave it to me, but I was wondering—is it, you know, full of facts and stuff? Is there too much history?"

Too much history! If only he were here today, listening to all that the Texas State Historical Association is doing to tell long-neglected stories, I believe he would realize that we need more history. More history of the sort you are practicing here is the only possible antidote to the deafening effects of history written by winners. It's the way to come to an understanding of who we were, where we've gone wrong, what we've done right, and who we might become. That's what history is when pursued with integrity and openness and with zest for the telling of untold stories.

There is something wonderfully democratic about an organization like this that nourishes and encourages all comers who bring with them a sense of curiosity. I am a regular reader of your quarterlies, essays, monographs, and books. With delight I have been plowing randomly through your new *Handbook of Texas History*. I am fascinated by the papers you are presenting here. You are exploring the lives of women as members of families and also as doctors and writers and historians and pilots. The lives of farmers, and the lives of ranchers. The life and work of Texas Baptists—an enormous task, as you know, because as my father used to say, there are more Baptists in Texas than people. And a prickly task, too. One of my seminary professors compared Baptists to jalapeño peppers: one or two make for a tasty dish, but a whole bunch of them together in one place brings tears to your eyes. You're also writing about the life and work of Texas Catholics. The music and art of Texas, and the police and National Guard of Texas. African Americans in Texas. Mexicans in Texas. Oilmen and immigrant laborers. Criminals, and segregationists, and filibusterers, and POWs, and the famously enigmatic Yellow Rose of Texas.

When I read what you're writing I daydream of re-creating myself as a journalist in other times—a Forrest Gump, or Zelig, with a press pass. The people who emerge from your research I would dearly love to have interviewed, to balance the understanding of the story promulgated earlier this century by *Texas History Movies*.

Imagine talking to Mary Rabb, one of the original three hundred colonists. A tall woman with dark eyes and black hair, riding to Texas on her iron-gray horse, Tormenter, her baby on her lap; moving from one place to another, the flies and mosquitoes so bad the women couldn't sew or churn, settling finally on Barton Springs near where we meet tonight; rising early in the morning, while her husband was away down the Brazos, to keep her new spinning wheel "whistling all day and into the night" so she wouldn't hear the strangers prowling outside the house. Imagine having a camera to record in person what Mary Rabb wrote with her pen:

> How many trials and troubles have we passed through together
> here in Texas, and no opportunity of going to church; Yet God

was mindful of us, and blessed us, and gave us his spirit, and made
us feel He was here.

Or Dilue Rose Harris, ten years old and fleeing with her family during the runaway scrape; I'd like to ask her how they managed to haul
their clothes, bedding, and provisions on a sleigh with one yoke of oxen,
and what they felt and feared those three days they waited to cross at the
Lynchburg Ferry, the children sickly with measles, sore eyes, and whoop-
ing cough.

Or Mathilde Wagner, whose poignant accounts of the cholera that
struck San Antonio in the 1870s are an antidote to nostalgia for the
good old days. People died by the scores, she reported. There were few
houses where death did not come. The carts traveled in the dark with
lanterns to light the way, and the drivers called out: "Any dead here?
Any dead here?" Sometimes, says Mathilde Wagner, when a poor fellow
was dying, the carters would sit by the wagon and wait, so they might
take his body away, warm in the sheet on which he died, to be buried in
one of the long, unmarked trenches filling with numberless bodies.

And Sylvia King. What an interview she would be! Born in Mo-
rocco, she was married with three children when she was stolen from her
home, drugged, and shipped in the bottom of a boat to New Orleans,
where blacksmiths pulled her teeth and she was stripped naked for
inspection by strangers. Sold on the block at auction and transported in
chains to Texas, to a master visited often by Sam Houston, a master in
whose service she spent cold winter nights spinning with two threads,
one in each hand and a foot on the pedal as her baby slept on her lap.
Sylvia King lived until she was nearly one hundred, well into our century.

Freeman Smalley is someone else I'd like to interview. He was the
first Baptist minister to preach in Texas, and his audiences were always
small because of his abolitionist views. How he kept his spirits up I don't
know, but Brother Smalley organized the first antislavery church just
north of here in Williamson County, and he stuck to his convictions
even during the Civil War as threats were made against his life and

thieves made off with his possessions. Thanks to a Texas historian, the "still small voice" of Freeman Smalley speaks across the years.

And Kicking Bird, the Kiowa chief who advocated peace and accommodation with whites, and suffered from both sides for it. Having led his braves to victory over the U.S. military in an engagement he didn't want to fight, Kicking Bird was then castigated as a traitor by those same warriors when he was forced to choose which of his tribesmen would go to an American prison in Florida. Kicking Bird died in 1875 after drinking a cup of coffee that was widely thought to have been poisoned. I wish I could have asked him what it was like to live between two worlds.

I just missed interviewing Christina Adair. Some of you may have known her. She was born in 1893, in Victoria, and after graduating from Prairie View taught elementary school in Edna where one of her students was Barbara Jordan's father. Her family had been Lincoln Republicans, but when Warren Harding campaigned in Texas, her students were standing right in front of the observation gate where Harding appeared during a whistle-stop. Warren Harding reached right over the black children to shake the white children's hands, and right then and there Christina Adair became a Democrat. She went on to become the first recording secretary of the first Houston chapter of the NAACP—and a longtime battler for civil rights. It was Christina Adair who bought a $27 girdle she didn't need and insisted on trying it on in the fitting room that was off-limits to black women. It was Christina Adair who with her allies crusaded to close down a notorious holding pen on the county line where black men were taken to be beaten beyond prying eyes. Then one day, Christina Adair was there at Hobby Airport when John Kennedy stopped on his fateful trip to Texas. As she pushed the children closer to see the president, one little boy was jostled until his cap fell off. The president of the United States picked it up—the president himself!—and handed it to the child, patting him on the head and saying, "You lost your cap, didn't you, sonny?" Christina Adair helped to change her times, and our history.

So did Octavia Garcia, who didn't learn to speak English until he was seventeen. After working on his father's ranch near Falfurria he decided to study medicine, and did so well at the medical school in St. Louis, where he had arrived purely by chance, that he emerged as a brilliant student, senior intern, and then chief resident at the University Hospital. He married a Jewish girl named Cecile and together they came down to McAllen looking for a place to settle after the Depression wiped out his father's holdings. A Mexican doctor with a Jewish wife. No hospital wanted him or would take his patients, and many physicians refused to assist him in surgery. Octavia Garcia persisted. His patients got better when others did not, and his reputation mounted. Skill triumphed over skin, and he became a hero in the community. "I don't want to please you," he told people. "I want to tell you the truth." Of all the diseases he fought, the worst was bigotry.

All this is solid and important history that I've learned from you. But it's something more. I suppose you could call it multicultural in outlook—but it's something more than that, too. It may even end up hurting people's feelings, not by willfully and cynically distorting the truth, as some of those old *Texas History Movies* did, but by facing and naming that sad reality that is a part of every people's public life—the reality that we don't always do right or justly.

On the other hand, sometimes we do. History also teaches us this. Twice I was privileged to interview Barbara Tuchman. She saw history as a story of folly and as a source of inspiration, and she liked reminding me that across the centuries men and women have pursued knowledge, exercised reason, sparked laughter, enjoyed pleasure, played games with zest; showed courage, heroism, honor, and decency; experienced love, comfort, contentment, and occasionally happiness; and made sacrifices for the good of others.

It was also my good fortune several times to interview the historian Henry Steele Commager. He insisted that to counter bouts of pessimism, I should read Huizinga's *History of the Middle Ages*. Huizinga reminds us how in those times it was bad form to praise the world and life openly. It was fashionable to see only the suffering and the misery, to discover everywhere the signs of decadence and the end. In short, to condemn the times and to despise them. Yet looking back we know that the Middle Ages were not only the end, they were the beginning—the prelude to that great and vibrant flowering of beauty, art, and intelligence known as the Renaissance, the soaring of the human spirit. History says to optimist and pessimist alike: Wait a minute, count to ten.

You are making a real world of the past, what Thomas Carlyle called "a void of grey haze." The people who live there are not ghosts but players in the unfolding drama of which we are the present cast.

Because your work honors the experiences and takes seriously the lives of so many different and diverse people, it says to everyone gathered in this room, and to others all over Texas, all over the country, as far as words can fly: history is all of us. Everyone is part of the life of this nation; everyone has a stake in the Big Story.

In the novel *The Irish Signorina*, by Julia O'Faolain, the protagonist is a young Irishwoman who demonstrates her knowledge and affection for Italian culture and makes a wry acknowledgment of its similarities to her native land when she says, "Our thoughts are ancient and recycled. Like coal, they're made up of old matter. They flame, but they're old stuff. The voice of the tribe speaks through us."

So it does. The one and many tribes.

For many of the examples cited in this chapter I am indebted to Jo Ella Powell Exley, whose *Texas Tears and Texas Sunshine* (Texas A&M Press, 1986) has provided my wife and me with hours of pleasurable reading.

12. | WHEN THE PAST MEETS THE PRESENT

The Committee of 100

MAY 5, 2000

I meant to call this speech "The Paradox of Success." The audience was Chinese American, gathered under the auspices of the Committee of 100, an organization founded by architect I. M. Pei to encourage contact between the professions in the United States and China and to encourage fuller Chinese American participation in all aspects of life in this country. I knew many on the committee by first name and had marveled at their personal stories. Many had arrived penniless on strange shores and against the odds had risen to the top. I met them when my wife, Judith, and our team of producers had set out to research a PBS series Becoming American: The Chinese Experience. *The series took on a sense of urgency for me when controversies involving two men whom I never met—John Huang and Wen Ho Lee—dominated the news for months. Huang had fled China for Taiwan with his family in 1949 when the Communists took over the country. Ambitious but broke, he came to the United States in 1969, studied statistics as a graduate student while* manning a factory lathe, and climbed swiftly in the world of international banking. Along the way he became so successful as a Democratic fund-raiser that President Clinton put him in charge of Asian trade matters at the Commerce Department. The Democratic National Committee recruited him to raise money for Clinton's reelection in 1996. With extraordinary access to the White House, he seemed destined for greater stardom when, suddenly, his world imploded. Charged with raising funds illegally from foreign sources, Huang pleaded guilty and, chastened, was sentenced to one year of probation and 500 hours of community service. That same year—1999—Wen Ho Lee, a nuclear scientist at Los Alamos, was arrested and held without bail in solitary confinement for 278 days on suspicion of having given secrets to China. I followed the case closely, was appalled at Lee's treatment by the government and by the national media, which, relying on unsubstantiated sources, made a spectacle of the story. It seemed to many of us that Lee had been singled out because of his Chinese heritage. No charge of espionage was ever brought against him and he was released after pleading guilty to mishandling classified information. From our research on the history of the Chinese in America, I realized that no matter the circumstances, both Huang and Lee had been caught up in a panorama of prejudice that began when the first Chinese arrived in this country looking for Gold Mountain. So I changed the title of my speech from "The Paradox of Success" to "When the Past Meets the Present."

* * *

What shall we make of the deluge of news about the scientist and the fund-raiser?

The fund-raiser, as everyone here knows, is John Huang. He has pleaded guilty to charges of making illegal contributions to President Clinton's reelection in the campaign of 1996.

The scientist is Wen Ho Lee, suspected, it would seem, of espionage. We do not know at the moment if he is guilty or innocent of the charges against him. What we do know is that the media spectacle that descended upon him assumed his guilt and made a mockery of due process.

Curious, isn't it? While John Huang did bring in big donations from the Asian American community, the Clinton administration looked the other way until the press revealed the foreign sources of the money. Huang was then fired and made the fall guy, proving in one way—a perverse way—that Chinese Americans have made it in this country. Politics is an arms race today, with money doing the work of missiles. Once you have made it in America, you are welcome in the race because it is presumed you can afford the dues. The Irish will tell you this. And the Jews. And the Italians. And the Pakistanis, who recently ponied up big money for a meeting with Hillary Clinton in an effort to persuade her husband, the president, to stop in their native country on his way to India. You are welcome in the arms race as long as you have the money. But remember, as John Huang surely remembers, the weapons can explode in your face.

There is another dimension to the story that I want to discuss with you today. I mean the intersection where the past meets the present. John Huang was made the fall guy for Democratic fund-raisers who want us to believe they had their eyes closed even as they had their hands out. But as Huang became the fall guy, others suffered the fallout. Investigators looking into sources of fraudulent contributions called only people with "Chinese-sounding" last names. In other words, there was more than a small hint of guilt by association—the tendency to judge the entire group by one of its members.

The Wen Ho Lee case takes us even deeper below the surface. I repeat: we don't know if he is guilty, but under our system he deserves the presumption of innocence until proven otherwise. And that presumption has been violated. Consider the following:

1. The former head of counterintelligence at Los Alamos, Robert Vrooman, participated in the investigation. He now tells *The Washington Post* that Wen Ho Lee was singled out because of his ethnicity. A lot of Caucasians—white folks—were not investigated although they had access to the same information and the same people in China as Lee did.

2. After being fired and branded as a suspected spy, Lee was arrested last December and indicted—but not for espionage. He was charged

on fifty-nine counts of illegally downloading classified information and transferring the data onto nineteen portable computer tapes, of which seven were missing. Not a smart thing to do if you work in a sensitive area. But not espionage. Yet Lee has been denied bail, held in solitary confinement, shackled at his waist, and allowed only one visit a week from his family. (Meanwhile, and in contrast, during his tenure as director of the CIA John Deutch transferred 1,700 pages of classified documents, some secret, onto his unsecured home computers which were attached to modems with access to the Internet, and therefore vulnerable to hackers. When the transfer was discovered, Deutch refused to be interviewed and dozens of the files in his computer were mysteriously deleted. No action was taken for a year; the CIA didn't even formally notify the Justice Department of the security breach. Deutch is now teaching at MIT.)

3. Two and a half months after Lee was fired from Los Alamos, but six months before he was indicted on something other than espionage, a House Select Committee chaired by Congressman Christopher Cox released a 909-page report on Chinese nuclear espionage. In addition to demonizing China as America's arch enemy (even as American entrepreneurs swarm over the country, looking for business), the Cox Report warned that "essentially all Chinese visitors to the U.S. are potential spies." Furthermore, all Chinese Americans are potential "sleeper agents" who may not be activated for a decade or more. By this measure, everyone in this room is a potential suspect, with all that implies for the need for surveillance, wiretaps, anonymous tips, and the onerous intrusions and abrasions of the cold war. For its June 7, 1999, issue, *Time* magazine put on its cover a Chinese eye peering through a star with a red background. The headline read THE NEXT COLD WAR?

The Cox Report has subsequently been widely discredited and denounced by scientists and policy intelligence experts. Notably, a Stanford University study condemned the report for its "sloppy research, factual errors, and weakly justified inferences." Less than a month after its public release, the President's Foreign Intelligence Advisory Board said that in the Cox Report "possible damage has been minted as probable disaster; workaday delay and bureaucratic confusion have been cast as diabolical conspiracies."

Even so, when the Cox Report was issued, the tabloids had a field day. You would have thought every American of Chinese descent is working for the Chinese government. The airwaves filled with toxic fumes from the wastelands of nativism, paranoia, and prejudice, suggesting that Chinese agents are embedded in all levels of our nation's most sensitive military facilities.

Listening to talk radio after the Cox Report, I heard something profoundly disturbing: the wrenching, grating, ear-piercing, soul-shaking sound of the past meeting the present. Those people I heard—hosts and callers—thought they were voicing their own opinions. But in fact their loathing, spite, and fear were echoes from the past. For the soil of American experience has been fertilized by two centuries of racist rhetoric and crude caricature whose memory traces are imbedded deeply in our social DNA.

And yet it didn't start that way. The founders of this nation were men of ideas; some were intellectuals. Although they didn't possess any firsthand knowledge of China, they were fascinated by what they learned from contemporary Europeans who celebrated China as a prosperous and harmonious nation of industrious peasants and craftsmen governed by benevolent and moral rulers.

Benjamin Franklin marveled at how the most populous country on earth still "clothes its inhabitants with silk, while it feeds them plentifully." Franklin even upheld the Chinese civilization as a model for the new country. "Could we be so fortunate as to introduce the industry of the Chinese, their arts of living and improvements in husbandry, America might become in time as populous as China," Franklin wrote. James Madison wanted to know all he could about Chinese agricultural techniques. James Monroe and Thomas Jefferson admired China's political disengagement as a mark of superiority and independence. Upper-class Americans prized Chinese wallpaper, silk canopies, vases, and lacquered screens. George Washington bought a porcelain dinner service from China traders in 1786.

But then tastes changed, and the young nation saw China less as a model than as a market. Americans needed money and wanted trade. But they had little to offer. Early in the nineteenth century, merchants finally found a profitable export for the China trade—opium. They realized they could do as the British were doing and redress our balance of trade by exporting opium. There was a hitch: America had no opium. Merchants had to go to India to buy it from the British. This cut profits substantially so the United States encouraged the peasants in Turkey and Persia to grow opium, which they did. (Now, two hundred years later, we are paying Turkish peasants not to grow opium. Call it poetic justice. Call it the long arm of the past.) Soon every American firm doing business with China was handling opium, with the most prominent firms in Boston becoming the lead traffickers. Among them were names that would become famous for other reasons: Abbott, Low, Forbes, Delano.

Government agents knew a good thing when they saw it. In 1812, Benjamin Wilcocks was appointed American consul in Canton, and three years later, he used his official seal to prevent the Chinese from searching an opium ship owned by his family.

Americans soon moved on from the opium trade to what was called the "pig trade." American ships began to transport indentured laborers from China to British colonial plantations in the Caribbean, including Cuba. They were called "coolies"—from the Hindi word *kuli*, meaning unskilled labor. Impoverished young Chinese peasants were tricked, or kidnapped, and made to sign dubious labor contracts. They were held in barracoons—pigpens—until they were packed onto ships, often in chains. The majority were brought to Latin America where they were simply worked to death. In 1855 alone, five American ships smuggled three thousand coolies from a southern Chinese port that was not officially open for foreign trade. In 1861, as the first shots were being fired in our Civil War, the American ship *Norway* made a harrowing journey from Macao to Havana carrying 1,037 Chinese men. During the voyage 130 died from dysentery and gunshot wounds. Historians tell us the survival rate among Chinese shipped to Cuba was about as low as that of the African slave trade.

Do you see how the ideology grew? We saw the Chinese as utilitarian objects instead of human beings. They became exotic curiosities for exploitation and amusement. P. T. Barnum opened a Chinese museum at 539 Broadway in lower Manhattan whose main attraction became a seventeen-year-old girl with tiny feet. Barnum advertised her as "the first Chinese lady that has yet visited Christendom."

American traders published their memoirs, describing Chinese merchants as "the greatest villains in the universe." Wrote a Portsmouth, New Hampshire, trader: "The Chinese of the present day are grossly superstitious . . . depraved and vicious gambling is universal . . . they use pernicious drugs . . . are gross gluttons . . . bloodthirsty and inhuman."

First trade, then religion. One of the first American missionaries to China wrote to his father: "I have been here a week . . . and in that short time have seen enough idolatries to call forth all the energies I have. To see the abominations practiced . . . and not to be affected with a deep sense of the depth to which this people have sunk, is impossible to a warm Christian man." A journal published in China for Western missionaries concluded that China was "a defective civilization."

Connect the dots: trade to religion to culture. In 1824, America's foremost philosopher rendered his judgment on a land he had never visited and a people he had never known. Ralph Waldo Emerson wrote:

> The closer contemplation we condescend to bestow, the more disgustful is that booby nation . . . I have no gift to see a meaning in the venerable vegetation of this extraordinary people. They are tools for other nations to use. Even miserable Africa can say I have hewn the wood and drawn the water to promote the civiliza-

tion of other lands. But China, Reverend Dullness, Hoary Ideot!
All she can say at the convocation of nations must be—"I made
the tea."

Connect the dots: trade, religion, culture, politics. In 1877 the
United States was in the fourth year of a major depression. On the
morning of July 16 railroad workers blocked a train in West Virginia to
protest a wage cut. The strike spread—Buffalo, Pittsburgh, Chicago,
Boston, Newark, the Midwest, the South. Federal troops joined the state
militia to put down the unrest. Newspaper headlines warned of anarchy
and revolution. Washington needed to mollify the workers. The powers
that be needed a scapegoat. Why not the Chinese? They were sub-
human, right? Opium smokers, "pig" workers, freaks, and heathens all.
Now Chinese exclusion—immigration restriction—became a political
panacea: to make the angry white workers think that their troubles were
the fault not of the politicians, speculators, and bankers but of a weak,
vulnerable minority of Chinese laborers.

Scapegoating had been hugely successful in California. During the
presidential campaign of 1876 both the Republican and Democratic parties needed to take California to win the election. Both decided they
couldn't win the White House without running against a demon. The
Chinese were an easy target. Republicans demanded a congressional investigation of the effects of Chinese immigration. The Democrats went
further, calling for legislation to "prevent further importation or immigration of the Mongolian race." Hateful invective filled the air, aimed at
Chinese workers.

The election that year produced the closest electoral margin in the
nation's history. The Republican—Rutherford B. Hayes—won by one
vote in the Electoral College. The press said he would never have carried California if there had not been an anti-Chinese plank in the platform. Both parties got the message: national political dominance would
require the California vote, and that meant running against the Chinese. And that meant demonizing a whole people.

Over the coming years the ideology took on an apocalyptic fervor.

Ambitious men became apostles of malice for their own gain. Preparing to run for the White House, Senator James G. Blaine converted to the cause. In a speech supporting the restriction to limit Chinese immigration, he said,

> The question lies in my mind thus: Either the Anglo-Saxon race will possess the Pacific slope or the Mongolians will . . . you cannot work a man who must have beer and bread, and would prefer beer, alongside of a man who can live on rice. It cannot be done.

In 1881 Republican senator John Miller of California introduced a bill in Congress to suspend immigration of Chinese laborers. He spoke for two hours on the Senate floor:

> The Chinese are inhabitants of another planet . . . machine-like . . . they are automatic engines of flesh and blood. Why not discriminate? Why aid in the increase and distribution over our domain of a degraded and inferior race, and the progenitors of an inferior sort of men . . . we ask you to secure to us American Anglo-Saxon civilization without contamination or adulteration. Let us keep pure the blood which circulates through our political system . . . and preserve our life from the gangrene of oriental civilization.

The New York Times called Miller's speech "A masterly statement . . . admirable in temper and judicial in fairness."

A popular cartoon that year replaced the Statue of Liberty in New York harbor with one of a Chinese radiating "Filth," "Immorality," "Diseases," and "Ruin to White Labor."

A widely circulated pamphlet proclaimed "The Last Days of the Nation." Chinese were depicted as invaders and conquerors.

There is an old proverb: "The fathers have eaten a sour grape, and the children's teeth are set on edge." When the news broke about John Huang and Wen Ho Lee, I listened to talk radio indict a whole people for the alleged transgressions of a few. In the angry voices of callers and the condescending snideness of the hosts, I heard echoes of Boston traders and Yankee missionaries, of P. T. Barnum and Ralph Waldo Emerson, James Blaine and John Miller. A virus spread through the molecular membranes of America's other GNP, our gross national psychology—those subterranean chambers, which send us their silent signals without our knowing their source.

Now you know why I want to tell the story of the Chinese experience in America. On PBS we've told the story of the Jews in America. The Irish in America, the English in America, the Italians in America, and the Africans in America. But not this story. It, too, is a story of terror and tragedy. But it is also one of triumph.

The Chinese fought back. A hundred years ago a twenty-two-year-old Chinese cook named Wong Kim Ark returned to San Francisco, the city of his birth, after visiting his parents in China. He was denied entry. Immigration officers declared that he was a laborer and could not enter the United States under the Chinese Exclusion Act. He sued, arguing that he was, by birth, a citizen. He took his case all the way to the Supreme Court. The United States government opposed him. The Solicitor General asked the Supreme Court: "Are Chinese children born in this country to share with the descendants of the patriots of the American Revolution to exacted qualification of being eligible to the presidency of the nation?"

To practically everyone's surprise, the Supreme Court said: "Yes." The Court decided for the cook. Chinese Americans went on to challenge the Chinese Exclusion Act with more than 7,000 petitions in state and federal courts—cases that profoundly affected the course of American jurisprudence and contributed to the molding of equal-protection jurisprudence under the Fourteenth Amendment.

Even as we meet here today, far away in New Haven, Connecticut, the president of Yale University is welcoming the Chinese minister of education and a select group of Yale alumni and friends. They are there, in the Grand Hall of one of America's oldest and most elite universities, to unveil a portrait of the first Chinese to earn a diploma from an American university. His name was Yung Wing. He graduated from Yale in 1854 at a time when Chinese were considered by many to be immoral heathens. Yet Yung Wing was highly regarded at Yale; he married a girl from a prominent Hartford family, befriended Mark Twain, became a naturalized citizen, and died here. He did this at a time in this country when Chinese were being massacred in western states and a Chinese man could put his life at risk by speaking to a white woman. Yet Yung Wing wasn't afraid to speak out or to fight the Chinese Exclusion Act. Only two states voted against that act—Massachusetts and Connecticut. Yung Wing's grandson says he can't help thinking that Yung Wing could have been a factor influencing that vote. He also established the Chinese Educational Mission and brought 120 young Chinese boys to America to study Western science and technology. Some of the descendants of those first students are at the unveiling today. So is Yung Wing's grandson.

You're part of this great story. The Committee of 100 reads like a who's who of Chinese descent in America. Your success in corporate and high-tech America and your leadership in politics, the arts, communications, and literature confirm the latest chapter of the Chinese experience in America. It's the story of how, in the last half of the twentieth century, Chinese not only entered the mainstream of American society but rose to its pinnacle. I don't know how many of you shared the experience of rejection and exclusion suffered by earlier generations, but all of you are beneficiaries of the sacrifices they endured as they struggled to make America their home. You stand on the shoulders of brave ghosts.

A personal note.

Thirty-five years ago President Lyndon Johnson descended from a helicopter at the base of the Statue of Liberty. There he signed into law the Immigration and Nationality Act, which removed the previous quota system that had favored northern and western European immigrants. His signature marked the true end of Chinese exclusion in America. I was on that helicopter with President Johnson. I was thirty-one at the time, one of his White House assistants who helped draft what he said that day. Let me read it to you:

This bill that we will sign today . . . is one of the most important acts of this Congress and this administration. For it does repair a very deep and painful flaw in the fabric of American justice. It corrects a cruel and enduring wrong in the conduct of the American Nation . . . This bill says simply that from this day forth those wishing to immigrate to America shall be admitted on the basis of their skills and their close relationship to those already here . . . The fairness of this standard is so self-evident . . . Yet the fact is that for over four decades the immigration policy of the United States has been twisted and distorted by the harsh injustice of the national origins quota system . . . This system violated the basic principle of American democracy . . . Today, with my signature, this system is abolished.*

And so it is. But we still have work to do if we are finally to throw off the yoke of prejudice that is our burden from the past.

---

*This was the system, embodied in legislation in 1924, that restricted immigration from southern and eastern Europe.

Part III

POLITICS

13. | A VISION OF THE FUTURE

*Keynote Address for the National Legislative Education
Foundation's Democratic Issues Conference*

MARCH 8, 1991

*When I left the White House in 1967 for journalism, I left partisanship be-
hind. As best I can remember, during these forty years my wife and I have
made two financial contributions in a partisan race—for close friends running for state office far from where we live. I vote—journalists are citizens,
and we allow the franchise of a civil muscle to atrophy at peril. So when the
invitation came to deliver the keynote speech at the Democratic Issues Conference in 1991, I declined. Overnight came a renewed plea in writing from
the organizers, explaining that the event was to be sponsored by the National
Legislative Education Foundation for the purpose of exposing Democrats to a
variety of opinions and ideas—conservative and Republican journalists and
analysts had also spoken over the years. I was persuaded. And I was grateful they persisted, because I had something on my mind. The right-wing assault on government that had been launched by Ronald Reagan, temporarily
sidetracked by George H. W. Bush, who was no antigovernment ideologue,*

was again gathering force. Furthermore, Democrats seemed at sea without ballast; they were no longer articulating the fundamental argument for the role of government. Bewildered by the antigovernment populism on the Right, Democrats were functioning less and less as a grassroots party devoted to mobilizing citizens for sustained participation in our political life. Instead, they had become essentially a fund-raising machine in the service of organized special interests, which only produced more scandals and gridlock that made ordinary people more skeptical, even cynical, that government could fulfill any of its critical promises. This, in turn, played into the hands of the corporate, political, and religious forces that were attempting to separate government from the people who were most in need of it. Those of us who believe government is essential to addressing the problems Americans face in common needed once again to affirm why politics is everybody's business. This is no partisan truth, but the party that claims it, I wanted to tell the Democrats, will own the future.

* * *

I was honored by your invitation and I am pleased to be here. The company of so many members of Congress recalls some of my happier memories from an earlier incarnation—memories of the Hill. I spent the summer of 1954 on the staff of Senator Lyndon Johnson. He took a fancy to letters I wrote on his behalf and when I finished graduate school, he invited me back in 1960. I was twenty-six. Since then, I have spent my entire adult life in and around public affairs, as a congressional and presidential assistant, as an organizer for the Peace Corps, a newspaper publisher, and a broadcaster.

I left partisanship behind when I left the White House in 1967 for journalism. But my roots are tangled with yours. In Texas I was nourished on mother's milk and FDR's speeches. I still cherish the party's defining stands. It was a Democratic president who inspired my father's generation to meet despair with courage and it was the same president who rallied the nation against Hitler and the warlords of Japan. Another Democratic president drew the line against expansion of the Soviet empire, committed us to the generous reconstruction of our vanquished foes, to the United Nations, and called on us to support the new state of Israel. Two Democratic presidents in the '60s roused us to reject poverty as an act of God and segregation as immutable, so that LBJ, in his finest hour, could stand before the Congress and the nation and declare, "We shall overcome."

Those are the moments I remember most proudly from this party's history in my time. But I remember other things, too. We went to war in Vietnam against a foe that refused to mass his troops for our convenience; we went without either the preparation or speed so decisive in battle, and without the global consensus President George H. W. Bush organized against Saddam Hussein, and we went to war without the confidence of the public that gives conviction to a cause and spares young soldiers from dying in a morass of ambiguity.

So we left our successors a lost cause and a bloody mess, with our leadership spent, our budget broken, the dollar weakened, and the public embittered. The country's faith in the Democrats' ability to govern was so shaken that soon it was not principle but survival which defined the party's mission.

Your adversaries delight in all this. For them, given their ideological appetite for conformity, one party is enough. When only one team shows up to play, the other forfeits the game. Just the other day *The Wall Street Journal* urged in an editorial that Democrats learn a lesson from the Persian Gulf. The lesson was that you should be more like Republicans. It criticized—and listed the names of—those members of Congress, most of them Democrats, who had voted against the use of force in the Gulf in favor of sustained international diplomacy and it suggested that no Democrat will ever win the White House until the party sheds its image as a bunch of pacifists opposed to a "strong U.S. role in the world." That, of course, is the usual cartoonist distortion of realities that we have come to expect from the Right.

Truth is, the Persian Gulf vote was an example of party politics at its best—exactly because there *were* two parties to choose from, parties with clear differences. Because there is always more than one possible answer to an issue, voters need to hear the choices forcefully argued, as they were in this case. The editorial suggested that the "central problem" for the Democrats who preferred continuing the embargo instead of using force is that they are "now seen to be so obviously wrong." Well, since the embargo was never given a chance to prove itself one way or another, no one knows whether the idea was *obviously* wrong. In fact, when the UN agreed on the sanctions against Iraq, it was a moment when an alternative to war was proposed and recognized and accepted by the world community. That George H. W. Bush chose war in no way diminishes the courage many of you demonstrated in framing a clear alternative to war. Furthermore, Americans were seriously divided over going to war in the Persian Gulf. As many did not want war as did. A political system that does not reflect the natural divisions of opinion will not long hold to its legitimacy. Your stand reflected at least half the American people and much of its leadership—including eight of nine former defense secretaries, two recent chairmen of the Joint Chiefs of Staff, and articulate liberal and conservative voices alike.

A principled stand remains honorable, no matter how politically vulnerable. Conscience, not conformity, defines America. Otherwise, we might still be British subjects. Who remembers the names in the crowd that voted *for* the Gulf of Tonkin Resolution, but who can forget the names of Wayne Morse and Ernest Gruening, who voted *against* it? It is an affront to democracy to require Americans to judge their political parties as if they were comparing identical twins. For ten years now, the other party has embraced the notion that "war is the health of the state," but in the long run, the future belongs to the party that knows that the health of the people precedes the health of the state.

In the last decade, America has experienced the worst recession since the '30s, the deterioration of our manufacturing base, a burst of speculation in stocks and bonds unequaled since 1929, and the biggest stock market collapse in nearly six decades. This is the landscape described by Kevin Phillips, the former Republican strategist, whose best-selling book *The Politics of Rich and Poor: Wealth and the American Electorate in the Reagan Aftermath* describes how America is dividing along cleavages of wealth, income, race, education, opportunity, and hope. For millions, says Phillips, the American dream is crumbling—not just in inner-city ghettoes and farm townships, but in blue-collar neighborhoods and even middle-class suburbs. He offers the statistics to back up his claim.

We are rightly concerned that the future of the newly emerging democracies of the dismantled East bloc lives up to its first bright promise. But the thirty to forty million Americans living in poverty are more in number than the entire population of East Germany and Hungary combined.

There are more Americans without health insurance than there are people living in all of Central America. Just look at today's lead story in *The Wall Street Journal:* thousands of West Virginians are left in dire straits by the collapse of Blue Cross and Blue Shield there. One of them is a thirty-two-year-old gas-line repairman who must now find a way to pay family medical bills of $36,000 on a yearly income from two jobs of $23,000. "I couldn't pay off $36,000 in a lifetime," he says.

Half of the children who enter our urban primary schools next fall will fail to finish school. Yet we spend four times as much on the Strategic Defense Initiative—Star Wars—than we do on the early-education program Head Start, which works.

In 1970, one in seven Americans experienced poverty in childhood or youth. In 1980, one in six. In 1990, one in five.

As always, the burdens of poverty are falling disproportionately on African American, Hispanics, and inner-city residents. It's outrageous that one in every five children is poor. But among black children, the percentage rises to nearly half. The population of poor black children in America is about equal to the entire population of Israel.

The United States is the most murderous nation in the world, with a homicide rate ten times as great as England or Japan. In many of our major cities crime, as John Lindsay famously said, "is a slow motion riot," committed by small armies of hustlers, fundamentally illiterate and disconnected from anything anybody understands as being American. Passing through those years without acquiring the capacity and motivation required by a regular job, they are likely to end up a ward of the government, a disability case, or a convicted criminal. Nine thousand black men are in prison in our nation's capital. Our prison population actually exceeds the number of Kuwaiti citizens.

Meanwhile, an epic is washing up on our shores—a new wave of immigrants from Asia, Central America, Africa, and the Caribbean. In the Los Angeles unified school district, Hispanics are 62 percent of the school population but four out of ten of those Hispanic kids will never make it through high school. By the turn of the century, according to one study, most Latinos will live in squalid towns without paved roads or electricity and stagger under heavy taxes to support Social Security and other old-age benefits for retired whites.

The income gap between rich and poor in America is greater than at any time since records were first kept forty years ago. By several measures, the United States in the late twentieth century leads all other major industrial nations in the gap dividing the upper fifth of the population from the lower. The richest 2.5 million American taxpayers will pocket as much money this year as the 100 million poorest combined. When Phillips and others recount such figures, reactionaries accuse them of fomenting "class warfare." But you don't have to advocate class warfare to advocate fairness in America.

The simple fact is that extremes of wealth and poverty undermine democracy. Poorly educated kids and illiterate adults get left out of democracy. Crime traumatizes democracy. And racism tribalizes democracy.

Together these forces prevent us from developing a dynamic society that creates opportunity for all Americans. It should be no secret to anyone that what the richest and strongest members of society want for their families is what all members of society want for theirs, too. They want their children to grow up and function independently. They want a place they call home. They want the means to cope with illness and other misfortunes. They want enough money for a sufficient living and a secure old age. They want to live freely as citizens without fear. And they want to contribute something to society.

A society whose economy cannot make these opportunities widely available is deeply in trouble, no matter how many glorious victories it wins over third-world dictators. As the Nobel laureate economist Kenneth Arrow has written, "The vast inequalities of income weaken a society's sense of mutual concern . . . The sense that we are all members of the social order is *vital* to the meaning of civilization."

Travel the country today and you hear in person what the pollsters report in percentages. People believe their government and its policy makers have failed them—that the system no longer produces solutions to our problems.

They are talking about the fact that schools are not adequately educating their children, that the environment is polluted, the federal deficit grows, the cost of health care keeps rising, and unfettered development threatens the quality of life in their communities. It's not surprising that millions of Americans are restless to get on with our revolution—working together to create "a more perfect union."

In their book *Starting with the People*, Daniel Yankelovich and Sidney Harman conclude that "People do not buy the premise that their role is merely to listen passively, absorb information the experts pass out, and then choose among the experts." The 1991 report *Citizens and Politics* by the Kettering Foundation concludes:

> When it comes to politics, Americans are both frustrated and downright angry. They argue that politics have been taken away from them—that they have been pushed out of the political process. This feeling of impotence is revealed for instance in a fervent belief that individual citizens can no longer have their voice heard on important public issues. That many, if not most public issues are talked about by experts in ways that neither connect with the concerns of citizens nor make any sense to them. It is revealed also in citizens' belief that they have been squeezed out of politics by a system dangerously spiraling out of control, a system made up of lobbyists, political action committees, special interest organizations, and the media . . . They sense that we risk losing

something precious to the meaning of the American experience . . . that the very meaning of the public good is disappearing
in a sea of self-seeking.

I travel frequently and widely as a journalist. I hear Americans talk
seriously about public life and our civic culture. I hear them saying they
want to signify morally and they want their country to signify morally,
too. Václav Havel talks about a need "to inject ideas of spirituality, mutual understanding, and mutual tolerance into the affairs of state." These
ideas exposed the hollowness of Soviet shibboleths and forged resistance
to one-party domination. They kept alive the notion of a participatory
public, of people accountable for their own destiny.

I find traces of these ideas in America today. Perhaps they are no
bigger at the moment than the mustard seed. But we know what happens
to the mustard seed. So I see two important stories are emerging in the
intersection between the secular and the spiritual, between God and
politics.

One is the attempt to find a new vision for America which has the
authority and power of a religious vision but which is inclusive—not
sectarian. At its best, religion's great accomplishment has been to create
social bonds based on love, justice, and mutual respect. In a pluralistic
and secular democracy, what gives us that energizing and organizing vision now? How can we be properly enthusiastic—how do we honor the
religious sense—without denying reason? What does it mean to be inspired? In other words, how is the hunger of the soul to be suitably filled?

The second story is the effort to rewrite our own history so that we
can tell the truth about America and still be proud of the country. Somewhere between the righteous Right and the cynical Left is a real country people can recognize and improve without having to deny the dark
side of one experience.

President Bush choked up the other day as he recalled the televised
scene of four terrified Iraqi soldiers, emerging from their bunkers to sur-
render to an American soldier who told them, "It's OK. You're all right
now. You're all right." The president said, "We are a good people, we are

a generous people." I thought: Yes, but what about all those Iraqi soldiers and civilians—people whose only offense was their inability to escape Saddam's tyranny and our technology—who were smashed to a pulp by American power? Saddam is said by psychologists to be the incarnation of "malignant narcissism"—willing to use others' pain for one's own purpose. We did his dirty work for him and made them pay the penalty for their leader's transgressions.

Following the president's address to Congress that same night, I saw another television report. A camera had recorded Los Angeles police swinging their nightsticks at a black motorist, jostling one another to take turns hitting and kicking him until he was battered and bruised and bleeding. Not long before, President Bush had praised the Los Angeles chief of police in one of those generalized benedictions that take no note of complex American realities. Yes indeed, while we can be "a good people, a generous people," our record is stained by cruelty, racism, and chauvinism. Dedicated to the proposition that all men are created equal, Americans still violently dispossessed the Indian and nurtured slavery in the cradle of liberty.

So what is the story we can write that does not deny our sin but does not end in cynicism? How can we write our story so that it is meaningful even when the truth is uncomfortable?

We begin by resurrecting the neglected side of the American story. Individual initiative succeeded only when it led to a strong system of mutual support. Laissez-faire had given England seven-day workweeks, twelve-hour workdays, and filthy, dangerous factories. But here in America, we would move beyond the philosophy of "live and let live" to the active and affirmative notion of "live and *help* live." I couldn't sit in my clearing while you sweated and strained alone to raise your barn. Neighbors came together to help. Barn raisings became a social occasion, a way of expressing solidarity and caring. You helped to deliver one another's babies. When a family was sick, you took turns sitting at the bedside or helping with the meals. You helped bury the dead.

Before my father died last year, we sat on his porch in Marshall, Texas, as he reminisced about his own childhood in a family of poor farmers living near the Red River between Oklahoma and Texas. He was fourteen when his father died during the flu epidemic of 1918. Neighbors washed his father's body, neighbors dug the grave, and neighbors laid my grandfather in the earth. Even as late as my high-school days, my father and others in the church would sit all night at the funeral home beside the corpse of a friend. I once asked him, "Why did you do that, knowing you had to work hard all the next day driving a truck?" He looked at me as if I were an ignoramus and answered, "Because it was just the thing we did."

Just the thing WE did.

I often remind audiences of the historical marker not far from where I grew up which records that in 1842, one John McGarrah brought his family to Texas and settled there, founding the town of Buckner. Soon a church was built, then a school, then a trading post—indications that neighbors had settled nearby. Four years later, on July 4, 1846, John Mc-Garrah and his neighbors elected their first public officials and opened a post office. The marker captures the story of civilization, the progression from solitary initiative to social cooperation. First the prime family unit; then the wagon train; then the church and the school for worship and learning; then a trading post for the goods of survival and comfort; then local government for roads and public order; then the post office for communications with others; then a public holiday for celebration and recreation.

Standing there, as I did hitchhiking to college, I began to understand the web of cooperation joining individuals to family, friends, communities, and country, creating in each a sense of reliance on the whole, a recognition of the self in companionship with others, sharing powerful loyalties. Robert Bellah speaks of "habits of the heart." Our challenge is to create a political culture that nurtures obligation, reciprocity, and trust, to bring about policies that have wide public support.

I can hear some of you say, "Moyers, you're just being romantic. The frontier is long gone. Let the dead bury the dead." In one sense, that's true. As Robert Reich tells us in *Tales of a New America*, we don't have communities and neighborhoods the way we used to. Rather, more

Americans lived on military bases in the '80s than in what could be called "neighborhoods" in the traditional sense—card games on the front porch, kids running over lawns and fields, corner soda fountains, etc. The majority today live in suburban subdivisions that extend helter-skelter in every direction, bordered by highways and punctuated by large shopping malls; or in condominiums, town houses, co-ops, and retirement communities that provide privacy and safety; or they inhabit dilapidated houses and apartments.

That old sense of community is gone, depriving us of shared loyalties and landmarks, making us more nervous, vulnerable, and amenable to nonsense and violence. Fearful and fragmented, we seek refuge in the comfortable lie rather than face the uncomfortable truth. The lie is John Wayne: the embodiment of the rugged individual as savior of the West. The truth is the wagon train: if we don't get there together, we won't get there at all.

At root this is a moral enterprise. Before John McGarrah could have a trading post, there had to be a community, and there couldn't be a community unless its members agreed on the difference between a horse trader and a horse thief. The distinction, as Edward Ericson says, is ethical. Without it, society is a war of all against all—a free market for wolves becomes a slaughter for the lambs. A stable system of law, clean and safe streets, secure pensions, and schools where children learn whether they live in rich neighborhoods or poor—all of this is part of the bargain we strike with one another. The myths notwithstanding, our society is dependent on a far-reaching and complex organizational and institutional network. Every personal need, every want we satisfy, practically every action we take, our very ability to survive depends on a tremendously complex production and delivery system that extends not only across the nation but sometimes across the entire world.

We live, in other words, in a highly complex country where we are all connected. Government has become bigger and more centralized, not because we have become careless of our freedoms or morally lazy in our commitment to individual values, but because the important tasks that need to be done in our nation today are beyond the reach of individual men and women. Making our society work—the flourishing of civilization—is everyone's business. It's what *we* do. Our individual freedom depends upon our participating membership in democracy. The party that translates this vision into politics will lead our country in the twenty-first century.

14. | SO GREAT A SOUL

Memorial Service for Barbara Jordan,
February 21, 1936–January 17, 1996

JANUARY 28, 1996

Barbara Jordan's booming voice mesmerized the nation in 1974 as the House
Judiciary Committee took up the impeachment of Richard Nixon: "My faith
in the Constitution is whole; it is complete; it is total. And I am not going to
sit here and be an idle spectator to the diminution, the subversion, the de-
struction, of the Constitution." Yet as she also said in that electrifying speech,
she had not been included in "We the People" when the Founding Fathers
drew up the nation's political compact. There is no more dramatic personal
story in the unfolding of the long struggle to fulfill that compact than Barbara,
the daughter of a warehouse clerk and Baptist preacher, who graduated
magna cum laude from college, obtained her law degree from Boston Univer-
sity, and came home to Houston to practice law out of her parents' home for
three years until she saved enough money to open an office. After winning
election to the Texas Senate, where she also won over her thirty white male
colleagues, she became the first black woman from a Southern state to serve

in Congress. She personified tenacity, mastered detail, and grasped compromise as the art of politics. We became friends after she left Congress to teach at the LBJ School of Public Affairs at the University of Texas, where, suffering from multiple sclerosis and operating from a wheelchair, she inspired young people to see that politics at its best, for all the wheeling and dealing, is the necessary and enabling means of democracy, requiring an ethical bond between the people and their representatives. At parties and salons no one could belt out an old Baptist hymn like Barbara. Only in her final hours did I know that she had asked me to speak when she would not be there to sing.

* * *

When Dean Max Sherman called to tell me that Barbara Jordan was dying and that she had asked me to speak at this service, I had been reading a story in that morning's *New York Times* about the discovery of forty billion new galaxies to go with the ten billion we already knew about. As I put the phone down, I thought: It will take an infinite cosmic vista to accommodate so great a soul. The universe has been getting ready for her.

Now, at last, she has an amplifying system equal to her voice. As we gather in her memory, I can imagine the cadences of her eloquence echoing at the speed of light past orbiting planets and pulsars, past black holes and white dwarfs and hundreds of millions of sunlike stars, until the whole cosmic spectrum stretching out to the far fringes of space toward the very origins of time resonates to her presence.

The day after her death, the headline in the *Houston Chronicle* read: A VOICE FOR JUSTICE DIES. And I thought: Not so. The *body*, yes: "dust to dust and ashes to ashes." But the *voice* that speaks for justice joins the music of the spheres. What does the universe even know of justice unless informed by a Barbara Jordan? Cock your ear toward the mysterious and invisible matter that shapes the galaxies and sustains their coherence, and you will hear nothing of justice. On matters of meaning and morality the universe is dumbstruck, the planets silent. Our notions of right and wrong, of how to live together, come from our prophets, not from the planets. It is the *human* voice that commands justice to roll down "like waters, and righteousness like a mighty stream."

And what a voice this was!

They say that after Theodore Roosevelt was in heaven a few days, he complained to St. Peter that the choir was weak and should be reorganized. "All right," said St. Peter, "reorganize it." And Teddy Roosevelt replied: "Well, I'll need 10,000 sopranos, 10,000 altos, and 10,000 tenors."

"And what about the basses?" asked St. Peter.

"Oh," said Teddy Roosevelt, "*I'll* sing bass."

Well, they can all retire in heaven now. Sopranos, altos, tenors—and Teddy, too. There's a new choir in town, and she's a Baptist from the Fifth Ward in Houston.

Barbara was singing the last time we were together. There were twoscore of us at Liz Carpenter's up on Skyline Drive, belting forth old favorites from the Broadman and Cokesbury hymnals. "Standing on the Promises," "Throw Out the Lifeline," "The Old Rugged Cross." And spirituals, too. "Swing Low, Sweet Chariot," "Deep River," "My Lord, What a Morning." Friends have said her music often eased the smarting wounds of her long battle with multiple sclerosis. But this night some other wellspring opened as she sang one of her favorite blues songs. Hands on the arms of her electric chariot, that big head tilted back, a mischievous gleam of light in her eyes, she sang "Nobody Knows You When You're Down and Out."

> It's mighty strange, without a doubt
> Nobody knows you when you're down and out
> I mean, when you're down and out

As I recall that moment now, the Barbara Jordan who appears in my mind's eye is *not* the mature, powerful, accomplished, and celebrated woman whose music filled our circle of fellowship that night. No, I see a small child in Houston looking up at a water fountain posted WHITES ONLY. I see a little girl riding in the back of the bus to a movie she has to enter through a side door to sit in the balcony as prescribed by law. I see a teenager in a segregated high school preparing to go, as expected, to an all-black college. And I see the young collegian leading the Texas Southern debating team and placing first in oratory against all white opponents but required, even in victory, to sleep in quarters and eat in restaurants "for coloreds only." I see a young woman coming back from Boston to open her law practice on the dining-room table of her parents' modest brick house at a time that no white firm would hire her. I see her running for office and losing. Running again—and losing. But each time, getting up and coming back without bitterness or rancor, and on her third time, winning. I see her arriving in Austin, a political oddity and outcast, and I see her just six years later, Speaker pro tem of the Texas Senate.

How does it happen that when "nobody knows you when you're down and out," Barbara knew herself? All along the way, with the shadow of Jim Crow falling across her every step like an eclipse of the sun, she knew herself. She knew her family, too—her mother, Arlyne, and father, Benjamin, who once told her: "I'll stick with you and go with you as far as you want to go." And Rosemary and Bennie—she knew her sisters and the songs they sang together. And she knew the people of Good Hope Missionary Baptist Church, where reportedly the Lord called often.

She knew her ancestors, too. Not only the bloodlines running back to the sharecroppers and tenant farmers and former slaves and proud Africans, but her political lineage as well.

Socrates was Barbara's kin; with him she believed you cannot have a healthy state when "you have one half the world triumphing and the other plunged in grief." And Plato was her kin, exhorting young people, as she did, to "take part in the great combat, which is the contest of life."

Montesquieu was her kin, who said the state of nature bestows on us equality that society then robs from us, and we recover it "only by the protection of the laws." With him, she would hold that "a government is like everything else; to preserve it, we must love it."

Edmund Burke was her kin, who held that "all persons possessing any portion of power ought to be strongly and awfully impressed with the idea that they act in trust; and that they are to account for their conduct in that trust to the one great Master, Author, and Founder of society."

And Lincoln—Lincoln was surely Barbara's kin, who said, "We will make converts day by day. And unless truth be a mockery and justice a hollow lie, we will be in the majority after a while . . ." Who also said, "The battle of freedom is to be fought out on principle."

Dead white males—from Greece, France, England, and Illinois. And a black woman from Houston. Kin. Not by blood. Not through the color of skin. Not from place of birth or tribe of origin. Not by station, rank, or office. No, kinship in this universal republic is forged from the love of truth, the passion for liberty, and the conviction that justice cannot long be denied if a people are to prosper.

What made Barbara so effective is the way she brought those ideas to down-home politics. True, she was an extraordinary speaker. (It was said of the famous Methodist preacher George Whitefield that "He could make men laugh or cry by pronouncing the single word 'Mesopotamia.' " Barbara could do it with the word "Constitution.") But her ambition was not a few lines of immortality in Bartlett's *Familiar Quotations*. Nor was she content just to capture your heart. She wanted your vote.

She began in Houston politics licking stamps and knocking on doors; they still talk about the time she organized the city's first black precinct drive for Kennedy and Johnson in 1960. Here in Austin, half the bills she submitted for consideration were enacted into law. In a legislature that was practically an oligarchy, she made things happen for laundry workers, domestic helpers, and farm laborers.

And up in Washington, for only three terms, she so mastered the process and details of procedure that not even the craftiest patriarchs of Congress could outfox her. Her 1975 campaign to hold Texas accountable to the Voting Rights Act was a triumph over entrenched and powerful opponents. A journalist colleague of mine said she was "as cozy as a pile driver, but considerably more impressive." But in her study of the parliamentary arts, she had clearly listened to the counsel of the experienced, which holds that "as with sailing, so with politics; make your cloth too taut, and your ship will dip and keel, but slacken off and trim your sails, and things head off again."

Maybe she got that from her political godfathers, Franklin Roosevelt and Lyndon Johnson. Roosevelt was a hero because her family owed to his election the little brick house that her grandfather was able to buy in Houston with help from the Home Finance Corporation. And LBJ showed her how to maneuver among movers and shakers without being moved and shaken from her own principles. Like both of them, she understood that America's development owed much of its story to the affirmative action of government. From the common purse, throughout our history, had poured money for just about every improvement you could name—canals, dams, roads, forts, river channels, mining and fishing rights, and even orange groves. So she argued, as both Roosevelt and Johnson had argued, that the fruits of democracy belonged on the table of the simplest home no less than in the banquet hall of the grandest mansion.

But she was no creature of government. She went, she served, and she came home. After just six years in office, she voluntarily imposed term limits upon her career in Congress, long before there was a national movement to make them mandatory. Woodrow Wilson had said, "Things get very lonely in Washington. The real voice of the great people of America sometimes sounds faint and distant in that strange city." Not for Barbara Jordan. She heard the voice of the people, and she gave the people a voice.

They held her in respect approaching reverence. After her death, people who had never met her poured out their personal eulogies. I came across one last Friday in a letter to the *Los Angeles Times* signed by a twenty-four-year-old immigrant from Chile named Fabio Escobar. He said:

> I did not grow up in the United States. I do not remember the
> Watergate Hearings or Jordan's keynote address at the 1976 Dem-

ocratic Convention. I only learned of her career while studying philosophy and political science at Cal State a few years ago. I never met her except through the books and tapes of her speeches. But I know Barbara Jordan's accomplishments extend far beyond the narrow scope of the political realm. She spoke for millions of individuals who yearned for leaders who would commit themselves to a core set of issues grounded not in polls, but in the solid footing of raw, personal conviction. No American politician of recent times has done that better than she did. She stood on conviction and fought for what she believed was right. This is the noblest and most difficult task a person can undertake, and she did it with exceptional quality.

This, from a young man whose native language was Spanish.

To people like Fabio Escobar, Barbara Jordan was an inspiration; to others, a hero; to the lucky, a friend. To me, she was all these things and something more. In 1987, she became my muse.

That summer was the two-hundredth anniversary of the Constitutional Convention in Philadelphia, where remarkable minds had talked the United States into being. That remembrance made the Constitution my "beat" on PBS that year. Some of the programs we were producing were unabashedly celebratory; I still marvel that any group of fifty-six prickly men, meeting in the breathless heat of an urban summer, could have agreed on anything, let alone a firm and lasting foundation for a new kind of nation no one had ever seen before. But some of our programs that summer were much less hopeful and much less inspiring— remember, in 1987, even as we were celebrating the making of the Constitution, we were also watching its attempted undoing as the Iran-Contra scandal revealed yet one more conspiracy to subvert the Constitution by those sworn to uphold it.

Reporting on that scandal, I kept close to my heart Barbara's stirring words during the Watergate hearings scarcely a decade earlier. She had electrified the nation when she had famously declared her whole and total faith in the Constitution despite having been excluded from it because of her race. The convention of 1787 had decided people like her were "60 percent a person," which is how slaves were to be enumerated for the purposes of representation. But the truth is, in her understanding of justice, Barbara Jordan would have fit right in with any of the 100 percent white men in that hall, two hundred years ago, in Philadelphia.

George Mason had asked: "Shall any man be above justice?"

Edmund Randolph had declared: "Guilt wherever found ought to be punished."

And Gouverneur Morris had said: "The Magistrate is not the King. The people are the King."

Here is what Barbara Jordan said: "If the society today allows wrongs to go unchallenged, the impression is created that those wrongs have the approval of the majority." And this: "Justice of the right is always to take precedence over might."

The founders would have been lucky to have had her in that Constitutional Convention. If she had been present, it would have taken far less time for Barbara Jordan to be recognized as a whole person in the sight of the law, or for this country to fulfill its promise.

As it is, the good fortune has been yours and mine. Just when we despaired of finding a hero, she showed up, to give the sign of democracy.

Do you know what the odds of this happening had to be? That in a universe existing billions of years, with fifty billion galaxies and more, on a planet of modest size, circling an ordinary sun in an unexceptional galaxy, that you and I would have arrived in the same time zone as Barbara Jordan, at such a moment of serendipity to be touched by this one woman's life, to encounter her spirit and her faith?

This is no small thing. Call it grace.

15. | MONEY TALKS

Sacramento Community Center

NOVEMBER 24, 1997

You would think the measure of any democratic system of politics would be its ability to address the problems that it has created for itself. But in America nothing seems to be working to anyone's satisfaction—except, that is, the wealth machine that keeps enriching the people at the top. For them, the system puts King Midas, with his golden touch, to shame. Merely to suggest this arrangement—"the system"—might not be producing the best results for the multitudes brings down opprobrium and charges of "class warfare" on the skeptic. So the multitudes go on faithfully voting (well, at least half of them do), knowing that the savior on the ballot likely will turn out to be one more pretender, making only nominal changes to a system that is costly and inefficient but thrives by rewarding the very people who have gamed it. You will even hear it argued that what ails us can't be cured by democracy. Alan Greenspan came down from Mount Olympus to tell The Wall Street Journal that "politics is less important, domestically, than it was, because globalization is taking over an ever increasing part of the decision-making process . . ." This prompted the old curmudgeon Nicholas von Hoffman to snort: "This is a fancy dancy way of saying, 'You foolish little persons can get all worked up as you wish about your candidates and their promises, but the power, the decisive power, no longer adheres to the now puny offices they are breaking their butts to get elected to.' " He is onto something: people are seized by a sense that everything is out of control and nobody can do anything about it. German funds hold American mortgages; hedge fund managers sneeze and American workers catch pneumonia; your grandmother is lying in her own waste at a nursing home whose staff has been cut by 20 percent because the private equity fund that owns the chain is squeezing every ounce of profit out of the business—and to them it is just a business—in order quickly to dump it for a huge return on investment. This, we're told, is simply the way the world has to work if capitalism is to be served. "Globalism is given to us as the ineluctable working out of the laws of nature, as though there is anything natural about a complex economic system erected by human beings, not according to the laws of anything but according to their own will, their pleasure, their confusions and their lusts," von Hoffman writes. It is a strange turn of events for a people who once sent the king's men packing. Perhaps—God forbid—it will take a costly calamity to shake us from the benign neglect of our own destiny. But there is an alternative to saying nothing: break the monopoly control of the moneyed interests that fund our politicians and buy the power to set our agenda. Public funding of elections is our only way to compete with the private money that pours into campaigns. It's no pipe dream. Several states and municipalities have shown us that public funding can help level the playing field once people understand the stakes. And there's plenty of evidence to convince them. Many of my speeches over the past ten years have been devoted to making that case based on what I found in my reporting of money and politics. Audiences respond fervently when they realize how they are affected by the money that fuels the system that they sense is heading for the cliff. The following two speeches were given ten years apart. During that decade the money chase became more frenzied and our system more dysfunctional. "We are asleep with compasses in our hands," writes the poet W. S. Merwin. And the cliffs are dead ahead.

* * *

When in doubt about whether or not money in politics matters to you, consider this.

It was just a couple of years ago that controversy erupted over the so-called date-rape drug Rohypnol. Rapists were found to be using it to drug and sedate their victims before exploiting them. Sparked by public indignation, members of Congress moved to designate the drug as a controlled substance, which would have meant stiff penalties for its abuse. Lobbyists for the pharmaceutical industry, which obviously does not condone rape but does oppose regulation that might interfere with its astronomical profits, killed the effort. They smothered it to death with money, big contributions to Republicans and Democrats alike. The money talked and the politicians shut up.

In 1996 President Clinton signed into law a raise in the minimum wage from $4.25 to $5.15. The White House made an elaborate ceremony of the signing, to underscore that finally Washington was giving America's working stiffs a break. Only later did we read the fine print. The bill actually contained a lot of gifts to multinational corporations— tax breaks for banks, tax breaks for newspaper publishers, tax breaks for the very wealthy. Guess what? They were big contributors to both Democrats and Republicans. In Washington you can't even give working people a modest raise without giving big contributors a windfall.

The cheers went up when Congress and the president recently agreed to balance the budget and cut taxes. Some lobbyists weren't around to cheer. They had skedaddled to the nearest bar to raise a glass to their own success. The bill contained billions of dollars in tax breaks for five industries that since 1995 contributed $35 million to members of Congress—to leaders in both parties who have the most influence over who wins and who loses in any legislation.

You ask: Money talks, what's new? And you're right. This is an old story. "There are two things that are important in politics," said the wealthy Ohio businessman Mark Hanna. "The first is money and I can't remember what the second one is." He said that a hundred years ago. Hanna was the first modern political fund-raiser. On behalf of presidential candidate William McKinley, he tapped the banks, insurance companies, railroads, and other industrial trusts of the late 1800s. The Democrats' William Jennings Bryan, who was perceived as a real challenge to organized wealth due to his Populist roots, raised one-tenth as much as Hanna did for McKinley. Bryan lost.

What's new is this: politics today has become an all-out arms race, with money doing the work of missiles. Federal elections last year cost $1.6 billion and that could double in the year 2000. The lid's off, and the biggest givers have a nuclear arsenal to unleash. In every escalation of this arms race, the ante gets raised.

Let's talk about the second thing, which Mark Hanna forgot: democracy.

One of the networks recently commissioned an interesting poll. Voters were asked, "Do you think our elected representatives are dedicated public servants or lying windbags?" The response: 44 percent—nearly half the public—said our elected officials were a bunch of lying windbags. Just 36 percent said they thought elected officials were dedicated public servants. And this was true of voters regardless of their party. The rank and file of both parties—as well as Independents—see a bunch of lying windbags in Washington, D.C. I wince at the term, but that's how the poll put the question.

When asked who really controls Washington, voters overwhelmingly answered: special interests. Nearly everyone thinks contributions affect the voting behavior of Congress. And three-quarters of the public says that elected officials care more about getting reelected than about doing what's best for the country. In another poll only 14 percent of the people give members of Congress a high rating for honesty and ethical standards.

Is this what politics has become: a bunch of self-interested, lying windbags on the take from moneyed special interests? I don't know whether to laugh or cry. On the one hand, these polls tell us that Americans are a pretty smart bunch and see through the surface reporting that passes for coverage of Washington. On the other hand, there is a terribly important warning here: Americans are disillusioned about democracy. They feel betrayed, sold out.

The anger, however, has produced apathy. Less than half of us bother to vote at all in our presidential elections—compared to 80 percent a century ago—and only about a third in our congressional elections. In 1996 fewer people bothered to watch the presidential debates or the parties' national conventions than ever before. Every now and then a reporter from one of our big newspapers ventures out to listen to voters in the heartland and brings back a headline like this one from *The New York Times*: THE BUZZ IN THE CAPITAL BRINGS A YAWN IN PEORIA. The reporter was trying to find out what voters thought about the hearings on campaign finance reform, and what he found is that people simply don't think Washington has much interest in what happens to them in their daily lives.

Some people don't think there's anything so terrible about this. Republican Senator Mitch McConnell, who gloats about defeating even the most modest efforts at political reform, thinks there's nothing at all to worry about in this great withdrawal from democracy. On the Senate floor he declared: "Low voter turnout shows that people are happy with the job we're doing in Washington." (As Jim Hightower says, "If he gets any dumber than that, we're going to have to start watering him twice a week.")

More than half of ordinary Americans are not satisfied with the state of things; millions believe there has been a hostile takeover of our electoral and governmental process. We're becoming two Americas, divided by our position in life and access to power. The important divide in politics is not Republicans versus Democrats but the "ins" versus the "outs." It's between the top 10 percent of Americans who own more than 60 percent of the entire nation's wealth and the more than 70 percent of people who have essentially no net worth. Between those whose children go to the best schools and those whose children grow up poor. Between those who are connected and those who feel pushed aside by a system dominated by professional politicians and their contributors and consultants. As a result, our democracy is becoming unresponsive and intractable in the face of radical capitalism—unfettered markets, tax flight, and deterioration of the public sphere.

I believe the soul of democracy to be the fundamental notion of political equality—"government of, by, and for the people," which means, as FDR once defined it, that "inside the polling booth every American man and woman stands as the equal of every other American man and woman. There they have no superiors. There they have no masters save their own minds and consciences."

Perhaps. But Roger Tamraz has his own take on representation. Tamraz is the oilman who paid $300,000 to the Democratic Party to get a moment at Bill Clinton's ear. He wanted the president to support a pipeline from Russia to the Mediterranean that would have given him control of exports from the Caspian Sea, the richest undeveloped pool of oil left on earth. Tamraz had also made large contributions to President Reagan—enough to earn him status as a "Republican Eagle." All of this got him called before the recent Senate hearings on campaign finance, where his candor made him the star. His money, he said, had produced potential benefits for him far beyond the pipeline project. He hoped it might someday lead to a foreign policy post. After all, he noted, "a lot of our cabinet ministers and a lot of our ambassadors" have been large donors—including, he said, Felix Rohatyn, now ambassador to France, and Secretary of the Treasury Robert Rubin. If you were watching the performance, you know the senators put on a good show. They fumed. They expressed outrage. At one point Senator Fred Thompson boomed: "Do you think you have a constitutional right to have your business deal considered personally by the president of the United States?" Tamraz looked right back at him and said, "Senator, I go to the outer limits. Why not? You set the rules and we're following. This is politics as usual."

And then the punch line. In a final effort to shake him one senator asked Tamraz if he had ever voted or registered to vote. No, he replied, "I think [money] is a bit more than a vote."

And there is the developer Angelo K. Tsakopoulos, here in Sacramento. In 1995 he was locked in a nasty fight over development of eight hundred acres of pasture in the southern part of the county. The federal government insisted on saving the wetlands and endangered species. Despite federal warnings, his work crews went forward—without the required permits. Now, Tsakopoulos is a longtime Democratic fundraiser—$165,000 in one year alone. So guess who got to sleep in the Lincoln Bedroom? R-i-g-h-t. And guess who winds up sipping coffee with the president and nine other guests in the same room where the course of World War II was charted? Right again! And unless you were born yesterday I'll bet you can predict what happened after he pressed his case at the White House. You got it. An Environmental Protection Agency official in Washington directed the West Coast office to forego any major fines or criminal sanctions against the developer. One EPA official on the West Coast admitted: "Mr. Tsakopoulos has a direct line to the White House." Said another, "He has clout, he has access . . . We're aware of it." The U.S. Wildlife Service even waived its own policy requiring landowners to restore wetlands they destroy.

I could go on. The chairman and CEO of Federal Express bought his way into the White House for a forty-five-minute one-on-one session with the president to discuss a trade issue important to his company's lucrative business in Asia. It was a legitimate issue, but even the White House had to concede that individual businessmen pressing such causes are rarely granted exclusive access to the president. Certainly people making minimum wage and hoping to raise it couldn't afford the same privilege.

Three weeks after the meeting Federal Express gave $100,000 to the Democratic National Committee. When I heard this, I thought of the judge who called one of the opposing lawyers in a civil suit to the bench and said, "Your opponent gave me $5,000 last night to decide the case his way. I'm an honest man and can't be influenced. So why don't you give me $5,000 and then I can decide it on the merits."

We have lost the ability to call the most basic transaction by its right name. If a baseball player stepping up to home plate were to lean over and hand the umpire a wad of bills before he called the pitch, we'd call that a bribe. But when a real estate developer buys his way into the

White House and gets a favorable government ruling that wouldn't be available to you or me, what do we call that? A "campaign contribution."

Let's call it what it is: a bribe.

A bribe is in effect what Newt Gingrich and Trent Lott got from the tobacco industry: more than $13 million in "soft money" to the Republican Party since 1995. Behold! Earlier this year, without any debate or even an acknowledged sponsor, Gingrich and Lott, with the complicity of the White House, slipped a $50 billion tax credit to the tobacco companies, which they were going to use to lower the cost of their pending settlement of all those state lawsuits. Only after it was exposed and there was a vast outcry did both houses of Congress rescind the giveaway. Another example: the founder of the Amway Corporation, Richard DeVos, gave more than a million dollars to the Republican Party in the last two years. Then Trent Lott and Newt Gingrich delivered a last-minute addition to the tax bill easing the burden on Amway's two Asian affiliates. It's estimated that tax break will cost you, the public, $280 million.

This is the same Newt Gingrich, by the way, who said in 1990: "Congress is increasingly a system of corruption in which money politics is defeating and driving out citizen politics." That was before he became Speaker. In the last election Speaker Gingrich raised more than $100 million for Republican House candidates. He raised more than $6 million for his own reelection—the most expensive House race of 1996—and another $1 million to cover legal bills related to ethics charges against him in the House. No wonder he's been called "the godfather of the new Republican Party."

Bribes work in odd ways. There's a tax-exempt organization called the Asia Pacific Exchange Foundation that sends members of Congress to Burma as guests of the country's military rulers. One of their stops is a remote mountain where the American oil company Unocal and a French company are building a natural-gas pipeline. The project could be in jeopardy if Washington imposes sanctions against Burma for human rights violations. Would you be surprised to learn that the tax-exempt organization that sponsors the junkets is underwritten by American companies with major financial reasons to oblige dictators, including, guess who? Unocal. Since the companies can make tax-deductible contributions to the foundation, you know who has to make up the lost tax revenue.

Politicians and press in Washington talk in euphemisms when it comes to the impact of money. It's time for a different language to describe more accurately the real terms of endearment inside the Beltway: cash constituents, cashing in, conflicts of interest, corruption, dialing for dollars, fat cats, honest graft, influence peddling, interested money, legalized bribery, loopholes, money chase, quid pro quo, regulatory exemptions, subsidies, tax breaks, vested interests, and the institution that makes it all possible, the wealth primary. If our elected representatives didn't first have to raise thousands, even millions of dollars from rich individuals and moneyed interests to finance their campaigns—the so-called wealth primary that determines who is a viable candidate and who is just a well-meaning person with some good ideas and a few friends—maybe people like you would have more of a voice in what goes on in Washington.

We're talking here about winners and losers—not just in political campaigns but in policy choices.

The Environmental Protection Agency estimates that its newly proposed national air pollution standards for ozone (smog) and fine particles (soot) will lead to 60,000 fewer cases of chronic bronchitis, 250,000 fewer cases of aggravated asthma in children and adults, 1.5 million fewer cases of significant breathing problems, and 20,000 saved lives.

Asthma alone is the leading serious chronic illness of children in the United States and the number-one cause of school absences attributed to chronic illness. Asthma attacks send an estimated 1.6 million Americans to emergency rooms each year and account for approximately one in six of all pediatric emergency room visits in the United States. The direct health costs from asthma are $9.8 billion a year.

We know why these kids are getting sick. In Utah Valley near Provo, researchers from Brigham Young University studied hospital admissions over a several-year period during which a local steel mill closed and then reopened. The steel mill was the source of nearly all the small particles in the local atmosphere. This is an area where very few people smoke, due to the influence of the Mormon Church. The researchers found that the opening of the mill coincided with a doubling and even a tripling (depending on the time of year) in hospital admissions for pneumonia, pleurisy, bronchitis, and asthma, especially among young people.

Despite this kind of evidence, some people argue that we have already done enough to improve the nation's air. These people happen to be associated with the American Automobile Manufacturers Association, the American Petroleum Institute, the American Electric Power Company, the National Mining Association, and the National Association of Manufacturers. The coalition fighting the new air standards is reported to have something like $30 million pooled in its war chest. The American Lung Association, by comparison, doesn't even have a political action committee.

In the House of Representatives, 192 members have signed on to legislation to force the EPA to delay the new standards for at least four years. These members of Congress have received nearly three times as much in campaign contributions from big air polluters than members who have not signed on to the bill. According to the Environmental Working Group, the more money a House member receives from major air polluters, the more likely that politician is to support anti–clean air legislation. By comparison, representing constituents in a heavily polluted area does not necessarily lead a House member to oppose the bill. As Roger Tamraz reminds us, the money matters more. And as David Corn writes in *The Nation,* "Soot and smog are not the only pollutants in the air of Capitol Hill. There is also money. So much, you can almost breathe it."

Here in California, which for many years has had one of the least-regulated systems of campaign finance in the country, the legislature has long been for sale. You don't have to take my word for it. You've got a former state senator out here who served two years in prison after pleading guilty to corruption charges. In a 1994 article by Kim Alexander for the *Sacramento News & Review*, here's what Alan Robbins had to say about how money works its way in the state capital:

> What goes on, every day, in Sacramento is that the same lobbyist comes in and on Monday he talks to you about how he's arranging for a campaign contribution to come from his client, and on Tuesday he comes back and asks you to vote on a piece of legislation for that same client. It doesn't take very long before the least-bright legislator figures out if he keeps ignoring the Tuesday request then the lobbyist is going to stop coming to his fundraisers. And especially when you talk about a lobbyist who controls over $1 million a year of campaign money, who can make or break one's career, it's very easy for legislators to come to the conclusion that his arguments are persuasive.

We all pay for a system rigged against us.

We pay at the grocery story because Congress has done sweetheart deals for major campaign contributors. The price of milk went up twenty cents a gallon in New England states last year because of a special subsidy for area dairy farmers passed by Congress. A five-pound bag of sugar costs fifty cents more than it should because year in and year out, contributions from the sugar lobby help keep alive sugar price support. When you buy a brand-name drug that isn't available in generic form, it may be because a pharmaceutical company maneuvered to keep the generic version off the market, with help from officials who have received campaign contributions from that company. An eighteen-ounce jar of peanut butter costs thirty-three cents more because Congress still allows a peanut subsidy program. Dairy farmers, sugar growers, the pharmaceutical industry, and peanut political action committees have all dumped millions of dollars into Congress, and it worked.

We pay higher bills for cable TV because the industry poured money into Congress prior to the passage of the Telecommunications Act of

1996. That bill ostensibly was to promote competition in the broadcast industry but it has allowed cable companies to raise their rates at three times the inflation rate since it was passed.

We pay in delays on the release of cheaper generic drugs, while companies that produce expensive name-brand products use their campaign contributions to buy extensions on their monopolies from Congress.

We pay for less-fuel-efficient cars and more dangerous roads.

We pay for high health insurance and restricted service from managed-care providers and insurance companies who block health-care reform with their campaign contributions.

We pay for corporate subsidies that the conservative representative John Kasich estimates cost at least $11 billion a year. The libertarian Cato Institute suggests the number is more like $65 billion in unnecessary programs supporting already profitable businesses. And this is not counting the plums in the new budget agreement.

Children pay, too. They don't vote and they don't lobby. They don't contribute to political campaigns and they don't pay for candidates' trips. They don't go to soirees on Capitol Hill and they don't do lunch. They don't respond to polls and they don't hold fund-raisers. About the only thing a child does for political candidates is provide a photo opportunity. And what do they get in return? Classrooms and schools and public libraries with peeling paint, leaky roofs, no heat in the winter and no air-conditioning in the summer, broken or boarded-up windows, electrical systems unable to handle computer networks. Children have no money to contribute, and they have gotten what they paid for.

Sometimes people pay with their lives. Think of Cynthia Chavez Wall, a single mother who worked at a textile factory near Hamlet, North Carolina, for thirteen years. She was making $8 an hour until she was abruptly fired one day for failing to come to work when her daughter was stricken with pneumonia. She then went to work at Imperial Food Products for $4.95 an hour, cutting up and preparing chicken parts that were sold to fast-food restaurants. She worked up against fryers with oil heated to 400 degrees. There was no air-conditioning or fans. She often went home with her hands bleeding from cuts.

In his book *There's Nothing in the Middle of the Road but Yellow Stripes and Dead Armadillos,* Jim Hightower continues the story:

> Then on the morning of September 3, 1991, women in one area of the plant began to yell, "Fire!" Flames flared and smoke billowed throughout the building, which had no sprinkler system, no evacuation plan, and only one fire extinguisher. As the fire spread quickly, panicked workers raced to the exits, but the people shoved on the closed doors to no avail. All but the very front doors had been padlocked from the outside. Company executives later said they did this to prevent chicken parts from being stolen. Trapped, twenty-five of the ninety employees died in the flames. More than fifty others were burned or injured. Cynthia Chavez Wall's body was found at one of the doors.

The media called it a "horrific accident." But Jim Hightower writes:

> These people were effectively placed in a death trap by their employer—a death trap that had never once in its eleven-year existence been inspected by safety officials, though it was regularly visited by U.S. Agriculture Department inspectors checking on the quality of the chicken meat. Earlier in the year the North Carolina legislature had rejected proposals to toughen the state's safety regulation; even though the system is so lax that the average North Carolina workplace is inspected once every seventy-five years. Under Reagan and Bush, Washington, too, had cut back on the number of federal inspectors, leaving us even today with fewer than 1,200 to check out 7 million American workplaces.

Two years after Cynthia Chavez Wall's death, two years after the media had scurried away to the next "big story" and the politicians had held their hearings and moved on, the watchdog Government Accountability Project revisited Hamlet and the surrounding area. Imperial Food Products is no longer there, but in other poultry plants nothing has changed. Assembly-line speedups continue to cause excessive injuries. Stifling heat and oppressive working conditions remain. Sick and injured employees are forced to stay on the line or be fired, and, yes, doors are still locked from the outside.

William Greider got it right in his book *Who Will Tell the People?* The hard questions of governance, he said, "are questions of how and why some interests are allowed to dominate the government's decision making while others are excluded." These rarely get explained to the public despite the fact that

> this is the reality of politics that matters to people in their everyday lives. [Yet] no one can hope to understand what is driving political behavior without grasping the internal facts of governing and asking the kind of gut-level questions that politicians ask themselves in private: "Who are the *winners* in this matter and who are the *losers*. Who gets the money and who has to *pay*? Who must be heard on this question and who can be *safely ignored*?"

Sadly, the larger problems facing our nation—increasing job insecurity, declining real wages and income, children living in poverty, inadequate and costly health insurance, increasing disparity of income and wealth, pollution and environmental degradation—cannot be seriously addressed by our politicians. To do so would offend the people who pay to play.

Here's the good news. While the political class scoffs at the notion that ordinary citizens really care, out across the country a different story is unfolding. At the end of October, some two thousand citizen activists fanned out across the state of Massachusetts carrying petitions seeking to put the Massachusetts Clean Elections Law on the ballot before the voters next year. By the end of the day, despite a cold, driving rainstorm, they had collected more than fifty thousand signatures—close to the total needed to qualify for the ballot. Clean Elections for Massachusetts wants to set up a system under which candidates who make a binding agreement to raise almost no private money and to abide by spending limits would receive competitive public financing, and no longer owe their victories to private campaign contributors. This goes beyond anything currently being talked about in Washington—but guess what? Polls show that even after hearing arguments against the proposal, Massachusetts voters backed it by more than a two-to-one margin.

The voters in Maine last November broke the mold of what activists thought was possible, becoming the first in the nation to enact clean-money financing of state elections. This June, Vermont lawmakers proved that such a reform could be enacted legislatively, with broad bipartisan support. But this isn't just a New England phenomenon. Now, in addition to Massachusetts, initiative campaigns aimed at the 1998 ballot are also gaining ground in Arizona, Idaho, Missouri, New York, and Washington State; recent polls in these places show strong support across the political spectrum. Legislatures in Connecticut, Illinois, and North Carolina are currently considering similar bills, and movements are under way in more than a dozen other states.

The basic idea is this: candidates who voluntarily agree to raise no private money and abide by spending limits, and can demonstrate that they have a basic level of support in their district, can opt to receive "clean money" from a public fund. This breaks the direct link between special interest donors and politicians that is proving so debilitating to our democracy.

Clean-money reform won't end the power of organized special interests in Washington, but with it candidates will have a choice about how to finance their campaigns that they do not have now. The money chase, which so many candidates find so exhausting, will be tempered. Good people who today choose not to run because they can't raise the money, or don't want to get on their knees before big donors, will have a fighting chance to run serious campaigns. The inherent conflicts of interest that arise when public servants are privately financed will be eliminated, restoring needed public confidence in the process. And at a minimum, the voters will finally have a real choice on Election Day.

Here we are between two centuries, facing what the scholar James Davison Hunter describes as "the never-ending work of democracy: the tedious, hard, perplexing, messy, and seemingly endless task of working through what kind of people we're going to be and what kind of communities we will live in." The work of democracy encompasses practically everything that we can and must do together . . . how we educate our children, design our communities and neighborhoods, feed ourselves and dispose of our wastes, how we care for the sick and elderly and poor, how we relate to the natural world, how we entertain and enlighten ourselves, how we defend ourselves and what values we seek to defend, what roles are chosen for us by virtue of our identity and what roles we create for ourselves.

These fundamental issues are for all of us to address, as free and equal citizens, through the political process. But when public servants are privately financed, ordinary people are shut out of politics. Elections are turned into auctions and access to public officials into a commodity available only to the highest bidders. Most of that money then goes to enrich the broadcasting industry through distorted political commercials, which in turn lead to what one longtime observer calls "the cynical acceptance of falsehood as a way of government and a way of life."

We must change the rules, and it won't be easy. Powerful entrenched interests write the rules to their own advantage.

But an aroused public can change this system. Nothing less than democracy is at stake.

16. | SAVING DEMOCRACY

Remarks on a Lecture Series in California
on the Issue of Money and Politics

FEBRUARY 2006

I was on a speaking tour in California when Vice President Cheney acciden-
tally shot one of his companions during a hunting trip in Texas. Fortunately,
the victim survived, and late-night comics lived off the incident for days. As
the details slowly emerged, however, they provided a rare glimpse into the
cozy world of power that is the nexus of money and politics today.

I

I will leave to Jon Stewart the rich threads of humor to pluck from
the hunting incident in Texas. All of us are relieved that the vice
president's friend has survived. We can accept Dick Cheney's word
that the accident was one of the worst moments of his life. What

intrigues me as a journalist is the rare glimpse we have serendipitously been offered into the tightly knit world of the elites who govern today.

The vice president was hunting on a fifty-thousand-acre ranch owned by a lobbyist friend who is the heiress to a family fortune of land, cattle, banking, and oil (ah, yes, the quickest and surest way to the American dream remains to choose your parents well).

The circumstances of the hunt and the identity of the hunters provoked a lament from *The Economist*. The most influential pro-business magazine in the world is concerned that hunting in America is becoming a matter of class: the rich are doing more, the working stiffs less. The annual loss of 1.5 million acres of wildlife habitat and 1 million acres of farm and ranchland to development and sprawl has come "at the expense of *The Deer Hunter* crowd in the small towns of the north-east, the rednecks of the south and the cowboys of the west." Their places, says *The Economist*, are being taken by the affluent who pay plenty for such conveniences as being driven to where the covey cooperatively awaits. The magazine (hardly a Marxist rag, remember) describes Mr. Cheney's own expedition as "a lot closer to *Gosford Park* than *The Deer Hunter*— a group of fat old toffs waiting for wildlife to be flushed towards them at huge expense."

We have here a metaphor of power. The vice president turned his host, Katharine Armstrong, the lobbyist who is also the ranch owner, into his de facto news manager. She would disclose the shooting only when Cheney was ready and only on his terms. Sure enough, nothing was made public for almost twenty hours until she finally leaked the authorized version to the local newspaper. Armstrong suggested the blame lay with the victim, who, she indicated, had failed to inform the vice president of his whereabouts and walked into a hail of friendly fire. Three days later Cheney revised the story and apologized.

It has been reported that someone from the hunting party was in touch with Karl Rove at the White House. For certain Rove's the kind of fellow you want on the other end of the line when great concoctions are being hatched, especially if you wish the victim to hang for the crime committed against him.

Watching these people work is a study of the inner circle at the top of American politics. The journalist Sidney Blumenthal, writing on Salon.com, reminds us of the relationship between the Armstrong dynasty and the Bush family and its retainers. Armstrong's father invested in Rove's political consulting firm, which managed George W. Bush's election as governor of Texas and as president. Anne Armstrong is a longtime Republican activist and donor. Ronald Reagan appointed her to the Foreign Intelligence Advisory Board after her tenure as ambassador to the United Kingdom under President Ford, whose chief of staff was a young Dick Cheney. Anne Armstrong served on the board of directors of Halliburton, which hired Cheney to run the company. Her daughter, Katharine, host of the hunting party, was once a lobbyist for the powerful Houston law firm founded by the family of James A. Baker III, who was chief of staff to Reagan, secretary of state under George H. W. Bush, and the man designated by the Bush family to make sure the younger Bush was named president in 2000 despite having lost the popular vote. According to Blumenthal, one of Katharine Armstrong's more recent lobbying jobs was with a large construction firm with contracts in Iraq.

It is a Dick Cheney world out there—a world where politicians and lobbyists hunt together, dine together, drink together, play together, pray together, and prey together, all the while carving up the world according to their own interests.

II

Two years ago, in a report entitled "American Democracy in an Age of Rising Inequality," the American Political Science Association concluded that progress toward realizing American ideals of democracy "may have stalled, and in some arenas reversed." Privileged Americans "roar with a clarity and consistency that policy-makers readily hear and routinely follow" while citizens "with lower or moderate incomes speak with a whisper."

The following year, on the eve of President George W. Bush's second inauguration, the editors of *The Economist,* reporting on inequality in America, concluded that the United States "risks calcifying into a European-style, class-based society."

As great wealth has accumulated at the top, the rest of society has not been benefiting proportionally. In 1960 the gap between the top 20 percent and the bottom 20 percent was thirtyfold. Now it is seventy-five-fold. A recent article in the *Financial Times* reports on a study by the American economist Robert J. Gordon, who finds "little long-term change in workers' share of U.S. income over the past half century." Middle-ranking Americans are being squeezed, he says, because the top 10 percent of earners have captured almost half the total income gains in the past four decades and the top 1 percent has gained the most of all—more in fact, than the entire bottom 50 percent.

No wonder working men and women and their families are strained to cope with the rising cost of health care, pharmaceutical drugs, housing, higher education, and public transportation—all of which have risen faster in price than typical family incomes. The recent book *Economic Apartheid in America* describes how "thirty zipcodes in America have become fabulously wealthy" while "whole urban and rural communities are languishing in unemployment, crumbling infrastructure, growing insecurity, and fear."

This is a profound transformation in a country whose DNA contains the inherent promise of an equal opportunity at life, liberty, and the pursuit of happiness and whose collective memory resonates with the hallowed idea—hallowed by blood—of government of the people, by the people, and for the people. The great progressive struggles in our history have been waged to make sure ordinary citizens, and not just the rich, share in the benefits of a free society. Yet as the public today supports such broad social goals as affordable medical coverage for all, decent wages for working people, safe working conditions, a secure retirement, and clean air and water, there is no government to deliver on those aspirations. Instead, our elections are bought out from under us and our public officials do the bidding of mercenaries. So powerfully has wealth shaped our political agenda that we cannot say America is working for all of America.

In the words of Louis Brandeis, one of the greatest of our Supreme Court justices: "You can have wealth concentrated in the hands of a few, or democracy, but you cannot have both." Money is choking democracy to death.

III

Some simple facts:

The cost of running for public office is skyrocketing. In 1996, $1.6 billion was spent on the congressional and presidential elections. Eight years later, that total had more than doubled, to $3.9 billion.

Thanks to our system of privately financed campaigns, millions of regular Americans are being priced out of any meaningful participation in democracy. Less than 0.5 percent of all Americans made a political contribution of $200 or more to a federal candidate in 2004. When the average cost of running and winning a seat in the House of Representatives has topped $1 million, we can no longer refer to that august chamber as the "People's House."

At the same time that the cost of getting elected is exploding beyond the reach of ordinary people, the business of gaining access to and influence with our elected representatives has become a growth industry. Six years ago, in his first campaign for president, George W. Bush promised he would "restore honor and integrity" to the government. Repeatedly, during his first campaign for president, he would raise his right hand and, as if taking an oath, tell voters that he would change how things were done in the nation's capital. "It's time to clean up the toxic environment in Washington, D.C.," he would say. His administration would ask "not only what is legal but what is right, not what the lawyers allow but what the public deserves."

Hardly.

Since Bush was elected the number of lobbyists registered to do business in Washington has more than doubled. That's 16,342 lobbyists in 2000 to 34,785 last year. Sixty-five lobbyists for every member of Congress.

The amount that lobbyists charge their new clients has increased by nearly 100 percent in that same period, according to *The Washington Post*, going up from $20,000 to $40,000 a month. Starting salaries have risen to nearly $300,000 a year for the best-connected people, those leaving Congress or the administration.

The total spent per month by special interests wining, dining, and seducing federal officials is now nearly $200 million. *Per month.*

But numbers don't tell the whole story. There has been a qualitative change as well. With pro-corporate business officials running both the executive and legislative branches, lobbying that was once reactive has gone on the offense, seeking huge windfalls from public policy and public monies.

One example cited by *The Washington Post* is Hewlett-Packard, the California computer maker. The company nearly doubled its budget for contract lobbyists in 2004 and took on an elite lobbying firm as its Washington arm. Its goal was to pass Republican-backed legislation that would enable the company to bring back to the United States, at a dramatically lowered tax rate, as much as $14.5 billion in profit from foreign subsidiaries. The extra lobbying paid off. The legislation passed and Hewlett-Packard can now reduce its contribution to the social contract. The company's director of government affairs was quite candid: "We're trying to take advantage of the fact that Republicans control the House, the Senate, and the White House." Whatever the company paid for the lobbying, the investment returned enormous dividends.

I believe in equal opportunity muckraking. When I left Washington for journalism I did not leave behind my conviction that government should see to it that we have a more level playing field with one set of rules for everyone, but I did leave behind my partisan affections. Anyone who saw the documentary my team and I produced a few years ago on the illegal fund-raising for Bill Clinton's reelection knows I am no fan of the Democratic money machine that helped tear the party away from whatever roots it once had in the daily lives and struggles of working people, turning it into a junior partner of the chamber of commerce. I mean people like Tony Coelho, who as a Democratic congressman from California in the 1980s realized that his party could milk the business community for money if they promised to "pay for play." I mean people like Terry McAuliffe, the former Democratic National Committee chairman, who gave Bill Clinton the idea of renting the Lincoln Bedroom out to donors, and who did such a good job raising big money for the Democrats that by the end of his reign, Democrats had fewer small donors than the Republicans and more fat cats writing them million-dollar checks.

But let's be realistic here. When the notorious Willie Sutton was asked why he robbed banks, he answered, "Because there is where the money is." If I seem to be singling out the Republicans, it's for one reason: that's where the power is. They have a monopoly over government. First they gained control of the House of Representatives in 1994, then their self-proclaimed revolution went into overdrive with their taking of the White House in 2000 and the Senate in 2002. Their revolution soon became a cash cow and Washington a one-party town ruled by money.

Look back at the bulk of legislation passed by Congress in the past decade: an energy bill that gave oil companies huge tax breaks at the same time that ExxonMobil just posted $36 billion in profits in 2005 and our gasoline and home heating bills are at an all-time high; a bankruptcy "reform" bill written by credit card companies to make it harder for poor debtors to escape the burdens of divorce or medical catastrophe; the deregulation of the banking, securities, and insurance sectors, which led to rampant corporate malfeasance and greed and the destruction of the retirement plans of millions of small investors; the deregulation of the telecommunications sector, which led to cable-industry price gouging and an undermining of news coverage; protection for rampant overpricing of pharmaceutical drugs; and the blocking of even the mildest attempt to prevent American corporations from dodging an estimated $50 billion in annual taxes by opening a post-office box in an offshore tax haven like Bermuda or the Cayman Islands.

In every case the pursuit of this legislation was driven by Big Money. Our public representatives, the holders of our trust, need huge sums to finance their campaigns, especially to pay for television advertising, and men and women who have mastered the money game have taken advantage of that weakness in our democracy to systematically sell it off to the highest bidders.

Let's start with the K Street Project. K Street is the Wall Street of lobbying, the address of many of Washington's biggest lobbying firms. The K Street Project was the brainchild of Tom DeLay and Grover Norquist, the right-wing strategist who famously said that his goal is to shrink government so that it can be "drowned in a bathtub." This, of course, would render it impotent to defend ordinary people against the large economic forces—the so-called free market—that Norquist and his pals believe should be running America.

Tom DeLay, meanwhile, was a businessman from Sugar Land, Texas, who ran a pest extermination business before he entered politics. He hated the government regulators who dared to tell him that some of the pesticides he used were dangerous—as, in fact, they were. He got himself elected to the Texas legislature at a time when the Republicans were becoming the majority in the once-solid Democratic South, and his reputation for joining in the wild parties around the state capital in Austin earned him the nickname "Hot Tub Tom." But early in his political career, and with exquisite timing and the help of some videos from right-wing political evangelist James Dobson, Tom DeLay found Jesus and became a full-fledged born-again Christian. He would later humbly acknowledge that God had chosen him to restore America to its biblical worldview. "God," said Tom DeLay, "has been walking me through an incredible journey . . . God is using me, all the time, everywhere . . . God is training me. God is working with me . . ."

Yes, indeed: God does work in mysterious ways.

In addition to finding Jesus, Tom DeLay also discovered a secular ally to serve his ambitions. "Money is not the root of all evil in politics," DeLay once said. "In fact, money is the lifeblood of politics." By raising more than $2 million from lobbyists and business groups and distributing the money to dozens of Republican candidates in 1994, the year of the Republican breakthrough in the House, DeLay bought the loyalty of many freshmen legislators and got himself elected majority whip, the number-three man in Newt Gingrich's "Gang of Seven" who ran the House.

Here's how they ran it. On the day before the Republicans formally took control of Congress on January 3, 1995, DeLay met in his office with a coterie of lobbyists from some of the biggest companies in America. The journalists Michael Weisskopf and David Maraniss report that "the session inaugurated an unambiguous collaboration of political and commercial interests, certainly not uncommon in Washington but remarkable this time for the ease and eagerness with which these allies combined."

DeLay virtually invited them to write the Republican agenda. What they wanted first was "Project Relief"—a wide-ranging moratorium on regulations that had originally been put into place for the health and safety of the public. For starters, they wanted "relief" from labor standards that protected workers from the physical injuries of repetitive work. They wanted "relief" from tougher rules on meat inspection. And they wanted "relief" from effective monitoring of hazardous air pollutants. Scores of companies were soon gorging on Tom DeLay's generosity, adding one juicy and expensive tidbit after another to the bill. According to Weisskopf and Maraniss, on the eve of the debate twenty major corporate groups advised lawmakers that "this was a key vote, one that would be considered in future campaign contributions." On the day of the vote lobbyists on Capitol Hill were still writing amendments on their laptops and forwarding them to House leaders.

Speaker of the House Newt Gingrich famously told the lobbyists: "If you are going to play in our revolution, you have to live by our rules." Tom DeLay became his enforcer.

The rules were simple and blunt. Contribute to Republicans only. Hire Republicans only. When the electronics industry ignored the warning and chose a Democratic member of Congress to run its trade association, DeLay played so rough—pulling from the calendar a bill that the industry had worked on two years, aimed at bringing most of the world in alignment with U.S. copyright law—that even the House Ethics Committee, the watchdog that seldom barks and rarely bites, stirred itself to rebuke him. Privately, of course.

DeLay wasn't fazed. Not only did he continue to make sure the lobbying jobs went to Republicans, he also saw to it that his own people got a lion's share of the best jobs. At least twenty-nine of his former employees landed major lobbying positions—the most of any congressional office. The journalist John Judis found that together ex-DeLay people represent around 350 firms, including thirteen of the biggest trade associations, most of the energy companies, the giants in finance and technology, the airlines, automakers, tobacco companies, and the largest health-care and pharmaceutical companies. When tobacco companies wanted to block the FDA from regulating cigarettes, they hired DeLay's man. When the pharmaceutical companies—Big Pharma—wanted to make sure companies wouldn't be forced to negotiate cheaper prices for drugs, they hired six of Tom DeLay's team, including his former chief of staff. The machine became a blitzkrieg, oiled by campaign contributions that poured in like a gusher.

Watching as DeLay became the virtual dictator of Capitol Hill, I was reminded of the cardsharp in Texas who said to his prey, "Now play the cards fair, Reuben, I know what I dealt you." Tom DeLay and his cronies were stacking the deck.

They centralized in their own hands the power to write legislation. Drastic revisions to major bills were often written at night, with lobbyists hovering over them, then rushed through as "emergency measures," giving members as little as half an hour to consider what they might be voting on.

The Democratic minority was locked out of conference committees where the House and Senate are supposed to iron out their differences with both parties in the loop. The Republican bosses even took upon themselves the power to rewrite a bill in secrecy and move it directly to a vote without any other hearings or public review.

Sometimes this meant overruling what the majority of House members really wanted. Consider what happened with the bill to provide Medicare prescription drug coverage, as analyzed by Robert Kuttner in *The American Prospect*. As the measure was coming to a vote, a majority of the full House was sympathetic to allowing cheaper imports from Canada and to giving the government the power to negotiate wholesale drug prices for Medicare beneficiaries. But DeLay and his cronies were working on behalf of Big Pharma and would have none of it. So they made sure there would be no amendments on the floor. They held off the final roll call a full three hours—well after midnight—in order to strong-arm members who wanted to vote against the bill.

It was not a pretty sight out there on the floor of the House. At one point DeLay marched over to one reluctant Republican—Representative Nick Smith, who opposed the Medicare bill—and attempted to change his mind. Smith, who was serving his final term in office, later alleged that he was offered $100,000 for his son's campaign to succeed him. When he subsequently retracted his accusation, the House Ethics Committee looked into the charges and countercharges and wound up admonishing both Smith and DeLay, who admitted that he had offered to endorse Smith's son in exchange for Smith's support but that no money or bribe was involved. Timothy Noah of Slate.com has mused about what DeLay's endorsement would nonetheless have meant in later campaign contributions if Smith had gone along. While the House Ethics Committee never did find out the true story, Noah asks: "Who did whisper '$100,000' in Smith's ear? The report is full of plausible suspects, including DeLay himself, but it lacks any evidence on this crucial finding. You get the feeling the authors would prefer to forget this mystery ever existed."

There are no victimless crimes in politics. The price of corruption is passed on to you. What came of all these shenanigans was a bill that gave industry what it wanted and taxpayers the shaft. The bill covers only a small share of drug expenses. It has a major gap in coverage—the so-called doughnut hole. It explicitly forbids beneficiaries from purchasing private coverage to fill in the gap and explicitly forbids the federal government from bargaining for lower drug prices. More than one consumer organization has estimated that most seniors could end up paying even more for prescription drugs than before the bill passed.

Furthermore, despite these large flaws the cost of the bill is horrendous—between $500 billion and $1 trillion in its first ten years. The chief actuary for Medicare calculated a realistic estimate of what the bill would cost, but he later testified before Congress that he was forbidden from releasing the information by his boss, Thomas Scully, the head of the Centers for Medicare and Medicaid Services, who was then negotiating for a lucrative job with the health-care industry. Sure enough, hardly had the prescription drug bill become law than Scully went to work for the largest private equity investor in health care and at a powerful law firm focusing on health care and regulatory matters.

One is reminded of Boies Penrose. Back in the Gilded Age, Penrose was a United States senator from Pennsylvania who had been put and kept in office by the railroad tycoons and oil barons. He assured the moguls: "I believe in the division of labor. You send us to Congress; we pass laws under which you make money . . . and out of your profits you further contribute to our campaign funds to send us back again to pass more laws to enable you to make more money."

Gilded ages—then and now—have one thing in common: audacious and shameless people for whom the very idea of the public trust is a cynical joke.

Tom DeLay was elected to Congress by the ordinary people of Sugar Land, Texas. They had the right to expect him to represent them. This expectation is the very soul of democracy. We can't all govern—not even tiny Switzerland practices pure democracy. So we Americans came to believe our best chance of responsible government lies in obtaining the considered judgments of those we elect to represent us. Having cast our ballots in the sanctity of the voting booth with its assurance of political equality, we go about our daily lives expecting the people we put in office to weigh the competing interests and decide to the best of their ability what is right.

Instead, they have given the American people reason to believe the conservative journalist P. J. O'Rourke was right in describing Congress as "a parliament of whores."

A recent CBS News–*New York Times* poll found that 70 percent of Americans believe lobbyists bribing members of Congress is the way things work. Fifty-seven percent think at least half of the members of Congress accept bribes or gifts that affect their votes. Findings like these underscore the fact that ordinary people believe their bonds with democracy are not only stretched but sundered.

You see the breach clearly with Tom DeLay. As he became the king of campaign fund-raising, the Associated Press writes, "He began to live a lifestyle his constituents back in Sugar Land would have a hard time ever imagining." Big corporations such as R. J. Reynolds, Philip Morris, Reliant Energy, El Paso, and Dynegy provided private jets to take him to places of luxury most Americans have never seen—places with "dazzling views, warm golden sunsets, golf, goose-down comforters, marble bathrooms and balconies overlooking the ocean." The AP reports that various organizations—campaign committees, political action committees, even a children's charity established by DeLay—paid more than $1 million on hotels, restaurants, golf resorts, and corporate jets on DeLay's behalf: at least forty-eight visits to golf clubs and resorts (the Ritz-Carlton in Jamaica, the Prince Hotel in Hawaii, the Michelangelo in New York, the Phoenician in Scottsdale, the El Conquistador in Puerto Rico, where villas average $1,300 a night); one hundred flights aboard corporate jets arranged by lobbyists; and five hundred meals at fancy restaurants, some averaging $200 for a dinner for two. There was even a $2,896 shopping spree at a boutique on Florida's Amelia Island offering "gourmet cookware, Sabatier cutlery and gadgets for your every need."

DeLay was a man on the move and on the take. But he needed help to sustain the cash flow. He found it in a fellow right-wing ideologue named Jack Abramoff. Abramoff personifies the Republican money machine of which DeLay, with the blessing of the House leadership, was the maestro. It was Abramoff who helped DeLay raise those millions of dollars from campaign donors that bought the support of other politicians and became the base for an empire of corruption. DeLay praised Abramoff as "one of my closest friends." Abramoff, in turn, told a convention of College Republicans, "Thank God Tom DeLay is majority leader of the house. Tom DeLay is who all of us want to be when we grow up."

Just last month Jack Abramoff pleaded guilty to fraud, tax evasion, and conspiracy to bribe public officials, a spectacular fall for a man whose rise to power began twenty-five years ago with his election as chairman of the College Republicans. Despite its innocuous name, the organization became a political attack machine for the far right and a launching pad for younger conservatives on the make. "Our job," the twenty-two-year-old Abramoff wrote after his first visit to the Reagan White House, "is to remove liberals from power permanently—[from] student newspaper and radio stations, student governments, and academia." Karl Rove had once held the same job as chairman. So did Grover Norquist, who ran Abramoff's campaign. A youthful $200-a-month intern named Ralph Reed was at their side. These were the rising young stars of the conservative movement who came to town to lead a revolution and stayed to run a racket.

They reeked of piety. Like DeLay, who had proclaimed himself God's messenger, Ralph Reed found Jesus, was born-again, and wound up running Pat Robertson's Christian Coalition, landing on the cover of *Time* as "the Right Hand of God." Reportedly after seeing *Fiddler on the Roof* Abramoff became an Orthodox religious Jew who finagled fake awards as "Scholar of Biblical and American History," "Distinguished Bible Scholar" (from an apparently nonexistent organization), the "Biblical Mercantile Award" allegedly from the Cascadian Business Institute through which money was funded for DeLay's famous visit to a plush Scottish golf club, and the National Order of Merit from the USA Foundation, whose chairman was . . . Jack Abramoff.

It is impossible to treat all the schemes and scams this crowd concocted to subvert democracy in the name of God and greed. But thanks to some superb reporting from the Associated Press and Knight Ridder, among others, we can touch on a few.

Abramoff made his name, so to speak, representing Indian tribes with gambling interests. As his partner he hired a DeLay crony named Michael Scanlon. Together they would bilk half a dozen Indian tribes who hired them to protect their tribal gambling interests from competition. What they had to offer, of course, were their well-known connections to the Republican power structure, including members of Congress, friends at the White House (Abramoff's personal assistant became Karl Rove's personal assistant), Christian Right activists like Ralph Reed, and right-wing ideologues like Grover Norquist (according to *The Texas Observer*, two lobbying clients of Abramoff paid $25,000 to Norquist's organization—Americans for Tax Reform—for a lunch date and meeting with President Bush in May 2001).

Abramoff and Scanlon came up with one scheme they called "Gimme Five." Abramoff would refer tribes to Scanlon for grassroots public relations work, and Scanlon would then kick back about 50 percent to Abramoff, all without the tribes' knowledge. Before it was over the tribes had paid them $82 million, much of it going directly into Abramoff's and Scanlon's pockets. And that doesn't count the thousands more that Abramoff directed the tribes to pay out in campaign contributions.

Some of the money found its way into an outfit called the Council of Republicans for Environmental Advocacy, founded by Gale Norton before she became secretary of the interior, the cabinet position most responsible for Indian gaming rights (as well as oil-and-gas issues, public lands and parks, and something else we'll get to in a moment).

Some of the money went to so-called charities set up by Abramoff and DeLay that filtered money for lavish trips for members of Congress and their staff, as well as salaries for congressional family members and DeLay's pet projects.

And some of the money found its way to the righteous folks of the religious Right. One who had his hand out was Ralph Reed, the Christian Coalition's poster boy against gambling. "We believe gambling is a cancer on the American body politic," Reed had said. "It is stealing food from the mouths of children . . . [and] turning wives into widows."

When he resigned from the Christian Coalition (just as it was coming under federal investigation and slipping into financial arrears), Reed sought a cut of the lucre flowing to Abramoff and Scanlon. He sent Abramoff an e-mail: "Now that I am leaving electoral politics, I need to start humping in corporate accounts . . . I'm counting on you to help me with some contacts."

Abramoff came through. According to *The Washington Post*'s Susan Schmidt and R. Jeffrey Smith, he and Scanlon paid Reed some $4 million to whip up Christian opposition to gambling initiatives that could cut into the profits of Jack Abramoff's clients. Reed called in some of the brightest stars in the Christian firmament—Pat Robertson, Jerry Falwell, James Dobson, Phyllis Schlafly—to participate in what became a ruse on Abramoff's behalf. They would oppose gambling on religious and moral grounds in strategic places at decisive moments when competitive challenges threatened Abramoff's clients. Bogus Christian fronts were part of the strategy. Baptist preachers in Texas rallied to Reed's appeals. Unsuspecting folks in Louisiana heard the voice of God on the radio—with Jerry Falwell and Pat Robertson doing the honors—thundering against a riverboat gambling scheme that one of Abramoff's clients feared would undermine its advantage. Reed even got James Dobson, whose nationwide radio "ministry" reaches millions of people, to deluge phone lines at the Department of the Interior and White House with calls from indignant Christians.

In 1999 Abramoff arranged for the Mississippi Choctaws, who were trying to stave off competition from other tribes, to contribute more than $1 million to Norquist's Americans for Tax Reform, which then passed the money along to the Alabama Christian Coalition and to another antigambling group Reed had duped into aiding the cause. It is unclear how much these Christian soldiers "marching as to war" knew about the true purpose of their crusade, but Ralph Reed knew all along that his money was coming from Abramoff. The e-mails between the two men read like *Elmer Gantry*.

It gets worse.

Some of Abramoff's money from lobbying went to start a nonprofit organization called the U.S. Family Network. Nice name, yes? An uplifting all-American name, like so many others that fly the conservative banner in Washington. Tom DeLay wrote a fund-raising letter in which he described the U.S. Family Network as "a powerful nationwide organization dedicated to restoring our government to citizen control." Fund-raising appeals warned that the American family "is being attacked from all sides: crime, drugs, pornography . . . and gambling." So help me, I'm not making this up. You can read R. Jeffrey Smith's mind-boggling account of it on *The Washington Post* Web site, where he writes that the organization did no discernable grassroots organizing and its money came from business groups with no demonstrated interest in the "moral fitness" agenda that was the network's professed aim.

Let's call it what it was: a scam—one more cog in the money-laundering machine controlled by DeLay and Abramoff. A former top assistant to DeLay founded the organization. It bought a town house just three blocks from DeLay's congressional quarters and provided him with fancy free office space where he would go to raise money. DeLay's wife also got a salary. But that's the least of it.

Working with Abramoff through a now-defunct law firm in London and an obscure offshore company in the Bahamas, Russian oil-and-gas executives were using the U.S. Family Network to funnel money to influence the majority leader of the House of Representatives—yes, that chamber of American government once known as the "People's House."

Our witness for this is the Christian pastor who served as the titular president of the U.S. Family Network, the Reverend Christopher Geeslin. He told *The Washington Post* that the founder of the organization, the former DeLay aide, told him that a million dollars was passed through from sources in Russia who wanted DeLay's support for legislation enabling the International Monetary Fund to bail out the faltering Russian economy without demanding that the country raise taxes on its energy industry. As Molly Ivins pointed out in a recent column, right on cue DeLay found his way onto *Fox News Sunday* to argue the Russian position. That same titular head of the U.S. Family Network, the Christian pastor, said DeLay's former chief of staff also told him, "This is the way things work in Washington."

This is the way things work in Washington.

Twenty-five years ago Grover Norquist had said that "What Republicans need is 50 Jack Abramoffs in Washington. Then this will be a different town."

Well, they got it, and the arc of the conservative takeover of government was completed. Abramoff had once said that his goal was to banish liberals from college campuses, and that "all of my political work is driven by philosophical interests, not by the desire to gain wealth." Now his intentions, as he admitted to Michael Crowley of *The New York Times*, were "to push the Republicans on K Street to be more helpful to the conservative movement." Money, politics, and ideology became one and the same in a juggernaut of power that crushed everything in sight, including core conservative principles.

Here we come to the heart of darkness.

One of Abramoff's first big lobbying clients was the Northern Mariana Islands in the Pacific. After World War II the Marianas became a trusteeship of the United Nations, administered by the U.S. government under the stewardship of the Department of the Interior. We should all remember that thousands of marines died there, fighting for our way of life and our freedoms. Today these islands are a haven for tourists—first-class hotels, beautiful beaches, a championship golf course. But the islands were exempted from U.S. labor and immigration laws, and over the years tens of thousands of people, primarily Chinese, mostly women, were brought there as garment workers. These so-called guest workers found themselves living in crowded barracks in miserable conditions. The main island, Saipan, became known as America's biggest sweatshop.

In 1998 a government report found workers there living in substandard conditions, suffering severe malnutrition and health problems, and subjected to unprovoked acts of violence. Many had signed "shadow contracts," which required them to pay up to $7,000 just to get a job. They also had to renounce their claim to basic human rights, including political and religious activities, socializing, and marrying. If they protested, they could be summarily deported. As Greg McDonald wrote in the *Houston Chronicle*, the garments produced on Saipan were manufactured for American companies from tariff-free Asian cloth and shipped duty- and quota-free to the United States. Some of the biggest names in the retail clothing industry—Levi Strauss, Gap, J.Crew, Eddie Bauer, Reebok, Polo, Tommy Hilfiger, Nordstrom, Lord & Taylor, Jones New York, and Liz Claiborne—had been able to slap a "made in the USA" label on the clothes and import them to America, while paying the workers practically nothing.

When these scandalous conditions began to attract attention, the sweatshop moguls fought all efforts at reform. Knowing that Jack Abramoff was close to Tom DeLay, they hired him to lobby for the islands. Conservative members of Congress lined up as Abramoff's team arranged for them to visit the islands on carefully guided junkets. Conservative intellectuals and journalists, for hire at rates considerably above what the women on the islands were making, also signed up for expense-free trips to the Marianas. They flew first-class, dined at posh restaurants, slept in comfort at the beachfront hotel, and returned to write and speak of the islands as "a true free market success story" and "a laboratory of liberty."

Abramoff took Tom DeLay and his wife there, too. DeLay practically swooned. He said the Marianas "represented what is best about America." He called them "my Galapagos"—"a perfect petri dish of capitalism."

These fellow travelers—right-wing members of Congress, their staffs, and their lapdogs in the right-wing press and think tanks—became a solid phalanx against any and all attempts to provide the workers on the islands with a living wage and decent conditions. When a liberal California Democrat, George Miller, and a conservative Alaskan senator, Frank Murkowski, indignant at the "appalling conditions," wanted to enact a bill to raise minimum wages on the islands and at least prevent summary deportation of the workers, DeLay and Abramoff stopped them cold. As Representative Miller told it, "They killed my reform bill year after year. And even when an immigration reform bill by Senator Frank Murkowski, a Republican, was approved by the full Senate, they blocked it repeatedly in the House."

After the 2000 election, when the spoils of victory were being divided up, Abramoff got himself named to the Bush transition team for the Department of the Interior. He wanted to make sure the right people wound up overseeing his clients, the Marianas. He enlisted Reed, who said he would raise the matter with Rove, to stop at least one appointment to the Department of the Interior that might prove troublesome. About this time Reed wrote an e-mail to Enron's top lobbyist touting his pal Abramoff as "arguably the most influential and effective GOP lobbyist in Congress. I share several clients with him and have yet to see him lose a battle. He also is very close to DeLay and could help enormously on that front. raised $ for bush . . . he [sic] assistant is Susan Ralston [who would become Rove's assistant]."

For his services to the Marianas Jack Abramoff was paid nearly $10 million, including the fees he charged for booking his guests on the golf courses and providing them copies of Newt Gingrich's book. One of the sweatshop moguls with whom Abramoff was particularly close contributed half a million dollars to—you guessed it—the U.S. Family Network that laundered money from Russian oligarchs to Tom DeLay.

To this day, workers on the Marianas are denied the federal minimum wage while working long hours for subsistence income in their little "perfect petri dish of capitalism."

Both ends of Pennsylvania Avenue were now in sync. George W. Bush had created his own version of the K Street Project. Remember how he emerged from the crowded field of Republican candidates in early 1999 and literally blew several of them out of the water? He did so by drowning his opponents with money. In just his first six months of fund-raising, Bush collected some $36 million—nine times more than his nearest opponent, John McCain. The money came from the titans of American business and lobbying who understood that their contributions would be rewarded. You've heard of the Pioneers and Rangers—people who raised at least $100,000 and $200,000 for Bush. Among them were people like Tom DeLay's brother, also a lobbyist; the CEO of Enron, Kenneth ("Kenny Boy") Lay; and hundreds of executives from the country's banks, investment houses, oil-and-gas companies, electric utilities, and other corporations.

While Tom DeLay kept a ledger on K Street, ranking lobbyists as friendly and unfriendly, the Bush campaign assigned a tracking number to every major contributor, making sure to know who was bringing in the bucks and where they were coming from. In May of 1999 the trade association for the electric utility industry sent a letter to potential contributors on Bush campaign stationery, reminding them that campaign managers "have stressed the importance of having our industry incorporate the tracking number in your fundraising efforts . . . it does ensure that our industry is credited and that your progress is listed . . ."

The bounty was plentiful. A score of Pioneers and Rangers were paid off with ambassadorships. At least thirty-seven were named to post-election transition teams, where they had a major say in selecting political appointees at key regulatory positions across the government. Remember the California energy crisis, when Enron traders boasted of gouging grandmothers to drive up the prices for energy? Well, Enron's Kenneth Lay had been Bush's biggest campaign funder over the years and what he asked now as a payoff was appointment to the Department of Energy transition team. This is how Enron's boss got to name two of the five members of the Federal Energy Regulatory Commission, who looked the other way while Enron rigged California's energy prices and looted billions right out of the pockets of California's citizens.

There are, repeat, no victimless crimes in politics. The cost of corruption is passed on to you. When the government of the United States falls under the thumb of the powerful and privileged, regular folks get squashed.

This week I visited for the first time the Museum of the Presidio in San Francisco. From there American troops shipped out to combat in the Pacific. Many never came back. On the walls of one corridor are photographs of some of those troops, a long way from home. Looking at them, I wondered: Is this what those marines died for on the Marianas—

for sweatshops, the plunder of our public trust, the corruption of democracy? Government of the Abramoffs, by the DeLays, and for the people who bribe them?

I don't think so.

But this crowd in charge has a vision sharply at odds with the American people. They would arrange Washington and the world for the convenience of themselves and the transnational corporations that pay for their elections. In the words of Al Meyeroff, the Los Angeles attorney who led a successful class action suit for the workers on Saipan, the people who control the U.S. government today want "a society run by the powerful, oblivious to the weak, free of any oversight, enjoying a cozy relationship with government, and thriving on crony capitalism."

America as their petri dish—the Marianas, many times over.

This is an old story and our continuing struggle. A century ago Theodore Roosevelt said the central fact of his time was that corporations had become so dominant they would chew up democracy and spit it out. His cousin Franklin Roosevelt warned that a government of money was as much to be feared as a government by mob. One was a progressive Republican, the other a liberal Democrat. Their sentiments were echoed by an icon of the conservative movement, Barry Goldwater, in 1985 during his statement before the Commission on National Elections:

> The fact that liberty depended on honest elections was of the utmost importance to the patriots who founded our nation and wrote the Constitution. They knew that corruption destroyed the prime requisite of Constitutional liberty, an independent legislature free from any influence other than that of the people . . . representative government assumes that elections will be controlled by the citizenry at large, not by those who give the most money. Electors must believe their vote counts. Elected officials must owe their allegiance to the people, not to their own wealth or to the wealth of interest groups who speak only for the selfish fringes of the whole community.

I have painted a bleak picture of our political process. I believe it is a true picture. But it is not a hopeless picture. Something can be done about it. Organized people have always had to take on organized money. If they had not, blacks would still be slaves, women wouldn't have the vote, workers couldn't organize, and children would still be working in the mines. Our democracy today is more inclusive than in the days of the founders because time and again, the people have organized themselves to insist that America become "a more perfect union."

It is time to fight again. These people in Washington have no right to be doing what they are doing. It's not their government, it's *your* government. They work for you. They're public employees—and if they let us down and sell us out, they should be fired. That goes for the lowliest bureaucrat in town to the senior leaders of Congress on up to the president of the United States.

They would have you believe this is just "a lobbying scandal." They would have you think that if they pass a few nominal reforms, put a little more distance between the politician and the lobbyist, you will think everything is okay and they can go back to business as usual.

They're trying it now. Just look at Congressman John Boehner, elected to replace Tom DeLay as House majority leader. Today he speaks the language of reform, but ten years ago Boehner was handing out checks from the tobacco executives on the floor of the House. He's been a full player in the K Street Project and DeLay's money machine, holding weekly meetings with some of the most powerful lobbyists in the Speaker's suite at the Capitol. He has thought nothing of hopping on corporate jets or cruising the Caribbean during winter breaks with high-powered lobbyists. Moreover, Congressman Roy Blunt has been elected to DeLay's first job as majority whip despite being deeply compromised by millions upon millions of dollars raised from the same interests that bought off DeLay.

And what now of DeLay? He's under indictment for money laundering in Texas and had to resign as majority leader. But just the other day the party bosses in Congress gave him a seat on the powerful House

Appropriations Committee where big contributors get their rewards. And—are you ready for this?—they put him on the subcommittee overseeing the Justice Department, which is investigating the Abramoff scandal, including Abramoff's connections to DeLay.

Business as usual. The usual rot.

You may say, "See? These forces can't be defeated. They're too rich, they're too powerful, they're too entrenched."

But look at what has happened in Connecticut, one of the most corrupt states in the Union. Rocked by multiple scandals that brought down a state treasurer, a state senator, and the governor himself with convictions of bribery, tax evasion, and worse, the people finally had enough. Although many of the parties had to be forced kicking and screaming to do it, last December the legislature passed clean-money reform and the new governor signed it into law. The bill bans campaign contributions from lobbyists and state contractors and makes Connecticut the very first state in the nation where the legislature and governor approved full public funding for their own races.

Connecticut isn't the only place where the link between public officials and private campaign contributions has been broken. Both Arizona and Maine offer full public financing of statewide and legislative races. New Jersey, New Mexico, North Carolina, and Vermont have clean-money systems for some races. The cities of Portland, Oregon, and Albuquerque, New Mexico, recently approved full public financing for citywide races.

In these places, candidates for public office—executive, legislative, and in some cases judicial—have the option of running on a limited and equal grant of full public funding, provided they take little or no private contributions. To qualify they have to pass a threshold by raising a large number of small contributions from voters in their district. The system allows candidates to run competitive campaigns for office even if they do not have ties to well-heeled donors or Big Money lobbyists, a near impossibility when public elections are privately funded.

In places where clean elections are law, we see more competition for legislative seats and a more diverse group of people running for office. And there are policy results as well. In Arizona, one of the first acts of Governor Janet Napolitano, elected under the state's public financing program, was to institute reforms establishing low-cost prescription drug subsidies for seniors. Compare that to the Medicare debacle going on at the national level. In Maine, where clean elections have been in place since 2000, there have also been advances in providing low-cost pharmaceutical drugs for residents, and in making sure that every state resident has medical coverage.

Why? Because the politicians can do what's right, not what they're paid to do by big donors. They, not the lobbyists, write the legislation.

California may soon follow Connecticut. Calling for the political equivalent of electroshock therapy, the *Los Angeles Times* recently urged Californians: "Forget half-measures. The cure is voluntary public financing of election campaigns." Already the Clean Money and Fair Elections bill has passed the state assembly and is headed for the senate.

Think about this: Californians could buy back their elected representatives at a cost of about $5 or $6 per resident. Nationally we could buy back our Congress and the White House with full public financing for about $10 per taxpayer per year. You can check this out on the Web site for Public Campaign (www.publicampaign.org).

Public funding won't solve all the problems. There's no way completely to legislate predators from abusing our trust. But it would go a long way to breaking the link between big donors and public officials and to restoring democracy to the people. Until we offer qualified candidates a different source of funding for their campaigns—clean, disinterested, accountable public money—the selling of America will go on. From scandal to scandal.

Representative Barney Frank says of Congress: "We are the only people in the world required by law to take large amounts of money from strangers and then act as if it has no effect on our behavior."

What law is he talking about? The unwritten law that says your congressman has to raise $2,000 per day from the day he or she is sworn in to the next Election Day—weekdays, Saturdays, Sundays, Christmas Eve, and the Fourth of July. As long as elected officials need that constant stream of cash, someone will run our country but it won't be you.

Even some business lobbyists are having second thoughts. One of them, Stanton Anderson, was recently quoted in *BusinessWeek*: "As a conservative, I've always opposed government involvement. But it seems to me the real answer is federal financing of Congressional elections."

Mr. Anderson understands this isn't about a few bad apples. This is about the system. We can change the system. But we have to believe democracy is worth fighting for.

Listen to what Theodore Roosevelt said in 1912 in Chicago when he took on the political bosses and Big Money of his time for committing "treason to the people":

> We are standing for the great fundamental rights upon which all successful free government must be based. We are standing for elementary decency in politics. We are fighting for honesty against naked robbery. It is not a partisan issue; it is more than a political issue; it is a great moral issue. If we condone political theft, if we do not resent the kinds of wrong and injustice that injuriously affect the whole nation, not merely our democratic form of government but our civilization itself cannot endure.

We need that fighting spirit today—the tough, outraged, and resilient spirit that knows we have been delivered the great and precious legacy, "government of, by, and for the people," and by God we're going to pass it on.

17. | AFTER 9/11

Keynote Address for the Environmental Grantmakers Association

OCTOBER 16, 2001

Before the terrorists struck on 9/11 I had been scheduled to speak to the Environmental Grantmakers Association on the impact of money in politics, one of my regular beats in journalism. When I went on the air with a daily broadcast after 9/11 I thought of canceling the speech, then five weeks away; it just didn't seem timely to talk about money and politics while the country was still in mourning. But I began to notice some items in the news that struck me as especially repugnant amid all the grief. In Washington, where environmentalists and other public-interest advocates had suspended normal political activities, corporate lobbyists were suddenly mounting a full-court press for special favors at taxpayer expense. There was no black crepe draped on the windows of K Street—the predatory epicenter of Washington; inside, visions of newfound gold danced in the heads of lobbyists. And in corporate suites across the country CEOs were waking up to the prospect of a bonanza born of tragedy. Within two weeks of 9/11 the business press was telling of corporate directors rushing to give bargain-priced stock options to their top executives. The Wall Street Journal* *would later piece the whole story to-gether: stocks had fallen sharply after the attacks, reaching a low on Septem-ber 21; families of 9/11 victims were still waiting for some piece of flesh or bone to confirm the loss of a loved one; soldiers were loading their gear for deployment to Afghanistan; and corporate executives were too busy counting their shekels to notice. As stock options grant executives the right to buy shares at that low price for years to come, the lower the price when options are awarded, the more lucrative they are. "Since the house is on fire, let us warm ourselves," goes an Italian proverb. Translated to English, it reads: "Grab the loot and run." Some CEOs didn't need reminding. During the last days of September, 511 top executives at 186 companies gobbled up stock-option grants—more than twice as many as in comparable periods in recent years. Almost 100 companies that did not regularly grant stock options in September now did so. One company—Teradyne—had begun laying off em-ployees just hours before the terrorists struck; the chairman, nonetheless, helped himself to 602,589 options just two weeks later, and when Journal re-porters wanted to ask about it, his spokesman said the CEO wouldn't be available for an interview because "I don't want to put him in the position of answering how does he feel about potentially benefiting from the 9/11 trag-edy." President Bush had already urged us to prove our patriotism by going shopping. New York mayor Rudy Giuliani went on television to say we should "step up to the plate right now and show the strength of the American economy." Giuliani himself would soon be hauling in a fortune exploiting his newfound celebrity to advise corporations on how to protect against terror-ism. And in Washington the marionettes of the military-industrial-security complex salivated at the prospect of windfall profits rising from the smolder-ing ruins. Grief would prove no match for greed. I decided not to cancel the speech.*

* * *

This isn't the speech I expected to give today. I intended something else.

For several years I've been taking every possible opportunity to talk

---

* See Charles Forelle, James Bandler, and Mark Maremont, "Executive Pay: The 9/11 Factor," The Wall Street Journal, July 15, 2006.

about the soul of democracy. "Something is deeply wrong with politics today," I told anyone who would listen. And I wasn't referring to the partisan mudslinging, or the negative TV ads, the excessive polling, or the empty campaigns. I was talking about something deeper, something troubling at the core of politics. The soul of democracy—government of, by, and for the people—has been drowning in a rising tide of money contributed by a narrow, unrepresentative elite that has betrayed Abraham Lincoln's vision of self-government.

This, to me, is the big political story of the last quarter century, and I started reporting it as a journalist in the late 1970s with the first television documentary about political action committees. I intended to talk about this today—about the soul of democracy—and then connect it to your environmental work. That was my intention. That's the speech I was working on six weeks ago. Before 9/11.

We've all been rocked on our heels by what happened. We have been reminded that while the clock and the calendar make it seem as if our lives unfold hour by hour, day by day, our passage is marked by events—of celebration and crisis. We share those in common. They create the memories which make us a people, a nation with a history.

Pearl Harbor was that event for my parents' generation. It changed their world, as it changed them. They never forgot the moment they heard the news. For my generation it was the assassinations of the Kennedys and Martin Luther King, the bombing of the Sixteenth Street Baptist Church, the dogs and fire hoses in Alabama. Those events broke our hearts.

For this present generation, that moment will be September 11, 2001. We will never forget it. In one sense, this is what terrorists intend. Terrorists don't want to own our land, wealth, monuments, buildings, fields, or streams. They're not after tangible property. Sure, they aim to annihilate the targets they strike. But their real goal is to get inside our heads, our psyche, and to deprive us—the survivors—of peace of mind, of trust, of faith, to prevent us from believing again in a world of mercy, justice, and love, or working to bring that better world to pass.

This is their real target, to turn our imaginations into private Afghanistans, where they can rule by fear. Once they possess us, they are hard to exorcise.

This summer our daughter and son-in-law adopted a baby boy. On September 11, our son-in-law passed through the shadow of the World Trade Center to his office up the block. He got there in time to see the eruption of fire and smoke. He saw the falling bodies. He saw the people jumping to their deaths. His building was evacuated and for long awful moments he couldn't reach his wife to say he was okay. She was in agony until he finally got through—and even then he couldn't get home to his family until the next morning. It took him several days to get his legs back fully. Now, in a matter-of-fact voice, our daughter tells us how she often lies awake at night, wondering where and when it might happen again, going to the computer at three in the morning—her baby asleep in the next room—to check out what she can about bioterrorism, germ warfare, anthrax, and the vulnerability of children. Beyond the carnage left by the sneak attack, terrorists create another kind of havoc, invading and despoiling a new mother's deepest space, holding her imagination hostage to the most dreadful possibilities.

The building where my wife and I produce our television programs is in midtown Manhattan, just over a mile from ground zero. It was evacuated immediately after the disaster although the two of us remained with other colleagues to help keep the station on the air. Our building was evacuated again late in the evening a day later because of a bomb scare at the nearby Empire State Building. We had just ended a live broadcast for PBS when the security officers swept through and ordered everyone out of the building. As we were making our way down the stairs I took Judith's arm and was suddenly struck by a thought: Is this the last time I'll touch her? Could our marriage of almost fifty years end here, on this dim and bare staircase? I ejected the thought forcibly from my mind; like a bouncer removing a rude intruder, I shoved it out of my consciousness by sheer force of will. But in the first hours of morning, the specter crept back.

Returning from Washington on the train last week, I looked up and for the first time in days saw a plane in the sky. And then another, and another—and every plane I saw invoked unwelcome images and terrifying thoughts. Unwelcome images, terrifying thoughts—embedded in our heads by terrorists.

I wish I could find the wisdom in this. But wisdom is a very elusive thing. Wisdom comes, if at all, slowly, painfully, and only after deep reflection. Perhaps when we gather next year the wisdom will have arranged itself like the colors of a kaleidoscope, and we will look back on September 11 and see it differently. But I haven't been ready for reflection. I have wanted to stay busy, on the go, or on the run, perhaps, from the need to cope with the reality that just a few subway stops south of where I get off at Penn Station in midtown Manhattan, three thousand people died in a matter of minutes. One minute they're pulling off their jackets, sipping their coffee, adjusting the picture of a child or sweetheart or spouse in a frame on their desk, booting up their computer— and in the next, their world ends.

Practically every day *The New York Times* has been running compelling profiles of the dead and missing, and I've been keeping them. Not out of some macabre desire to stare at death, but to see if I might recognize a face, a name, some old acquaintance, a former colleague, even a stranger I might have seen occasionally on the subway or street. That was my original purpose. But as the file has grown I realize what an amazing montage it is of life, a portrait of the America those terrorists wanted to shatter. I study each little story for its contribution to the mosaic of my country, its particular revelation about the nature of democracy, the people with whom we share it.

Ivhan Luis Carpio Bautista: It was his birthday, and he had the day off from Windows on the World, the restaurant high atop the World Trade Center. But back home in Peru his family depended on Luis for the money he had been sending them since he arrived in New York two years ago speaking only Spanish, and there was the tuition he would soon be paying to study at John Jay College of Criminal Justice. So on September 11, Luis Bautista was putting in overtime. He was twenty-four.

William Steckman: For thirty-five of his fifty-six years he took care of the NBC transmitter at One World Trade Center, working the night shift because it let him spend time during the day with his five children and fix things up around the house. His shift ended at six a.m. but this morning his boss asked him to stay on to help install some new equipment, and William Steckman said sure.

Elizabeth Holmes: She lived in Harlem with her son and jogged every morning around Central Park where I often go walking, and I have been wondering if Elizabeth Holmes and I perhaps crossed paths early one day. I figure we were kindred souls; she, too, was a Baptist, and sang in the choir at the Canaan Baptist Church. She was expecting a ring from her fiancé at Christmas.

Linda Luzzicone and Ralph Gerhardt: They were planning their wedding, too. They had their parents come to New York in August to meet for the first time and talk about the plans. They had discovered each other in nearby cubicles on the 104th floor of One World Trade Center and fell in love. They were working there when the terrorists struck.

Mon Gjonbalaj: He came here from Albania. Because his name was hard to pronounce his friends called him by the Cajun "Jambalaya" and he grew to like it. He lived with his three sons in the Bronx and was to have retired when he turned sixty-five last year, but he was so attached to the building and so enjoyed the company of the other janitors that he often showed up an hour before work just to shoot the bull. In my mind's eye I can see him that morning, horsing around with his buddies.

Fred Scheffold: He liked his job, too—chief of the twelfth battalion of firefighters in Harlem. He loved his men. But he never told his daughters in the suburbs about the bad stuff in all the fires he had fought over the years. He didn't want to worry them. This morning, his shift had just ended and he was starting home when the alarm rang. He jumped into the truck with the others and at One World Trade Center he pushed through the crowds to the staircase, heading for the top. The last time anyone saw him alive he was heading up the stairs. As hundreds poured past him going down, Fred Scheffold just kept going up through the flames and smoke.

Now you know why I can't give the speech I was working on. Talking about my work in television would be too parochial. And what's happened since the attacks would seem to put the lie to my fears about the soul of democracy. Americans rallied together in a way that I cannot remember since World War II. In real and instinctive ways we have felt touched—singed—by the fires that brought down those buildings, even those of us who did not directly lose a loved one. Great and ordinary alike, we have been humbled by a renewed sense of our common mortality. Those planes the terrorists turned into suicide bombers cut through a complete cross-section of America—stockbrokers and dishwashers, bankers and secretaries, lawyers and janitors, Hollywood producers and new immigrants, urbanites and suburbanites alike. One community near where I live in New Jersey lost twenty-three residents. A single church near our home lost eleven members of the congregation. Eighty nations are represented among the dead. This catastrophe has reminded us of a basic truth at the heart of our democracy: no matter our wealth or status or faith, we are all equal before the law, in the voting booth, and when death rains down from the sky.

We have also been reminded that despite years of scandals and political corruption, despite the stream of stories of personal greed and lobbyists scamming the treasury, despite the retreat from the public sphere and the race toward private privilege, despite squalor for the poor and gated communities for the rich, we have been reminded that Americans have not yet given up on the idea of "We the People." They have refused to accept the notion, promoted so diligently by right-wingers, that government—the public service—should be shrunk to a size where they can drown it in the bathtub, as Grover Norquist said is their goal. These right-wingers teamed up after 9/11 with deep-pocket bankers to stop the United States from cracking down on terrorist money havens. As *Time* magazine reports, thirty industrial nations were ready to tighten the screws on offshore financial centers whose banks have the potential to hide and often help launder billions of dollars for drug cartels, global crime syndicates—not to mention groups like Osama bin Laden's al Qaeda organization. Not all offshore money is linked to crime or terrorism; much of it comes from wealthy people who are hiding money to avoid taxation. And right-wingers believe in nothing if not in avoiding taxation. So they and the bankers' lobbyists went to work to stop the American government from participating in the crackdown on dirty money, arguing that closing tax havens in effect leads to higher taxes on the people trying to hide their money. The president of the Heritage Foundation spent an hour, according to *The New York Times*, with Secretary of the Treasury Paul O'Neill, Texas bankers pulled their strings at the White House, and presto!—the Bush administration pulled out of the international campaign against tax havens.

How about that for patriotism? Better terrorists get their dirty money than tax cheaters be prevented from hiding their money. And this from people who wrap themselves in the flag and sing "The Star-Spangled Banner" with gusto. H. L. Mencken got it right when he said that when you hear some men talk about their love of country, it's a sign they expect to be paid for it.

But today's heroes are public servants. Those brave firefighters and policemen and Port Authority workers and emergency rescue personnel were public employees all, most of them drawing a modest middle-class income for extremely dangerous work. They command our imaginations not only because of their heroic deeds but because we know so many people like them, people we took for granted. For once, our TV screens have been filled with the modest declarations of average Americans coming to each other's aid.

I find this thrilling and sobering. It could offer a new beginning, a renewal of civil values that could leave our society stronger and more together than ever, working on common goals for the public good. In a 1991 interview in *Theater Week*, the playwright Tony Kushner wrote:

> There are moments in history when the fabric of everyday life unravels, and there is this unstable dynamism that allows for incred-

ible social change in short periods of time. People and the world they're living in can be utterly transformed, either for the good or the bad, or some mixture of the two.

This is such a moment, and it could go either way. Here's one sighting. In the wake of September 11 there's been a heartening change in how Americans view their government. For the first time in more than thirty years a majority of people say we trust the federal government to do the right thing "just about always" or at least "most of the time." It's as if the clock has been rolled back to the early sixties, before Vietnam and Watergate took such a toll on the gross national psychology. This newfound hope for public collaboration is based in part on how people view what the government has done in response to the attacks. President Bush acted with commendable resolve and restraint in those early days. But this is a case where yet again the people are ahead of the politicians. They're expressing greater faith in government right now because the long-standing gap between our ruling elites and ordinary citizens has seemingly disappeared. To most Americans, government right now doesn't mean a faceless bureaucrat or a politician auctioning access to the highest bidder. It means a courageous rescuer or brave soldier. Instead of representatives spending their evenings clinking glasses with fat cats, they are out walking among the wounded. In Washington it seemed momentarily possible that the political class had been jolted out of old habits. Some old partisan rivalries and arguments fell by the wayside as our representatives acted decisively on a fund to rebuild New York. Adversaries like Dennis Hastert and Dick Gephardt were linking arms. There was even a ten-day moratorium on political fund-raisers. I was beginning to be optimistic that the mercenary culture of Washington might finally be on its knees in repentance.

Alas, it was not to be. There are other sightings to report. It doesn't take long for the wartime opportunists—the mercenaries of Washington, the lobbyists, lawyers, and political fund-raisers—to emerge from their offices on K Street to grab what they can for their clients. While in New York we are still attending memorial services for firemen and police, while everywhere Americans' cheeks are still stained with tears, while the president calls for patriotism, prayers, and piety, the predators of Washington are up to their old tricks in the pursuit of private plunder at public expense. In the wake of this awful tragedy wrought by terrorism, they are cashing in.

How would they honor the thousands of people who died in the attacks? How do they propose to fight the long and costly campaign America must now undertake against terrorists?

Why, restore the three-martini lunch—surely that will strike fear in the heart of Osama bin Laden! You think I'm kidding, but bringing back the deductible lunch is one of the proposals on the table in Washington right now in the aftermath of 9/11. There are members of Congress who believe you should sacrifice in this time of crisis by paying for lobbyists' long lunches.

And cut capital gains for the wealthy, naturally—that's America's patriotic duty, too. And while we're at it, don't forget to eliminate the corporate alternative minimum tax, enacted fifteen years ago to prevent corporations from taking so many credits and deductions that they owed little if any taxes. But don't just repeal their minimum tax, give those corporations a refund for all the minimum tax they have ever been assessed. You look incredulous. But these proposals are being pushed hard in Washington right now in an effort to exploit the trauma of 9/11.

What else can America do to strike at the terrorists? Why, slip in a special tax break for poor General Electric while everyone's distracted, and torpedo the recent order to clean the Hudson River of PCBs. Don't worry about NBC, CNBC, or MSNBC reporting it; they're all in the GE family.

It's time for Churchillian courage, we're told. So how to assure that future generations will look back and say, "This was our finest hour"? That's easy. Give coal producers more freedom to pollute. Shovel generous tax breaks to those giant energy companies. Open the Alaskan wilderness to drilling. And while the red, white, and blue waves at half-mast over the land of the free and the home of the brave, give the president the power to discard open debate and the rule of law concerning controversial trade agreements, and set up secret tribunals to run roughshod over local communities trying to protect their environment and their health. It's happening as we meet.

If I sound a little bitter about this, I am. The president rightly appeals every day for sacrifice. But to these mercenaries sacrifice is for suckers. I am angry, yes, but my sadness is greater than my anger. Our business and political class owes us better than this. They're on top. If ever they were going to put patriotism over profits, if ever they were going to practice the magnanimity of winners, this was the moment. To hide now behind the flag while ripping off a country in crisis fatally separates them from the common course of American life.

Understandably, in the hours after the attacks many environmental organizations stepped down from aggressively pressing their issues. Greenpeace canceled its thirtieth-anniversary celebration. The Sierra Club stopped all advertising, phone banks, and mailing. The Environmental Working Group postponed a national report on chlorination in drinking water. That was the proper way to observe a period of mourning.

But the polluters and their political cronies accepted no such constraints. Just one day after the attack, one day into the maelstrom of horror, loss, and grief, many senators called for prompt consideration of the president's proposal to subsidize the country's largest and richest energy companies. While America was mourning they were marauding. One congressman even suggested that ecoterrorists might be behind the attacks. And with that smear he and his kind went on the offensive in Congress, attempting to attach to a defense bill massive subsidies for the oil, coal, gas, and nuclear companies.

To a defense bill! What an insult to the sacrifice of our men and women in uniform! To pile corporate welfare totaling billions of dollars onto a defense bill in an emergency like this is repugnant to the nostrils and a scandal against democracy.

They're counting on patriotism to distract you from their plunder.

They're counting on you to stand at attention with your hand over your heart, pledging allegiance to the flag, while they pick your pocket!

Let's face it: the predators of the Republic present citizens with no options but to climb back in the ring. We are in what educators call "a teachable moment." And we'll lose it if we roll over. Democracy wasn't canceled on September 11, but democracy won't survive if citizens turn into lemmings. Yes, the president is our commander in chief, and in hunting down the terrorists in Afghanistan who attacked us, he deserves our support. But we are not the president's minions. If in the name of the war on terrorism President Bush hands the state over to the most powerful interests circling Washington, it's every patriot's duty to join the loyal opposition. If the mercenaries try to exploit America's good faith to grab what they wouldn't get through fairly in peacetime, the disloyalty will not be our dissent but our subservience. The greatest sedition would be our silence.

Yes, there's a fight going on—against terrorists abroad, but just as certainly there's a fight going on here at home, to decide the kind of country this will be during the war on terrorism.

During two recent trips to Washington I heard people talking mostly about economic stimulus and the national security. How do we renew our economy and safeguard our nation? Those are the issues you are here to address, and you are uniquely equipped to address them with powerful leadership and persuasive argument.

If you want to fight for the environment, don't hug a tree, hug an economist. Hug the economist who tells you that fossil fuels are not only the third most heavily subsidized economic sector after road transportation and agriculture but that they also promote vast inefficiencies. Hug the economist who tells you that the most efficient investment of a dollar is not in fossil fuels but in renewable energy sources that not only provide new jobs but cost less over time. Hug the economist who tells you that the price system matters; it's potentially the most potent tool of all for creating social change. Look what California did this summer in responding to its recent energy crisis with a price structure that rewards those who conserve and punishes those who don't. Californians cut their electric consumption by up to 15 percent.

Do we want to send the terrorists a message? Go for conservation. Go for clean, homegrown energy. And go for public health. If we reduce emissions from fossil fuel, we will cut the rate of asthma among children. Healthier children and a healthier economy—how about that as a response to the terrorists?

As for national security, well, it's time to expose the energy plan before Congress for the dinosaur it is. Everyone knows America needs to reduce our reliance on fossil fuel. But this energy plan is more of the same: more subsidies for the rich, more pollution, more waste, more inefficiency. Get the message out.

Start with John Adams's wake-up call. The head of the Natural Resources Defense Council says the terrorist attacks spell out in frightful terms that America's unchecked consumption of oil has become our Achilles' heel. It constrains our military options in the face of terror. It leaves our economy dangerously vulnerable to price shocks. It invites environmental degradation, ecological disasters, and potentially catastrophic climate change.

Go to TomPaine.com and you will find the two simple facts we need to get to the American people: first, the money we pay at the gasoline pump helps prop up oil-rich sponsors of terrorism like Saddam Hussein and Muammar al-Qaddafi; and second, a big reason we spend so much money policing the Middle East—$30 billion every year, by one reckoning—has to do with our dependence on the oil there. The single most important thing environmentalists can do to ensure America's national security is to fight to reduce our nation's dependence on oil, whether imported or domestic.

You see the magnitude of the challenge. You understand the work that we must do. It's why you must not lose heart. Your adversaries will call you unpatriotic for speaking the truth when conformity reigns. Ideologues will smear you for challenging their spin. Mainstream media will ignore you, and those gasbags on cable TV and the radio talk shows will ridicule and vilify you. But I urge you to hold to these words: "In the course of fighting the present fire, we must not abandon our efforts to create fire-resistant structures of the future." Those words were written by the activist Randy Kehler more than ten years ago, as America geared up to fight the Gulf War. They ring as true today. Those fire-resistant structures must include an electoral system that is no longer dominated by Big Money, where the voices and problems of average people are attended on a fair and equal basis. They must include an energy system that is more sustainable and less dangerous. And they must include a press that takes its responsibility to inform us as seriously as its interest in entertaining us.

My own personal response to Osama bin Laden is not grand, or rousing, or dramatic. All I know to do is to keep practicing as best I can the craft that has been my calling for most of my adult life. My colleagues and I have rededicated ourselves to the production of several environmental reports that were in progress before September 11. As a result of our two specials this year—*Trade Secrets* and *Earth on Edge*—PBS is asking all of public television's production teams to focus on the environment for two weeks around Earth Day next April. Our documentaries will anchor that endeavor. One will report on how an obscure provision in the North American Free Trade Agreement can turn the rule of law upside down and undermine a community's health and environment. Our four-part series *America's First River* looks at how the Hudson River shaped America's conservation movement a century ago and, more recently, the modern environmental movement. We're producing another documentary on the search for alternative energy sources, and another on children and the environment—the questions scientists, researchers, and pediatricians are asking about children's vulnerability to hazards in the environment.

What does Osama bin Laden have to do with these? He has given me not one but three thousand and more reasons for journalism to signify on issues that matter. I began this talk with the names of some of them—the victims who died on September 11. I did so because I never want to forget the humanity lost in the horror. I never want to forget the e-mail sent by a doomed employee in the World Trade Center who, just before his life was over, wrote his comrade: "Thank you for being such a great friend." I never want to forget the man and woman holding hands as they leaped together to their death. I never want to forget those firemen who just kept going up; they just kept going up. And I never want to forget that the very worst of which human beings are capable can bring out the very best.

In response to the sneak attack on Pearl Harbor, my parents' generation waged and won a long war, then came home to establish a more prosperous and just America.

We will follow in their footsteps if we rise to the spiritual and moral challenge of 9/11. Michael Berenbaum has defined that challenge for me. As president of the Survivors of the Shoah Visual History Foundation, he worked with people who escaped the Holocaust. Here's what he says:

> The question is what to do with the very fact of survival. Over time survivors will be able to answer that question not by a statement about the past but by what they do with the future. Because they have faced death, many will have learned what is more important: life itself, love, family, community. The simple things we have all taken for granted will bear witness to that reality. The survivors will not be defined by the lives they have led until now but by the lives that they will lead from now on. For the experience of near death to have ultimate meaning, it must take shape in how one rebuilds from the ashes. Such for the individual; so, too, for the nation.

We are survivors, you and I. We will be defined not by the lives we led until September 11, but by the lives we will lead from now on.

So go home and make the best grants you've ever made. And the biggest—time is too precious to pinch pennies. Back the most committed and courageous people and back them with media to spread their message. Stick your own neck out. Let your work be charged with passion and your life with a mission. For when all is said and done, the most important grant you'll ever make is the gift of yourself to the work at hand.

18. | AMERICA 101

Council of the Great City Schools Fiftieth Anniversary
Fall Conference

OCTOBER 27, 2006

Our children are being cheated of their revolutionary heritage. Go to urban schools with high concentrations of poor and minority children and you can understand what it must have meant to Native Americans to be segregated on reservations—isolated, powerless, shorn of any chance to participate in shaping your destiny in the larger world. In 1976, filming a series on the bicentennial of the American Revolution, and again in 1986, filming for the bicentennial of the Constitution, and steadily over the last decade while making documentaries about education, kids in peril, and life in the inner city, I realized how little we teach children the true story of America—how the outcome of that story is in their hands, if only they are charged to claim it. Their imaginations are disenfranchised. They do not know that the whole course of our history can be seen as a long journey of different struggles to make democracy more vibrant and America more just. No one has told them that they are written into the Declaration of Independence: created equal, in value, as citizens, before the law. They are not told that of the twenty-six amendments to the Constitution, one deals with the judiciary, two with Prohibition, three with the presidency, and twenty with some extension of democracy. So they do not know that every generation must struggle to make the Constitution more consonant with the Declaration—to claim it as their own. No one has read them Thomas Wolfe:

> I believe that we are lost here in America, but I believe we shall be found . . . I think the true discovery of America is before us. I think the true fulfillment of our spirit, of our people, of our mighty and immortal land, is yet to come. I think the true discovery of our democracy is still before us.

Just about everywhere we turn the next generation is being indoctrinated to think of themselves narrowly as producers, employees, spectators, and consumers—everything but citizens. The least among us especially need to hear a different message. I have no solutions to the particular challenges facing urban schools—achievement scores, learning disabilities, teacher shortages—but I know we must change the curriculum in order to change the metaphor of our children from orphans of democracy to its rightful sons and daughters. Who will teach them that they, too, can mount a Boston Tea Party? When the Council of the Great City Schools, representing sixty-six large city school districts, asked me to give the keynote address at its annual conference, I said yes, knowing that in the audience I might find more than a few Paul Reveres, poised to teach their students the words of a ballad popular in 1776:

> Great nature's law inspires,
> All freeborn souls unite,
> While common interest fires
> Us to defend our rights.

* * *

When we talk about "urban education" we are talking about the poorest and most vulnerable children in America—kids for whom "at risk" has come to describe their fate and not simply their circumstances.

Their education should be the centerpiece of a great and diverse

America made stronger by equality and shared prosperity. It has instead become the epitome of public neglect, perpetuated by a class divide so permeated by race that it mocks the bedrock principles of the American promise.

George Bernard Shaw said the mark of a truly educated person is to be deeply moved by statistics. If so, America's governing class should be knocked off their feet by the fact that more than 70 percent of black children are now attending schools that are overwhelmingly nonwhite. In 1980 that figure was 63 percent. Latino students are even more isolated. *Brown v. Board of Education*'s "all deliberate speed" of 1954 has become slow motion in reverse. In Richard Kahlenberg's words, "With the law in retreat, geography takes command."

Not just the kids suffer. A nation that devalues poor children also demeans their teachers. For the life of me I cannot fathom why we expect so much from teachers and provide them so little in return. In 1940, the average pay of a male teacher was actually 3.6 percent more than what other college-educated men earned. Today it is 60 percent lower. Women teachers now earn 16 percent less than other college-educated women. This bewilders me. Children aren't born lawyers, corporate executives, engineers, and doctors. Their achievements bear the imprint of their teachers. There was no Plato without Socrates, and no John Coltrane without Miles Davis. Is there anyone here whose path was not marked by the inspiration of some teacher? Mary Sullivan, Bessie Bryant, Miss White, the Brotze sisters, Inez Hughes—I cannot imagine my life without them. Their classrooms were my world, and each one of them kept enlarging it.

Yet teachers now are expected to staff the permanent emergency rooms of our country's dysfunctional social order. They are expected to compensate for what families, communities, and culture fail to do. Like our soldiers in Iraq, they are sent into urban combat zones, on impossible missions under inhospitable conditions, and then abandoned by politicians and policy makers who have already cut and run, leaving teachers on their own.

One morning I opened *The New York Times* to read that tuition at

Manhattan's elite private schools had reached $26,000 a year, starting in kindergarten. On that same page was another story about a school in Mount Vernon, just across the city line from the Bronx, where 97 percent of the students are black and 90 percent of those are so impoverished they are eligible for free lunches. During Black History Month, a sixth grader researching Langston Hughes could not find a single book by Hughes in the library. This wasn't an oversight: there were virtually no books relevant to black history in that library. Most of the books on the shelves dated back to the 1950s and 1960s. A child's primer on work begins with a youngster learning to be a telegraph delivery boy!

It has taken constant litigation to bring to light this chronic neglect of basic learning in poor communities. In 1999, the Department of Education estimated that $127 billion were needed to bring "the nation's school facilities into good overall condition." The National Education Association puts the figure at $268 billion. Now the New York State Court of Appeals has ruled that the New York City school system alone is due approximately $15 billion "to provide students with their constitutional right to the opportunity to receive a sound basic education."

Surely this inexcusable underinvestment is one significant reason why, despite a national gross domestic product (GDP) higher than virtually all of Europe combined, American students as a whole fare so poorly compared to their counterparts in other advanced countries. In 2003, the United States ranked twenty-fourth out of twenty-nine advanced countries in combined mathematical literacy, according to the Programme for International Student Assessment. A better ranking in combined reading literacy—fifteenth out of twenty-seven Organisation for Economic Co-operation and Development countries in 2000—might be counted a success when compared to our abysmal math performance, but this can hardly be comforting if we consider that students are performing significantly better in countries without America's vast wealth.

The neglect of urban education—a capital moral offense in its own right—is but a symptom of what is happening in America. We are retreating from our social compact all down the line.

Our country is falling apart. Literally. In 2005 the American Society of Civil Engineers issued a report on our crumbling infrastructure. The engineers said we are "failing to maintain even substandard conditions" in our highway system—with significant economic effects. Poor road conditions cost motorists $54 billion a year in repairs and operating costs, and the 3.5 billion hours per year Americans spend stuck in traffic costs the economy more than $67 billion annually in lost productivity and wasted fuel.

The report said the country's power grid is likewise "in urgent need of modernization" as maintenance spending on transmission facilities has declined 1 percent annually since 1992, while growth in demand has risen 2.4 percent annually over the same period. In 2002, the Department of Energy warned that system "bottlenecks" due to transmission constraints were adding to consumer costs and threatening blackouts. In August of 2003 a blackout blanketed the Midwest and Northeast, leaving fifty million people in the dark, some for days, costing billions of dollars in lost commerce and production.

Even our much-touted technological superiority is in doubt. As my colleagues and I reported on my most recent PBS special, *The Net at Risk,* Asian and European countries have raced ahead of us in broadband speed—pushing America from fourth to twelfth place on the information superhighway. The Japanese, for example, have near-universal access to high-speed broadband connections, averaging sixteen times faster than U.S. connections at a much lower cost.

Connect the dots: neglected schools, crumbling roads, permanent environmental "dead zones," inadequate emergency systems, understaffed hospitals, library cutbacks, the lack of affordable housing, incompetent government agencies (whether FEMA or state bureaucracies charged with protecting helpless children)—these are characteristic features of our public sector today. Partly it's about money; little noticed amid all the concern about growing deficits and entitlement spending is this fact: nondefense discretionary spending declined 38 percent between 1980 and 1999 as a share of GDP. According to economists Barry Bluestone and Bennett Harrison, federal investment in nondefense capacities, including research and education, plummeted—from more than 2.5 percent of GDP in the 1980s to only 1.5 percent in the late 1990s.

All this comes at a point when American workers are losing ground in the marketplace as cheaper labor overseas becomes increasingly available through globalization, trade agreements, foreign investment, and technological outsourcing.

Rub the crystal ball: in the next few decades, when the huge liabilities start coming due from Social Security and Medicare, there will be a dogfight for public needs like education, highways, disaster relief, social services, and national health care.

Small wonder that the Wall Street investor Pete Peterson, a lifelong Republican who served as President Nixon's commerce secretary, says our children's future is being ruined by a reckless fiscal "theology."

Theology asserts propositions that are believed whether or not they meet the test of reality. Not only do our governing elites act as if there's no tomorrow, but they behave as if there is no reality. Alas, they won't be around to feel our grandchildren's pain.

In his recent book, *Collapse: How Societies Choose to Fail or Succeed*, the Pulitzer Prize–winning anthropologist Jared Diamond writes about how governing elites throughout history isolate and delude themselves until it is too late. He reminds us that the change people inflict on their environment was one of the main factors in the decline of earlier societies. For example: the Mayan natives on the Yucatán peninsula who suffered as their forests disappeared, their soil eroded, and their water supply deteriorated. Chronic warfare made matters worse as they exhausted dwindling resources. Although Mayan kings could see their forests vanishing and their hills eroding, they were able to insulate themselves from the rest of society. By extracting wealth from commoners, they could remain well-fed while everyone else was slowly starving. Realizing too late that they could not reverse their deteriorating environment, they became casualties of their own privilege.

Any society contains a built-in blueprint for failure, Diamond warns, if elites insulate themselves from the consequences of their decisions. He goes on to describe an America in which elites have cocooned themselves in gated communities, guarded by private security patrols and filled with people who drink bottled water, depend on private pensions, and send their children to private schools. Gradually they lose their motivation to support the police force, the municipal water supply, social security, and public schools.

The isolation of our schools, the crumbling of our infrastructure, and the reckless disregard of our fiscal affairs signal a retreat from the social compact that made America unique among nations. Our culture of democracy derived from the rooted experience of shared values, common dreams, and mutual aspirations that are proclaimed in the most disregarded section in the Constitution—the preamble—which announces a moral contract among "We the People of the United States." Yes, I know: when those words were written "We the People" didn't include slaves, or women, or exploited workers, or unwelcome immigrants. But the very idea of it, the vision of it, the potential power of "We the People" let loose by the American Revolution was to change the consciousness of the world. How radical it was to imagine citizens as political equals sharing in the consent required for self-government and in the great experiment of nation building.

Abraham Lincoln understood this. He recognized that freedom requires an economic system in which individuals can enjoy the fruits of their labor, and that the job of government was to keep the playing field level. Lincoln fought to preserve the Union because he knew government "of the people, by the people, and for the people" rested on economic opportunity, social mobility, and shared prosperity. America's great strength, in his eyes, derived from a unique and balanced blend of democracy and capitalism, and as the president of the Rockefeller Brothers Fund, Stephen Heinz, recently put it, "It is hard to imagine either democracy or capitalism functioning at peak performance without the other."

But look around: the great ideals of the American Revolution as articulated in the preamble to the Constitution are being sacrificed to the Gospel of Wealth.

The evidence abounds. Despite continued growth in the economy, real median household income declined between 2000 and 2004. Between 1980 and 2004, real wages in manufacturing fell 1 percent while the real income of the richest 1 percent rose by 135 percent. In 1976 the top 1 percent of Americans owned 22 percent of our total wealth. Today, the top 1 percent controls 38 percent of our total wealth. In 1960 the gap in terms of wealth between the top 20 percent and the bottom 20 percent was thirtyfold. Now it is seventy-five-fold. In 1996 there were just thirteen billionaires in America. Now there are more than one thousand. According to one study, the combined wealth of American millionaires—$30 *trillion*—more than equals the aggregated GDP of the European Union, Japan, China, Russia, and Brazil.

Such concentrations of wealth would be far less of an issue if the rest of society were benefiting proportionately. But that's not the case. The Census Bureau reports that Americans have become progressively less likely to advance up the socioeconomic ladder. One study cited by Stephen Heinz concludes, "The rich are likely to remain rich and the poor are likely to remain poor."

Aristotle thought injustice resulted from *pleonexia*, literally, "having more." A class of people having more than their share of the common wealth was the characteristic feature of an unjust society. Plato thought that the common good required a ratio of only five to one between the richest and poorest members of a society. Even J. P. Morgan thought bosses should only get twenty times more than their workers, at most. How quaint: in 2005 the average CEO earned 262 times what the average worker got.

As hard as it is to believe, the average real weekly wage for blue-collar workers, adjusted for rising costs of living, was about $278 a week in 2004 (in constant 1982 dollars). In 1972, it was $332 a week. That's not a slight downward trend—it's a significant and steady decline. So what of the argument that the rising tide lifts all boats? What we are seeing today is closer to the old view of class struggle. A recent Goldman Sachs report says it outright: "The most important contributor to higher profit margins over the past five years has been a decline in labor's share of national income."

Yet in a country where the press now represents the dominant class through an unprecedented concentration of media ownership, instead of this remarkable divergence of profits and wages making news, what grabs the headlines is the daily momentum of the stock market. Rarely does the corporate media note that the share of GDP going to wages is now at the lowest point since 1947, when the government started measuring things. Those who look fondly on "market discipline" that keeps wages down ignore the deep distortions built into a system in which capital is highly organized and workers are not.

So it is that to make ends meet in the face of stagnant or declining incomes, regular Americans have gone deeper and deeper in debt—with credit card debt nearly tripling since 1989. Poor kids are dropping out of high school and college at alarming rates. The middle class and working poor have been hit hard by a housing squeeze. Forty-five million or more Americans—eight out of ten of them in working families—are without health insurance. "The strain on working people," says the economist Jeffrey Madrick, "has become significant. Working families and the poor are losing ground under economic pressures that deeply affect household stability, family dynamics, social mobility, political participation, and civic life."

The American dream—on life support.

This wasn't meant to be. America was not intended to be a country where the winner takes all. Our system of checks and balances—read the Federalist Papers—was meant to keep an equilibrium in how power works and for whom. As Madrick reminds us, because equitable access to public resources is the lifeblood of democracy, Americans made primary schooling free to all. Because everyone deserves a second chance, debtors—especially the relatively poor—were protected by state law against rich creditors. Charters to establish corporations were not restricted to elites. Government encouraged Americans to own their own piece of land, and even supported squatters' rights. In my lifetime, equal access to opportunity began to materialize for millions of us, especially in the period following World War II, when the rising tide of our economy began to lift all boats more or less equally. The incomes of the bottom 80 percent grew faster than the incomes of the top 1 percent, and those at the bottom grew most rapidly of all. America was indeed becoming a shared project.

I don't need to tell you that a profound transformation is occurring in America. And it's man-made. Over the last thirty years a well-funded and closely coordinated coalition of corporate elites, power-hungry preachers, and hard-line ideologues has mounted an aggressive drive to dismantle the public foundations and philosophy of shared prosperity and fairness in America.

It's all right there in such essential reading as William Simon's *A Time for Truth*. He argued that "funds generated by business" would have to "rush by multimillions" into conservative causes to uproot the institutions and the "heretical" morality of the New Deal. An "alliance" between right-wing leaders and "men of action in the capitalist world" must mount a "veritable crusade" against everything brought forth by the long struggle for a progressive America. Reading right out of the new reactionary playbook, the business press somberly concluded that "some people will obviously have to do with less . . . It will be a bitter pill for many Americans to swallow the idea of doing with less so that big business can have more."

They succeeded beyond expectations. Instead of a level playing field, government now favors the powerful and privileged. Public institutions, laws and regulations, the ideas, norms, and beliefs which aimed to protect the common good and helped to create America's iconic middle class are now greatly weakened and increasingly vulnerable to attack. The Nobel laureate economist Robert Solow sums it up succinctly. What it's all about, he says, "is the redistribution of wealth in favor of the wealthy and of power in favor of the powerful."

Walking out of Union Station in Washington the other day toward the huge dome of the Capitol, I was struck by the realization that there's not a stone in that building that isn't owned by the people who make the big contributions. They own both ends of Pennsylvania Avenue lock, stock, and barrel. The simple proposition of the common good that might balance the influence of organized wealth with the interests of ordinary people—the most basic assumption of all political teaching since ancient Greece—is being written out of Washington life.

Here's an example of the difference it makes, reported by the tax journalist David Cay Johnston.

Maritza Reyes cleans houses in East Los Angeles. She scrubs toilets and mops floors for about $7,000 a year. She is also a liar and a fraud, if you believe the IRS after agents audited her tax returns. They didn't find unreported income or mysterious deductions on her returns; no, they found an address they thought made her ineligible to claim an Earned Income Tax Credit. She was ordered to return several years' credits, equal to nearly a year's worth of her wages.

The Earned Income Tax Credit is for the working poor, mainly those with children. First enacted in 1975, praised by Ronald Reagan and significantly expanded under President Clinton, it helps lift working-poor families out of poverty by reducing their income taxes below zero and thus supplying a refund. It is essentially a form of wage support. Without it we would have many millions more in poverty today.

But after Clinton expanded the credit, the self-styled revolutionaries who took over Congress in 1994 started to attack it as "backdoor welfare," or, as Oklahoma senator Don Nickles put it, as an "income redistribution program." To save it, Clinton cut a deal with the Republicans that gave them more than $100 million a year for IRS audits of people who file for the credit. It was hard for the radicals to repeal a tax policy that rewarded work when they were trying to abolish welfare for rewarding indolence. So they changed their drumbeat to fraud and deceit, making a cottage industry of attacking the credit as a haven for tax cheats.

The IRS said Reyes was cheating because she had an address that made it appear she lived with her husband. In fact, they were separated and she lived in a cottage at the back of his lot with their younger son— probably one step away from homelessness. Under the law, she is eligible for the Earned Income Tax Credit as a single "head of household" with children, but the IRS set out to prove that she was really living high off the hog under her husband's roof and her head-of-household filing was a charade designed to bilk the government.

But when the tax court judge came to Los Angeles in 2000, IRS lawyers had no evidence to disprove Reyes's claims that she was head of a separate household on her husband's lot. A student from Chapman University Law School helped her prevail before the tax judge, noting that "if just one person had taken the time to listen to her they would have seen what the judge did." To Frank Doti, head of Chapman's legal clinic for poor people, Reyes's case is typical of what he's seen in recent years: government comes down hardest on the easiest targets—those without resources and power to defend themselves.

How does this measure on the scales of justice?

In 2001, 397,000 people who applied for the Earned Income Tax Credit were audited, one out of every forty-seven returns. That's a rate eight times higher than the rate for people earning $100,000 or more. Only one out of every 366 returns of wealthy households was audited. Over the previous eleven years, in fact, audit rates for the poor increased by a third, while the wealthiest enjoyed a 90 percent decline in IRS scrutiny. Of all the 744,000 tax returns audited by the IRS in 2002, more than half, Johnston finds, were filed by the working poor. More than half of IRS audits targeted people who account for less than 20 percent of taxpayers, the poorest 20 percent.

It doesn't make sense, by the logic of justice, to spend $100 million a year of taxpayer money to audit the working poor, while actively foregoing billions in revenue from the wealthy who hide or defer their income! But of course the government piles much, much more onto the rich man's side of the scale: every year, as much as $70 billion is legally sheltered from taxation in offshore trusts and other financial devices. Big accounting firms like Ernst & Young actually sell tax shelters for a good share of their own huge profits. One of their "products" costs $5 million and, in exchange, the client gets up to $20 million in tax obligations wiped out. There's an entire new cottage industry devoted to making tax obligations disappear, helping the rich get richer at the expense of those who have no choice but to pay their fair share—and mostly feel obligated to do so anyway.

It's stunning. All told, we have a "tax gap"—the difference between taxes owed and taxes paid—of more than $345 billion a year, more than nine times our entire Department of Homeland Security budget. Make no mistake; every foregone dollar the rich owe is one you ultimately pay for in either higher taxes or fewer services down the road. When our tax code permits such public larceny, you know who writes the laws in this country. Consider: more than eighty-two companies paid no tax at all in at least one of the first three years of the present Bush administration. When I was in college in the 1950s the proportion of federal income from corporate taxes was 33 percent; by 2003 it was just 7.4 percent, as more and more companies—the tax system rigged by their highly paid Washington lobbyists—went AWOL from social responsibility.

Even those who break the law have less and less to fear. Last summer the IRS quietly moved to eliminate the jobs of nearly half of its estate tax auditors, a move that one IRS lawyer described as a "backdoor way for the Bush administration to achieve what it cannot get from Congress, which is repeal of the estate tax."

The journalist of the American Revolution, Thomas Paine, described the United States of his day as the Archimedean point of democratic liberty. He invoked the Greek proverb: "Had we a place to stand upon, we might raise the world." To Paine, that place was America. Here citizens would fight for their rights against imperial government and arbitrary power, agitate for social justice, and stand up against domination by organized wealth. Today that revolution has been blunted by the reactionaries of the last thirty years celebrating ostentatious wealth, inequality, and social Darwinism. The egalitarian creed of the American promise is mocked in all but name, and the bar of tolerance for inequality is now brought so low that genetic sorting in the human population is once again "respectfully" debated as a leading cause. The dominant elites in America today—corporate executives, wealthy contributors, and the officials they have bankrolled into office—possess a degree of influence and privilege befitting a true ruling class. They are the Mayan elites of our time who would have us accept as immutable their preferred vision of the world.

What these thirty years of redistributing wealth upward have done to America is documented in a growing literature on inequality and its social consequences. But the spiritual costs—lost faith in democracy, failing empathy, growing distrust and division—may be greater.

We know from history what can happen when people say "Enough's enough." History tells us that the Jeffersonian "second revolution" of the 1790s, the Populist revolt of the 1890s, the Progressive Era of reform, the powerful electoral ratification of the New Deal, the equally powerful re-jection of discrimination in the 1960s—all moved America closer to the egalitarian values of democracy.

So I have a practical suggestion for those of you who are principals, superintendents, school-board members, and teachers: Go home from here and revise your core curriculum. Yes, teach the three Rs and the ABCs. Make sure your kids learn algebra, biology, and calculus. But teach them about the American Revolution—that it isn't just about white men in powdered wigs carrying muskets in a time long gone. It's about slaves who rose up and women who wouldn't be denied and un-welcome immigrants and exploited workers who against great odds claimed the Revolution as their own and breathed life into it. Teach your kids they don't have to accept what they have been handed. Teach them that they are not only equal citizens under the law but equal sons and daughters—heirs, every one—of that Revolution, and that it is their right to claim it as their own. Teach them to shake the torpor that has been prescribed for them by elders and ideologues. Teach them that there is only one force strong enough to counter the power of organized money today, and that is the power of organized people. They are wait-ing for this message. The kids in your schools have been made to feel like victims—powerless, ashamed, inferior, and disenfranchised. Tell them that despite their poverty, circumstances, and the long odds they are handed, they have the power to make the world over again.

Yesterday I visited the Museum of the Presidio in San Francisco.

That former military enclave beneath the Golden Gate Bridge is now a marvelous center of vital commerce and civic purpose—saved from exploitation and despoliation by citizens who rose up on its behalf. On the wall of one of the main buildings I came upon a painting of an enormous deep blue wave with whitecaps against an equally blue sky. The artist's inscription beneath the painting reads: "This human wave expresses the concept of people at the bottom rungs of society waking up to using their united strength to claim their universal rights to economic, social, and environmental justice."

Put that in your core curriculum. America 101.

Part IV

——————|——————

THE MEDIA

19. | TIME TO TELL

International Documentary Association Awards Dinner

NOVEMBER 2, 1991

My father and I were visiting the place of his youth and my birth in Oklahoma when I told him about my new job: senior correspondent for CBS Reports, the documentary unit established by Edward R. Murrow and Fred Friendly. He put down the barbecue sandwich, wiped his lips with a napkin, and said, "Exactly what is a documentary?" I was flummoxed. It was a good question for which I had no satisfactory answer. I had watched many documentaries but couldn't come up with a neat description that encompassed all that I had seen. Even now, after years of practicing the form, I am certain there is no one answer. Go to www.filmsite.org/docfilms and you will read that documentaries are "non-fictional, 'slice of life' factual works of art—and sometimes known as cinema verite." But journalism is not art, and some of the best documentaries ever made are journalistically driven. The people who first made them thought of documentaries as "life caught unawares," but that happens rarely, as "life caught unawares" is usually mundane, if not boring, and tells us very little unless embedded in a story. In 1928 the Russian filmmaker

Dziga Vertov filmed a typical day in Moscow from dawn to dusk, but even an excerpt of it that I once saw was boring and unrevealing. Vertov said the future of the form would depend on reporting the truth, but as Stalin's film censors would insist, only the "official" truth. A school of scrutiny has grown up around Robert Flaherty's Nanook of the North, *usually mentioned as the first feature-length documentary. Flaherty re-created some of the scenes to make the life of the indigenous hero more . . . well, more interesting than Nanook himself probably thought it was. Some of the most powerful documentaries were made solely for propaganda. While creating a series about the twentieth century my colleagues and I took one sequence from Leni Riefenstahl's* Triumph of the Will—*filmed at the Nazi Party rally in 1934 as propaganda for Hitler—and just for sport used it to make the Nazis look silly as opposed to Riefenstahl's portrait of them as superior. The Nazis were neither silly nor superior; the truth lay somewhere else. About the time Riefenstahl was creating documentaries for Hitler, the Roosevelt administration was turning to film to sell the New Deal. The documentaries were technically sophisticated but still propaganda—the only peacetime production of government films for commercial release. With the outbreak of war Roosevelt recruited the Hollywood film director Frank Capra to create propaganda to help Americans understand—the series was called* Why We Fight. *When I met Capra many years later, I told him that I had seen his films—made with the help of some of Hollywood's legendary directors—and was nervous at how effectively the form could be used to nurture the response sought by government. He had worried over it, too, and said that he had only decided the series was justified when at the end of the war he had seen photographs of Auschwitz and Buchenwald and Treblinka. By the time the International Documentary Association invited me to receive its lifetime achievement award, I still didn't have a sure answer for my father's question. Documentaries, I realized, are like nitroglycerin: they can be turned into dynamite to blow things up, or into medicine for an ailing heart. It's the form I still prefer after almost forty years as a journalist. Our aim is to get as close as possible to the verifiable truth, and the truth can be mighty powerful when supported by the coupling of word and image.*

* * *

I wish I could wave a wand and turn this microphone into a megaphone that would reach beyond this room to producers, directors, cameramen and -women, sound men, engineers, editors, researchers, and others who have made it possible for me to be here. I have been their front man, and I relish this work because it is a collaborative medium.

When I wandered into documentary television twenty years ago, I was a greenhorn. I knew something about the power of documentaries to tell stories because I had been deeply moved by CBS's *Harvest of Shame* and by NBC's *The Tunnel,* which told of the escape to the West of Germans digging beneath the Berlin Wall. But I knew next to nothing about how to tell such stories myself. My new colleagues at WNET in New York, all of them veterans of the craft, assured me not to worry. It's only television, they said; it's not brain surgery. As I've learned in the last twenty years, they were wrong. It is brain surgery.

Just three days ago, in the operating room of a hospital in Beijing, I stood beside a team of surgeons as they removed a tumor from the brain of a thirty-seven-year-old schoolteacher. She and the doctors had agreed to let us film the operation for a documentary on traditional Chinese medicine.

Because the surgeons wanted the patient's cooperation during the delicate operation, they used for anesthesia a combination of Western sedatives, about half the dosage that would otherwise have been necessary, and acupuncture—needles inserted at strategic points in the young woman's head and feet. Her pain was interrupted and diminished even as she remained conscious throughout the surgery. Not only did the doctors talk to her as they performed the operation, so did I. As they removed half of the flesh of her forehead and half of her scalp, and began to probe deep into the tissues of her brain for that black intruder of a tumor, she and I carried on a halting conversation. I asked her how she was doing, and to describe what she was experiencing. She was ever so cordial, as if lying on a table with forceps inside her cranium and two cameras poised above her head was something she did every morning after rice dumplings and tea. I was the nervous one. The surgeons and patient were fine.

I have often said that journalism has been for me a continuing course in adult education. This world's capacity to amuse, please, provoke, and challenge its tenants has been abundantly revealed to me over these years, and my own surprises, the eurekas that kept exploding in my own head when joy, knowledge, humor, sorrow, or wisdom presented themselves to me, have been moments that this medium enabled me to share with millions of others.

The democracy of experience is the documentary's chief claim to legitimacy. Whether we are reliving the Civil War, revealing the secret government, getting inside an American family or Chinese surgery, or seeing how others live or cells divide or the rocket flies, the documentary brings close what was distant, making bold what was hidden, and putting into the hand of many knowledge that was once possessed by the few.

In this metaphoric sense, the documentary is a kind of brain surgery. It can remove a cancerous prejudice, a toxic stereotype, or a morbid fear. Just as those Chinese doctors took out of that teacher an ugly growth that was strangling her good cells, film can take out barriers in the mind that isolate us from one another.

In this era of shrinking attention spans, dwindling sound bites, and shriveling news budgets, the survival of this long form of journalism cannot be taken for granted. The irony is that the documentary's greatest strength is exactly the quality that most imperils its survival. Time is the hardest commodity to come by these days. And time is the best thing that the documentary has going for it. Time confers a perspective that is hard to achieve in the chaotic daily world of news, print or broadcast. Not all of us can take years for a single project, as Ken Burns did with *The Civil War* or Barbara Kopple with *American Dream*. But that the documentary provides us the luxury of plotting our deadlines on the calendar instead of on the watch, in weeks or months rather than hours, is a rare boon.

George Bernard Shaw complained that reporters are unable seemingly to discriminate between a bicycle accident and the collapse of civilization. But some of history's most epic collapses started out looking very much like a bicycle accident. A young man named Paris ran off with a beautiful woman who was married to someone else, and the civilization of Troy began to unwind. A middle-aged black seamstress, riding in a Montgomery bus, had tired feet, and an ugly social order began to collapse. A night guard at an office complex in Washington, D.C., found masking tape on a doorjamb, and a presidency began to unravel. What journalist, writing on deadline, could have imagined the walloping kick that Rosa Parks's tired feet would give to the entrenched institution of segregation? Who could have fantasized that a third-rate burglary on a dark night could do to Richard Nixon what Hubert Humphrey and George McGovern never came close to managing?

Only time can help us disentangle the Schwinn from cataclysm. Only the documentary gives the journalist the freedom of time. But time does something else. Not only does time free the journalist, it also frees the story. Time gives the story a chance to tell itself.

Probably the most famous television documentary of the 1950s was the CBS documentary on Senator Joseph McCarthy. We remember it as the instrument Edward R. Murrow used to skewer a red-baiting senator, but when you watch that broadcast again, you're struck with how little of Murrow is in it. He and Fred Friendly made the brilliant decision to let McCarthy speak for himself, not to use a script but to feature McCarthy's own bullying words, an entire broadcast's worth, not just a couple of minutes. And McCarthy obligingly hanged himself on national television far more effectively and fatally than anyone else's words could.

It's only through this unhurried honoring of reality that we can even approach the myriad and messy truths of the human heart. They cannot be hurried, scripted, forced. They must be nurtured.

It is nearly a century now since the Lumière brothers invented a camera that would capture the world's memory in motion. They started by documenting the intimate drama of daily life: trains arriving, children swimming, employees playing at a picnic. But within a year of their invention, they also discovered that their cameras could capture the world's mistakes, tragedies, and injustices in motion, too.

A Lumière photographer traveled to Russia to film the ceremonial installation of the newly crowned Czar Nicholas II. As police tried to beat back the massive crowd that surged around the czar clamoring for gifts, an improvised viewing platform gave way. Thousands of people died in the panic. Officials confiscated the cameraman's camera and destroyed his film, and no word of the tragedy was published. But for the first time, those in power came up against an even greater power: the living record of their own deeds, a competing vision of truth.

It's happened often since then, this attempt by authority to direct the people's moral sight line. That's why French government officials kept *The Sorrow and the Pity* off French television. The film challenged the myth that French people mounted a steadfast, noble, and unified campaign of resistance against the Nazi occupiers; certain myths, said officials, must not be destroyed. That's why the U.S. State Department tried to pressure PBS not to air a documentary on the execution of a Saudi princess and her lover for committing adultery. Officials said it might "offend the Saudis" and Mobil Oil, which joined in the pressure campaign. That's why it took twenty-five years, and a ruling from the Massachusetts Superior Court, to overturn a ban on the airing of *Titicut Follies*, Frederick Wiseman's harrowing film about conditions in a correctional institution for the criminally insane. It might, said the authorities, invade the privacy of the inmates it portrayed, the pitiful and brutalized inmates whose privacy was the greatest protection their brutalizers had.

Shamefully, however, sometimes pressure comes not from outside but from inside, not from authority but from ourselves, from the executives of our own industry. That's why Jon Alpert's footage of the devastation inflicted on Iraq was not shown on commercial television.

All the more reason to keep at it.

The journalist Martha Gellhorn, who covered combat from the Spanish Civil War through Vietnam, recently said that she no longer believes that simply telling the truth, simply pointing out dishonor and injustice, will compel people to demand the saving action, the punishment of wrongdoers, or care for the innocent. She concluded that "No behavior is final . . . Victory and defeat are both passing moments. There are no ends, there are only means, and journalism is a means . . . I now think that the act of keeping the record straight is valuable in and of itself."

Thanks to all of you for honoring our craft by helping to keep the record straight.

20. | REMEMBERING FRED W. FRIENDLY

Eulogy for Fred W. Friendly,
October 30, 1916–March 13, 1998

MARCH 1998

Broadcast news might have been saved if we had figured out how to clone Fred Friendly. Despite the platoons of protégés he discharged into the field over a sixty-year groundbreaking career in broadcasting, it was virtually inevitable that the commercial forces against which he had waged a long-running battle would eventually triumph. Even as Fred and Edward R. Murrow were molding CBS News in their image in the 1950s, the network, fearing the loss of advertising revenues, refused to carry the landmark Army-McCarthy hearings into the disreputable tactics of the junior senator from Wisconsin, Joseph McCarthy. Fred ground his teeth over that one but he kept fighting for CBS News to signify. Without him I doubt Edward R. Murrow would have made the transition from radio icon to television's most formidable on-air journalist. The two of them created See It Now and CBS Reports, setting the standard for investigative reporting and documentaries of

unprecedented power and impact. They pooled their personal funds to pro-
mote the broadcast that used McCarthy's own words and deeds to turn mil-
lions of Americans against his demagoguery—something for which the Right
has never forgiven the "Communist Broadcasting System." In 1966 Fred re-
signed the job he had relished—CBS News president—when the network re-
fused to carry live Senate hearings on the Vietnam War, choosing instead to
run a repeat of I Love Lucy. *As an adviser to the Ford Foundation he be-*
came the prime mover in the creation of the Corporation for Public Broad-
casting, which he envisioned as being "free of commercials and commercial
values." His own Fred Friendly Seminars on public television demonstrated
how "to make the agony of decision-making so intense that you can escape
only by thinking." His death in 1998 was more than the felling of a great oak;
we lost the forest. At his memorial service I saw tears in the eyes of some
crusty old journalists.

* * *

When Fred Friendly was president of CBS News and I was the White
House press secretary, he would come down from New York on the shut-
tle and slip in the back door of the White House and along the hall past
the Cabinet Room to the private entrance to my office for an hour-or-so
chat. Occasionally the president would stop by. Watching each of them
take the other's measure was like watching King Kong and Godzilla simultaneously squeeze through the same airport metal detector.

The president sized Friendly up as a straight shooter and took a lik-
ing to him, all the more so when he discovered Fred wasn't just "another
Harvard graduate." I realized this because of something that happened in
late 1965. I had not sought or welcomed the press job and was always
lobbying LBJ for my release. The president would have none of it, until
one day, after I had written yet another petition requesting a parole, he
burst into my office waving the note, slapped it down on my desk, and
announced: "All right, you can leave—on one condition. I'll let you go
if you persuade Fred Friendly to succeed you."

I took him at his word and began to plot my escape. I called Fred in
New York and told him I needed to see him. He came down the next af-

ternoon. When I explained the scheme to him he didn't blink. He just looked me straight in the eye and said, "I'm flattered, Bill, but leaving CBS News to come to the White House would be a step down. Unless, of course, the president offered me *his* job." I dutifully reported this to the president that evening as he shoveled down his tapioca. He glowered and grumbled something to the effect that I should remind the arrogant SOB that every CBS station license would be coming up for renewal on our watch and a little humility on Fred's part might spare Bill Paley (the founder of CBS) a stroke. Obviously I deep-sixed that suggestion. Several months later when Fred resigned from CBS News over a dispute about airing the Senate hearings on Vietnam, the president called me and said, "You tell him he should be glad I didn't take him up on his offer. He can quit his job and I can't."

Over the next several months, Fred came down to Washington several times to meet with McGeorge Bundy, who was leaving his job as national security adviser to run the Ford Foundation and had engaged Friendly as adviser. The two of them were hatching plans to transform educational television. I had done some preliminary work at the Office of Education in 1964 on the future of public television, and I soon recognized Fred as a true believer. He and Bundy were by the office one day and Fred was soaring. He went on and on about television "that dignifies instead of debases" and about the potential importance of "at least one channel free of commercials and commercial values." He was public television's Johnny Appleseed in those formative days, and he persuaded the Ford Foundation to put its money where his mind was.

I eventually wound up on public television myself, anchoring a weekly broadcast with Fred's first teaching assistant, Martin Clancy, as my star producer; it was usually one of Fred's people who taught me the most about our craft. When I left for CBS the first time, he cheered me on. He welcomed me back to public television two years later. Then, when CBS beckoned again, he urged me to try again. No one understood better than Fred the grounds for my vagrancy. Five years later, when it was no longer possible to do at CBS what I wanted to do, Fred told me: "You're never going to do the work you most want to do until you do it for yourself." So I quit and headed for the life of an independent producer.

It's remarkable how often he was right. Remarkable how often he was there for us. When I later realized how many protégés he had, how many aspirants, acolytes, and apprentices were being nurtured by him, I wondered how he found time for all of us. But time to Fred was life, and life was to be shared.

I miss his calls. Sometimes they were subtle persuasions. Sometimes they were assault and battery. When I missed the mark with a broadcast, he said so. When I came close, he gave me the high sign. One night as one of my specials was ending—it was almost eleven—I got up from the chair and started for the hall. "Where are you going?" Judith asked. "To answer the phone," I said. "It's not ringing," she said. "It will," I said. And it did. Fred was calling. Sometimes he called just to commiserate, lament, or protest. "We're inventing the wheel on the way to the guillotine," he would say. I could mouth the words with him: "Because television can make so much money doing its worst, it often cannot afford to do its best." And he would say, "To turn a movie theater into a burlesque house may be an owner's prerogative, but a civilized society doesn't do that to its civic center!"

There's hardly one of us here today singing his praises who didn't once break his heart. But he never gave up on us. Journalism was a mission to him, not a business, so he grew more forlorn and frustrated as he watched news and public affairs morph into entertainment. Even his own offspring, public television—his last best hope for a civic center in this multichannel nation—could let him down, as he and Ruth found it harder and harder to secure prime time for their beloved Socratic seminars featuring many of the country's finest thinkers as participants.

Once he called—early on a Saturday morning—to protest something he had seen the night before on the air, something that he had found trivializing and a waste of precious airtime. Awakened from a deep sleep, I said in exasperation: "Fred, didn't anyone ever tell you all things

human given time, go badly? Why should television be any different?"
There was a long silence. And then he said softly: "What kind of world
would it be if we settled on just being human?"

So this overbearing, gruff, flawed, restless, brilliant, temperamental,
driven man, whose convictions were as stout as his heart—this cross between Jeremiah, Mark Hopkins, and Thomas Paine—turns out to be our
better angel, perhaps our last better angel, who until the very end was
trying to wake us from our slumber.

Excuse me, I hear the phone ringing.

21. | THE FIGHT FOR PUBLIC BROADCASTING

National Conference for Media Reform

MAY 15, 2005

You might have thought the Bush administration would have been more than satisfied. Here was Fox News functioning as the Republican Ministry of Truth, and Rush Limbaugh and a host of wannabes constituting an OPEC of right-wing agitprop, and the Beltway press according the White House a measure of deference surpassed only by that paid the Kremlin by Izvestia: Karl Rove could look at a media map of America and boast of it as occupied territory. Why bother about the sliver of the spectrum held by PBS, and especially about a single hour allocated once a week, on Friday nights, to a lone public affairs broadcast that would surely show up as a mere pinprick—no larger than, say, Guam—on Rove's wall map? Yet not a sparrow took wing in the media aerie that the Bush White House didn't want to politicize. My broadcast became the target of a campaign to intimidate PBS, waged secretly, at first, by a right-wing ideologue who occupied the very office that had been charged with protecting public broadcasting from political interference. In the great scheme of this administration's imperial designs on the Bill of Rights, this was a mere skirmish. But the story would prove to be revealing of the insatiable and unrestrained appetite of a regime that was not content just to control all three branches of government and bring the press to its knees. Their attempted coup of public broadcasting failed thanks to some vigilant members of Congress, an unimpeachable inspector general, and the chief plotter's own excesses. But even after I retired—voluntarily—from my broadcast at the end of 2004, the bizarre details continued to emerge. Here they are as I recounted the story in two speeches the following year, the first to the National Conference for Media Reform.

* * *

I can't imagine better company on this beautiful Sunday morning in St. Louis. There's no congregation in the country where I would be more likely to find more kindred souls than are gathered here.

What joins us all is our commitment to public media. Patricia Aufderheide wrote in the recent issue of *In These Times*:

> This is a moment when public media outlets can make a powerful case for themselves. Public radio, public TV, cable access, public DBS channels, media arts centers, youth media projects, nonprofit Internet news services . . . low-power radio and webcasting are all part of a nearly-invisible feature of today's media map: the public media sector. They exist not to make a profit, not to push an ideology, not to serve customers, but to create a public—a group of people who can talk productively with people who don't share their views, and defend the interests of the people who have to live with the consequences of corporate and governmental power.

In that spirit I've come to share with you a story that goes to the core of our belief that the quality of democracy and the quality of journalism are deeply entwined. I can tell this story because I've been living it. It's been in the news this week, including reports of more attacks on a single journalist—yours truly—by the right-wing media and their allies at the Corporation for Public Broadcasting. They've been demonizing me for years now, and I haven't given up although I retired more than six months ago. I have learned to take their partisan assaults in stride, but I should put my detractors on notice: they might just compel me out of the rocking chair and back into the anchor chair.

As some of you know, CPB was established almost forty years ago to set broad policy for public broadcasting and to be a firewall between political influence and program content. What some on this board are now doing today—led by its chairman, Kenneth Tomlinson—is wholly at odds with that mission.

We're seeing unfold a contemporary example of the age-old ambition of power and ideology to squelch and punish journalists who tell the stories that make princes and priests uncomfortable.

Who are they? They are the apologists for the people in power. I mean the people who are hollowing out middle-class security even as they enlist the sons and daughters of the working class in a war started under false pretenses. I mean the people who turn faith-based initiatives into a slush fund and encourage the pious to look heavenward and pray so as not to see the long arm of privilege and power picking their pockets. I mean the people who would discredit dissent and present their ideology as the official view of reality from which any deviation becomes unpatriotic heresy.

That's who I mean. And if that's editorializing, so be it. A free press is one where it's okay to state the conclusion you're led to by the evidence.

These apologists for power have come after my colleagues and me because we didn't play by the conventional rules of Beltway journalism. Those rules divide the world into Democrats and Republicans, liberals and conservatives, and allow journalists to pretend they have done their job if, instead of reporting the truth behind the news, they merely give each side an opportunity to spin the news.

Jonathan Mermin writes about this in a recent essay in *World Policy Journal* and in his book *Debating War and Peace: Media Coverage of U.S. Intervention in the Post-Vietnam Era*.

Mermin quotes David Ignatius of *The Washington Post* on why the deep interests of the American public are so poorly served by establishment journalism. The "rules of our game," says Ignatius, "make it hard for us to tee up an issue . . . without a news peg." He offers a case in point: the debacle of America's occupation of Iraq. "If Senator so and so hasn't criticized post-war planning for Iraq," says Ignatius, "then it's hard for a reporter to write a story about that."

Mermin also quotes public television's Jim Lehrer. Why were journalists not discussing the occupation of Iraq? Because, Lehrer said, "the word occupation . . . was never mentioned in the run-up to the war." Washington talked about the invasion as a war of liberation, not a war of occupation, and as a consequence "those of us in journalism never even looked at the issue of occupation."

Mermin takes this to mean that "if the government isn't talking about it, we don't report it." And he concludes:

> [Lehrer's] somewhat jarring declaration, one of many recent admissions by journalists that their reporting failed to prepare the public for the calamitous occupation that has followed the "liberation" of Iraq, reveals just how far the actual practice of American journalism has deviated from the First Amendment ideal of a press that is independent of the government.

Consider the witness of Charles J. Hanley, the Pulitzer Prize–winning reporter for the Associated Press, whose 2003 story on the torture of Iraqis in American prisons, which appeared before a U.S. Army report and photographs documenting the abuse surfaced, was ignored by major American newspapers. Hanley attributes this indifference to the fact that "it was not an officially sanctioned story that begins with a handout from an official source." Furthermore, Iraqis recounting their own personal experience of Abu Ghraib simply did not have the credibility with

Beltway journalists of American officials denying that such things happened. Judith Miller of *The New York Times*, among others, relied on the credibility of official but unnamed sources when she served essentially as a stenographer for neo-conservative and government claims that Iraq possessed weapons of mass destruction.

These "rules of the game" allow Washington officials to set the agenda for journalism, with journalists essentially left to recount what they are told instead of subjecting official words and deeds to critical scrutiny. Instead of acting as filters for readers and viewers, sifting the truth from the propaganda, the press transcribes both sides of the spin, invariably failing to provide context, background, or any sense of which claims hold up and which are misleading.

I realized long ago that this wasn't healthy for democracy. Objectivity is not satisfied by two opposing people offering competing opinions, leaving the viewer to split the difference. Over the years—in documentaries on the Watergate scandals, the Clinton administration's illegal fund-raising scandals, the Iran-Contra scandal, and the chemical industry's long and despicable withholding from workers and consumers critical data about its toxic products—I realized that investigative journalism is not a collaboration between the journalist and the subject.

Without a trace of irony, the powers that be have appropriated the Newspeak vernacular of George Orwell's *1984*.

One of Orwell's characters in *1984* is Syme, whose job is to help produce the totalitarian society's dictionary. He explains to the protagonist Winston,

> "Don't you see that the whole aim of Newspeak is to narrow the range of thought? . . . Has it ever occurred to you, Winston, that by the year 2050, at the very latest, not a single human being will be alive who could understand such a conversation as we are having now? The whole climate of thought will be different. In fact there will be no thought, as we understand it now. Orthodoxy means not thinking—not needing to think. Orthodoxy is unconsciousness."

An unconscious people, an indoctrinated people, a people fed only on partisan information and opinion that confirm their own bias, a people made morbidly obese in mind and spirit by the junk food of propaganda is less inclined to put up a fight, to ask questions and be skeptical.

I learned about this the hard way. I grew up in the South where the truth about slavery, race, and segregation had been driven from the pulpits, the classrooms, and the newsrooms. It took a bloody Civil War to bring the truth home and then it took another hundred years for the truth to make us free.

In the Johnson administration where I served, we circled the wagons to keep out evidence at odds with our arguments for war. The results were devastating.

These experiences shaped my resolve after 9/11 when PBS asked me to start a new weekly broadcast. We were urged to make it different from anything else on the air—commercial or public broadcasting—to tell stories no one else was reporting and to offer a venue to people who might not otherwise be heard. That wasn't a hard sell. Scholarly studies of the content of public television over the previous decade found that political discussions on our public affairs programs were generally restricted to a limited set of voices and a narrow range of perspectives. According to this research, public affairs programs on PBS stations were populated by the standard set of elite news sources. Whether the talk was about politics or the economy, public television was offering the same kind of discussions and a similar brand of insider discourse that was featured regularly on commercial television. Alternative perspectives were rare and were effectively drowned out by government, expert, and corporate views. The experts who got most of the airtime came primarily from mainstream news organizations and Washington think tanks. Economic news, for example, was almost entirely refracted through the views of business people, investors, and business journalists. Voices outside the corporate–Wall Street universe—blue-collar workers, labor representatives, consumer advocates, and the general public—were infrequently heard.

All this was contrary to the Public Broadcasting Act of 1967 that created the Corporation for Public Broadcasting. I know. I was there. As a policy assistant to President Johnson, I had attended meetings in the office of the commissioner of education in 1964 to explore the future of public television. I know firsthand that the Public Broadcasting Act was meant to provide an alternative to commercial television and to reflect a much greater diversity of people, ideas, and opinions.

This, too, was on my mind when we assembled the team for *NOW with Bill Moyers* soon after the terrorist attacks of 9/11. We decided on two priorities. First, we would talk to people from across the spectrum—left, right, and center. This meant poets, philosophers, politicians, scientists, sages, and scribblers. It meant the novelist Isabel Allende and columnist for the *Financial Times* Amity Shlaes. It meant the former nun and best-selling author Karen Armstrong, and it meant the right-wing evangelical columnist Cal Thomas. It meant Arundhati Roy from India, Doris Lessing and Will Hutton from London, and David Suzuki from Canada. It also meant two successive editors of *The Wall Street Journal*, Robert Bartley and Paul Gigot; the editor of *The Economist*, Bill Emmett; *The Nation*'s Katrina vanden Heuvel; and the *LA Weekly*'s John Powers. It meant liberals like Ossie Davis and Gregory Nava and conservatives like Frank Gaffney, Grover Norquist, and Richard Viguerie. It meant Archbishop Desmond Tutu and Bishop Wilton Gregory of the Catholic Bishops Conference in this country. It meant the conservative Christian activist and lobbyist Ralph Reed, and the liberal Catholic Sister Joan Chittister.

In other words, we threw the conversation of democracy open to all comers. Typical of the response was a letter I received from the Republican congressman from Texas, Ron Paul, after he had been on the broadcast: "I have received hundreds of positive e-mails from your viewers. I appreciate the format of your program which allows time for a full discussion of ideas . . . I'm tired of political shows featuring two guests shouting over each other and offering the same arguments . . . *NOW* was truly refreshing."

Hold your applause because that's not the point of the story.

We had a second priority: strong, honest, and accurate reporting of stories we knew people in high places wouldn't like.

I told our producers and correspondents that our job in covering Washington was to get as close as possible to the verifiable truth. This was all the more imperative in the aftermath of the terrorist attacks. America could be entering a long war against an elusive and stateless enemy with no definable measure of victory and no limit to its duration, cost, or foreboding fear. The rise of a homeland security state meant government could justify extraordinary measures in exchange for protecting citizens against unnamed, even unproven, threats.

Furthermore, increased spending during a national emergency can produce a spectacle of corruption behind a smokescreen of secrecy. I reminded our team of the news photographer in Tom Stoppard's play who said, "People do terrible things to each other, but it's worse when everyone is kept in the dark."

So we went about reporting on government as no one else in broadcasting was doing. We reported on the expansion of the Justice Department's power of surveillance; on the escalating Pentagon budget and expensive weapons that didn't work; on how campaign contributions influenced legislation and policy to skew resources to the comfortable and well connected while our troops were fighting in Afghanistan and Iraq with inadequate training and armor. We reported on how the Bush administration was shredding the Freedom of Information Act; how closed-door decisions in Washington were costing ordinary workers and taxpayers their livelihood and security; and on offshore tax havens that enable wealthy Americans to avoid paying their fair share of the cost of national security and the social contract.

Because what Americans know depends on who owns the press, we kept coming back in our reporting to the media business itself, to how mega-media corporations were pushing journalism further and further down the hierarchy of values, how giant radio cartels were silencing critics while shutting communities off from essential information, and how the media giants were lobbying the FCC for approval of even greater concentration of ownership.

The broadcast caught on. Our ratings grew every year. For a spell we were the only public affairs broadcast on PBS whose audience was going up instead of down.

Our journalistic peers took notice. The *Los Angeles Times* said, "*NOW*'s team of reporters has regularly put the rest of the media to shame, pursuing stories few others bother to touch."

The Philadelphia Inquirer said our segments on the sciences, the arts, politics, and the economy were "provocative public television at its best."

The *Austin American-Statesman* called *NOW* "the perfect antidote to today's high-pitched decibel level—a smart, calm, timely news program."

Frazier Moore of the Associated Press said we were "hard-edged when appropriate but never *Hardball*. Don't expect combat. Civility reigns."

And the *Baton Rouge Advocate* said, "*NOW* invites viewers to consider the deeper implication of the daily headlines," drawing on "a wide range of viewpoints which transcend the typical labels of the political left or right."

Let me repeat that: *NOW* draws on "a wide range of viewpoints which transcend the typical labels of the political left or right." The reviewer had not failed to note the appearance on our broadcast of such right-wing stalwarts as Paul Gigot, Richard Viguerie, Grover Norquist, Ralph Reed, and David Keene, among others, as well as guests who defied the traditional television labels of Democrat or Republican, liberal or conservative.

The Public Broadcasting Act of 1967 had been prophetic. Offer diverse interests, ideas, and voices, be fearless in your belief in democracy, and the public will respond.

Hold your applause—that's not the point of the story.

The point of the story is that a backlash was building in Washington against our reporting. The more we investigated noncompetitive Halliburton contracts, corruption at the Department of the Interior, the government's failure to provide U.S. troops with adequate matériel and wounded veterans with adequate care, lobbyists writing legislation, and political favors to insiders, the more offended officials complained to PBS executives. We were reporting the very stories that partisans in high places did not want told, and we were getting the stories right; in only three stories in three years did we err factually, and in each case we corrected the errors as soon as we confirmed their inaccuracy.

The problem was that we were getting it right, not right-wing.

My analysis of events was a case in power. The powerful Republican senator Trent Lott roared in protest when the week after the midterm elections in 2002 I described the probable agenda of the party that now controlled all three branches of government. Rather than celebrating their victory as Fox News, Rush Limbaugh, and other right-wing partisans were doing, I provided a different analysis of what the victory meant. And I did it the old-fashioned way: I looked at the record, took the winners at their word, and drew the logical conclusion as to the agenda the new conservative regime was likely to pursue.

Here is what I said:

> Way back in the 1950s when I first tasted politics and journalism, Republicans briefly controlled the White House and Congress. With the exception of Joseph McCarthy and his vicious ilk, they were a reasonable lot, presided over by that giant war hero Dwight Eisenhower, who was conservative by temperament and moderate in the use of power.
>
> That brand of Republican is gone. And for the first time in the memory of anyone alive, the entire federal government—the Congress, the executive, the judiciary—is united behind a right-wing agenda for which George W. Bush believes he now has a mandate.
>
> That mandate includes the power of the state to force pregnant women to give control over their own lives.
>
> It includes using the taxing power to transfer wealth from working people to the rich.

It includes giving corporations a free hand to eviscerate the environment and control the regulatory agencies meant to hold them accountable.

And it includes secrecy on a scale you cannot imagine. Above all, it means judges with a political agenda appointed for life. If you liked the Supreme Court that put George W. Bush in the White House, you will swoon over what's coming.

And if you like God in government, get ready for the Rapture. These folks don't even mind you referring to the GOP as the party of God. Why else would the new House majority leader say that the Almighty is using him to promote "a biblical worldview" in American politics?

So it is a heady time in Washington—a heady time for piety, profits, and military power, all joined at the hip to ideology and money.

Don't forget the money. It came pouring into this election, to both parties, from corporate America and others who expect the payback. Republicans out-raised Democrats by $184 million. And came up with the big prize—monopoly control of the American government, and the power of the state to turn their ideology into the law of the land. Quite a bargain at any price.

Events of course confirmed the accuracy of that analysis, but, being right, as I said, is exactly what the Right doesn't want journalists to be.

Strange things began to happen. Friends in Washington called to say there were muttered threats being heard about Congress holding up on renewed funding of PBS "unless Moyers is dealt with." The chairman of the Corporation for Public Broadcasting, Kenneth Tomlinson, a die-hard right-wing Republican, was reportedly quite agitated. One source at CPB called to tell me that she had heard Tomlinson say that his mission was to "get Moyers." Then came the last straw. There was apoplexy in the right-wing aerie when on the air I put an American flag in my lapel and said—well, here's exactly what I said:

I wore my flag tonight. First time. Until now I haven't thought it necessary to display a little metallic icon of patriotism for everyone to see. It was enough to vote, pay my taxes, perform my civic duties, speak my mind, and do my best to raise our kids to be good Americans.

Sometimes I would offer a small prayer of gratitude that I had been born in a country whose institutions sustained me, whose armed forces protected me, and whose ideals inspired me; I offered my heart's affections in return. It no more occurred to me to flaunt the flag on my chest than it did to pin my mother's picture on my lapel to prove her son's love. Mother knew where I stood; so does my country. I even tuck a valentine in my tax returns on April 15.

So what's this doing here? Well, I put it on to take it back. The flag's been hijacked and turned into a logo—the trademark of a monopoly on patriotism. On those Sunday morning talk shows, official chests appear adorned with the flag as if it is the Good Housekeeping Seal of Approval. During the State of the Union, did you notice Bush and Cheney wearing the flag? How come? No administration's patriotism is ever in doubt, only its policies. And the flag bestows no immunity from error. When I see flags sprouting on official lapels, I think of the time in China when I saw Mao's little red book on every official's desk, omnipresent and unread.

But more galling than anything are all those moralistic ideologues in Washington sporting the flag on their lapels while writing books and running Web sites and publishing magazines attacking dissenters as un-American. They are people whose ardor for war grows disproportionately to their distance from the fighting. They're in the same league as those swarms of corporate lobbyists wearing flags and prowling Capitol Hill for tax breaks even as they call for more spending on war.

So I put this on as a modest riposte to men with flags on their lapels who shoot missiles from the safety of Washington think tanks, or argue that sacrifice is good as long as they don't have to make it, or approve of bribing governments to join the coalition of the willing (after they first stash the cash). I put it on to remind myself that not every patriot thinks we should do to the people of Baghdad what Osama bin Laden did to us. The flag belongs to the country, not to the government. And it reminds me that it's not un-American to think that war—except in self-defense—is a failure of moral imagination, political nerve, and diplomacy. Come to think of it, standing up to your government can mean standing up for your country.

That did it.

At hearings in Congress Senator Lott protested that the Corporation for Public Broadcasting—controlled by his own party—"has not seemed willing to deal with Bill Moyers." President Bush's new appointee to the board, the Republican fund-raiser Cheryl Halperin, told Lott that CPB needed more power to do just that sort of thing, leaving no doubt that she thought journalistic malefactors should be brought to heel.

I asked to meet with the board. Having been present at the creation and part of the system for almost forty years, I wanted to remind them that CPB had been established as a heat shield to protect public broadcasters from exactly this kind of political intimidation. I had seen what had happened when that shield was removed. Early on public television had been feisty and irreverent, and often targeted for attacks. A Woody Allen special that poked fun at Henry Kissinger had been canceled. The Nixon White House had been so outraged over the documentary *The Banks and the Poor* that PBS was driven to adopt new guidelines. That didn't satisfy Nixon, and when public television hired NBC reporters Robert MacNeil and Sander Vanocur to co-anchor some news broadcasts, Nixon exploded. According to White House memos at the time, he was determined to "get the left-wing commentators who are cutting us up off public television at once—indeed, yesterday if possible."

Sound familiar?

Nixon vetoed the authorization for CPB with a message written in part by his sidekick Pat Buchanan, who had privately castigated Vanocur, MacNeil, *Washington Week in Review, Black Journal,* and Bill Moyers as "unbalanced against the administration."

Familiar, indeed.

Buchanan and Nixon managed to cut CPB funding for almost all public affairs programming. They knocked out multiyear funding for the National Public Affairs Center for Television, otherwise known as NPACT. And they managed to take away from the PBS staff the ultimate responsibility for the production of programming.

But in those days—and this is what I wanted to share with Kenneth Tomlinson and his partisan loyalists on the CPB board—there were still Republicans in America who stood on principle against politicizing public television. The chairman of the public station in Dallas was an industrialist, a Republican but no party hack, who saw the White House intimidation as an assault on freedom of the press and led a nationwide effort to stop it. The chairman of CPB was the former Republican congressman Thomas Curtis, also a principled man, who resigned rather than do Nixon's bidding. And the public rallied behind public television.

Within a few months, the crisis was over. CPB maintained its independence, PBS grew in strength, and President Nixon would soon face impeachment and resign for violating the public trust, not just public broadcasting. Paradoxically, the very National Public Affairs Center for Television that Nixon had tried to kill put PBS on the map by broadcasting the daily Watergate hearings, drawing huge ratings night after night and affirming public television's ability to serve the public interest.

That was thirty-three years ago. I figured the current CPB board, led by Kenneth Tomlinson, would like to hear and talk about the importance of standing up to political interference. I was wrong. They wouldn't meet with me. Three times I tried, but to no avail. I invited Tomlinson to come on the air to discuss the issues publicly. He declined, but he did go on Fox News to deny that he was following a White House mandate or that he had ever had any conversations with any Bush administration official about PBS. But *The New York Times* reported that he had enlisted the help of Karl Rove to help kill one proposal affecting the CPB board and that "on the recommendation of administration officials" had hired a White House flack named Mary Catherine Andrews as a senior CPB staff member. While she was still reporting to Karl Rove at the White House, Ms. Andrews set up CPB's new ombudsman's office and had a hand in hiring the two people who will fill it, one of whom once worked for . . . Kenneth Tomlinson.

I would like to give Mr. Tomlinson the benefit of the doubt, but I can't. According to a book written about *Reader's Digest* when he was its editor in chief, he surrounded himself with other right-wingers—a pattern he's now following at the Corporation for Public Broadcasting.

As everyone now knows, he also put up a considerable sum of public funds, reportedly more than $5 million, for a new weekly broadcast featuring the editorial board of *The Wall Street Journal* and its editor, Paul Gigot. I had Gigot on *NOW* as a guest several times and even proposed that he become a regular contributor to the broadcast. But I confess to some puzzlement that *The Wall Street Journal*, which over the years had editorialized to cut PBS off from the public tap, would now be subsidized by American taxpayers although its parent company, Dow Jones, had revenues in just the first quarter of this year of $400 million. I had always thought public television was an alternative to commercial media, not a funder of it.

But in this weird deal, you get a glimpse of the kind of programming preferred by the very partisan and ideological Kenneth Tomlinson. Alone of the big major newspapers, *The Wall Street Journal* has no op-ed page where different opinions can compete with its right-wing editorials. (Gigot would bring this practice to *The Wall Street Journal*'s new PBS broadcast, where right-wingers talked only to each other.)

There's more. Two weeks ago we learned that Tomlinson had spent $10,000 last year to hire one of his pals who would watch my show and report on political bias. That's right. The chairman of CPB spent $10,000 of your money to find out who my guests were and what my stories were.

Ten thousand dollars.

Gee, Ken, for $2.50 a week, you could pick up a copy of *TV Guide* on the newsstand. A subscription is even cheaper, and I would have sent you a coupon that can save you up to 62 percent.

For that matter, all you had to do was watch the show yourself. Or you could have gone online where the listings are posted. Hell, you could have called me—collect—and I would have told you.

But having paid someone else to find out for him, what did he learn? Only Mr. Tomlinson knows. He decided not to share the results with his staff or his board. The public paid for the monitoring, but Ken Tomlinson acts as if he owns it. In a recent op-ed piece in the conservative *Washington Times*, he maintained that he had not released the findings because he did not want to "damage public broadcasting's image with controversy." Where I come from in Texas, we shovel that kind of stuff every day.

As we learned just this week, that's not the only news Mr. Tomlinson tried to keep to himself. It turns out that CPB commissioned two surveys designed to probe what people think about public broadcasting. When the surveys were completed, however, they were not released to the media—not even to PBS and NPR! According to a source who talked to Salon.com, "the first results were too good and [Tomlinson] didn't believe them. After the Iraq War, the board commissioned another round of polling and they thought they'd get worse results."

But they didn't.

The data revealed that public broadcasting has an 80 percent favorable rating and that "the majority of the U.S. adult population does not believe that the news and information programming on public broadcasting is biased." More than half believed PBS provided more in-depth and trustworthy news and information than the networks and 55 percent said PBS was "fair and balanced."

Now consider this: Ken Tomlinson was the man running the Voice of America back in 1984 when a Republican partisan named Charlie Wick was politicizing the United States Information Agency (of which Voice of America was a part). Someone high up developed a blacklist of names that had been removed from the list of prominent Americans sent abroad to lecture on behalf of America and the USIA. Among those on the lists of journalists, writers, scholars, and politicians were dangerous subversives like Walter Cronkite, James Baldwin, Gary Hart, Ralph Nader, Ben Bradlee, Coretta Scott King, and David Brinkley. What's more, more than seven hundred documents had been shredded that contained evidence as to how those people were chosen to be blacklisted.

The right-winger who took the fall for the blacklist resigned. Shortly thereafter, so did Kenneth Tomlinson, who had been one of the people in the agency with the authority to see the lists of potential speakers and allowed to strike people's names.

Let me be clear about this: there is no record, apparently, of what Ken Tomlinson did. We don't know whether he supported or protested the blacklisting of so many American liberals. Or what he thinks of it now.

But I had hoped Bill O'Reilly would have asked him about this when Tomlinson appeared on *The O'Reilly Factor* this week. He didn't. Instead, with O'Reilly egging him on, Tomlinson kept up his attacks on me, denying all the time that he was carrying out a partisan mandate despite published reports to the contrary. The only time you could be sure Tomlinson was telling the truth was at the end of the broadcast when he said to O'Reilly, "We love your show."

"We love your show." No kidding!

There is one other thing in particular I wanted to ask Tomlinson. In an op-ed essay this week in *The Washington Times*, he tells of a phone call from an old friend complaining about bias on public television—about Moyers in particular. Tomlinson wrote: "The friend explained that the foundation he heads made a six-figure contribution to his local public television station for digital conversion. But he declared there would be no more contributions until something was done about the network's bias."

Apparently that's Kenneth Tomlinson's desired method of governance. Money talks, stations grovel.

I would ask him to listen to a different voice.

This letter came to me last year from a woman in New York—five handwritten pages. She said, among other things, that "After the worst sneak attack in our history, there's not been a moment to reflect, a moment to let the horror resonate, a moment to feel the pain and regroup as humans. No, since I lost my husband on 9/11, not only our family's world, but the whole world seems to have gotten even worse than that tragic day."

She told me her husband had not been on duty that day. "He was home with me having coffee. My daughter and grandson, living only five blocks from the Towers, had to be evacuated with masks—terror all around . . . my other daughter, near the Brooklyn Bridge . . . my son in high school. But my Charlie took off like a lightning bolt to be with his men from the Special Operations Command. 'Bring my gear to the plaza,' he told his aide immediately after the first plane struck the North Tower . . . He took action based on the responsibility he felt for his job and his men and for those Towers that he loved."

In the Fire Department of New York, she continued, chain-of-command rules extend to every captain of every firehouse in the city. "If anything happens in the firehouse—at any time—even if the captain isn't on duty or on vacation—that captain is responsible for everything that goes on there 24/7." Then she asked: "Why is this administration responsible for nothing? All that they do is pass the blame. This is not leadership . . . Watch everyone pass the blame again in this recent torture case [Abu Ghraib] of Iraqi prisons . . ."

And then she wrote: "We need more programs to wake America up . . . Such programs must continue amidst the sea of false images and name calling that divide America now . . . Such programs give us hope that the search will continue to get this imperfect human condition on to a higher plane. So thank you and all of those who work with you. Without public broadcasting, all we would call news would be merely carefully controlled propaganda."

Enclosed with the letter was a check made out to "Channel 13—NOW" for $500.

I keep a copy of that check above my desk to remind me who I am working for.

John Steinbeck once wrote: "There used to be a thing or a commodity we put great store by. It was called the people."

Kenneth Tomlinson has his demanding donors.

I'll take the widow's mite any day.

Kenneth Tomlinson resigned from the CPB Board of Directors on November 3, 2005, one day after CPB's inspector general released a scathing report critical of his leadership and alleging that he violated agency procedures, federal laws, and the Director's Code of Ethics. Among other things, the inspector general found that Tomlinson had been strongly motivated by political ideology and used "political tests" as a major criteria to recruit a president and chief executive officer for CPB in violation of statutory prohibitions against such tests.

22. | PENGUINS AND THE POLITICS OF DENIAL

Annual Conference of the
Society of Environmental Journalists

OCTOBER 1, 2005

The fiercest critics on the Right have labeled people like me "Bush haters." As apologists for a disastrous war and a failed administration, it's the best they can do. Truth is, I don't know George W. Bush well enough to hate him. I have never even met him. And hatred is a poison whose first victim is the hater; it's no way to spend your energy or day. No, the emotion I feel observing this administration is sadness. The president has turned the Oval Office into a cocoon where a war is hatched from fiction, people struggling to make a living are invisible, and the future doesn't count. A government is never more dangerous than when it is separated from reality. Six years into the Bush presidency, the writer Bill McKibben remarked that it is possible to forget just how radical the group of men and women running our country really is. Their perceptions of the world are without roots in lived experience, and, as McKibben puts it, "they've changed the setting for our political life so comprehensively that indignation slowly gives way to a kind of numbed head-shaking." Exhibit number one for McKibben, who is noted for his writing on the environment, is the administration's hostility toward the facts of climate change. Despite the steady outpouring of scientific data pointing to one of the greatest threats in human history, the administration has tried to thwart every international effort to take it seriously. At the Montreal conference of representatives from the developed world, which aimed to take larger steps toward controlling carbon emissions, the U.S. delegation opposed any new agreements—even more conferences to address the crisis. The Americans walked out of the meeting when former president Bill Clinton—not exactly a radical on the subject of the environment—was allowed to speak. Our government's delegation was led by Harlan Watson, who got his job, according to uncovered faxes, quoted by McKibben, at the "forceful urging of ExxonMobil." Think about it: the U.S. representative on global warming in fact was representing the petrochemical giant that has long cast global warming as a myth and has spent large sums of money to discredit the science that confirms the threat. God only knows the consequences of this refusal to face the facts because they will come due after George W. Bush has gone home, leaving his successors to wrestle with the consequences of his denial of reality. Fortunately, many in his own base of evangelical Christians have broken with the president over this issue. In the last two years, despite opposition from the White House and its network of right-wing religious operatives, scores of evangelical leaders have signed on to a major initiative to fight global warming as an act of stewardship for the earth. As I said in this speech to the Society of Environmental Journalists, faithful believers are desperately needed if we are to close the gap between policy and reality.

* * *

Thank you for counting me as a colleague. I don't fit neatly into the job description of an environmental journalist although I have returned to the beat ever since my first documentary on the subject some thirty years ago. That was a story about how the Republican governor of Oregon, Tom McCall, set out to prove that the economy and the environment could share the center lane on the highway to the future.

Those were optimistic years for the emerging environmental movement. Rachel Carson had rattled the cage with *Silent Spring,* and on the first Earth Day in 1970 twenty million Americans rose from the grass roots to speak for the planet. Even Richard Nixon couldn't say no to so powerful a subpoena by public opinion, and he put his signature to some far-reaching measures for environmental protection.

I shared that optimism and believed journalism would help to fulfill it. I thought that when people saw a good example they would imitate it, that if Americans knew the facts and possibilities they would act on them. After all, half a century ago as a student I had walked every day across the campus of the University of Texas and could look up at the inscription on the main tower: YOU SHALL KNOW THE TRUTH AND THE TRUTH SHALL SET YOU FREE. I believed we were really on the way toward the third American Revolution. The first had won our independence as a nation. The second had finally opened the promise of civil rights to all Americans. Now the third American Revolution was to be the Green Revolution for a healthy, safe, and sustainable future.

Sometimes in a moment of reverie I imagine that it happened. I imagine that we had brought forth a new paradigm for nurturing and protecting our global life-support system, that we had faced up to the greatest ecological challenge in human history and conquered it with clean renewable energy, efficient transportation and agriculture, and the nontoxic production and protection of our forests, oceans, grasslands, and wetlands. I imagine us leading the world on a new path of sustainability.

Alas, it is only a reverie. Rather than leading the world in finding solutions to the global environmental crises, the United States is a re-calcitrant naysayer and backslider. Our government and its corporate allies have turned against America's environmental visionaries. They have set out to eviscerate just about every significant gain of the past generation, and while they are at it they have managed to blame the environmental movement itself for the failure of the Green Revolution. If environmentalism isn't dead, they say, it should be. And they will gladly lead the cortege to the grave.

Yes, I know: the environmental community has stumbled on many fronts. All of us in this room have heard and reported the charges—that the rhetoric is alarmist and the ideology polarizing; that command-and-control regulation produces bureaucratic bungles, slows economic growth, and delays technological advances that save lives; that what began as a grassroots movement has now become an entrenched green bureaucracy precariously hanging on in occupied Washington while passionate citizens across the country are starved for financial resources. There is some truth in these charges; all movements flounder and must periodically regroup.

Before we consider the case closed, however, let me urge you to take a hard look at the backlash. If the Green Revolution is a bloody pulp today, it is not just because the environmental movement mugged itself. It is because the corporate, political, and religious Right ganged up on it. Big companies fund a relentless assault on green values and policies. Political ideologues press countless campaigns to strip from government all its functions except those that reward their rich benefactors. And the religious Right is more obsessed with demonizing gay people than with saving Earth.

I failed to reckon with how ruthless the reactionaries would be. What the chemical companies did to Rachel Carson when *Silent Spring* appeared in 1962 has been honed to a sharp edge aimed at the jugular of anyone who challenges them.

An antienvironmental crowd now runs the government. President Bush has turned the agencies charged with environmental protection over to people who don't believe in it. To manage the Department of the Interior he chose a longtime defender of polluters who has opposed laws to safeguard wildlife, habitat, and public lands. To run the Forest Service he chose a timber-industry lobbyist. To oversee our public lands he named a mining-industry lobbyist who believes public lands are unconstitutional. To run the Superfund he chose a woman who made a living advising corporate polluters how to evade the Superfund. And in the White House Office of Environmental Policy the president placed a lobbyist from the American Petroleum Institute whose mission was to make sure the government's scientific reports on global warming didn't contradict the party line and the interest of oil companies. Everywhere you look, the foxes occupy the chicken coop.

No, if the environmental movement is pronounced dead, it won't be from self-inflicted wounds. We don't blame slavery on the slaves, the Trail of Tears on the Cherokees, or the Srebrenica massacre on the bodies in the grave. The lethal threat to the environmental movement comes from the predatory power of money and the pathological enmity of ideology.

Theodore Roosevelt warned a century ago of the subversive influence of money over public policy. He said the central fact in his time was that big business had become so dominant it would chew up democracy and spit it out. The power of corporations, he said, had to be balanced with the interest of the general public. But a hundred years later corporations are once again the undisputed overlords of government. Follow the money and you are inside the inner sanctum of the Business Roundtable, the National Association of Manufacturers, and the American Petroleum Institute. As a result, America, once the leader in cutting-edge environmental policies and technologies and awareness, is now eclipsed. As the scientific evidence grows about global warming, our government has become an impediment to action, not a leader. Earlier this year the White House even conducted an extraordinary secret campaign to scupper the British government's attempt to tackle global warming—and then to undermine the United Nation's effort to stabilize greenhouse gas emissions. President Bush's failure to lead on global warming means that even if we were dramatically to decrease greenhouse gases overnight we have already condemned ourselves and generations to come to a warming planet.

You surely saw those reports a few days ago that the Arctic has suffered another record loss of sea ice. This summer, satellites monitoring the region found that ice reached its lowest monthly point on record— the fourth year in a row it has fallen below the monthly downward trend. The anticipated effects are well known: as the Arctic region absorbs more heat from the sun, causing the ice to melt still further, the relentless cycle of melting and heating will shrink the massive land glaciers of

Greenland and dramatically raise sea levels. Scientists said that with this new acceleration of melt the northern hemisphere may have crossed a critical threshold beyond which the climate cannot recover.

Nonetheless, last year a Gallup poll found that nearly half of Americans worry "only a little" or "not at all" about global warming or the greenhouse effect. In July of this year, ABC News reported that 66 percent of the people in a new survey said they don't think global warming will affect their lives. Denial is the only explanation for the gap between the threat and the response.

If you've seen the film *March of the Penguins*, you know it is a delight to the eye and a tug at the heart. The camera follows the flocks as they trek back and forth over the ice to their breeding ground. You see them huddle together to protect their eggs in temperatures that average seventy degrees below zero Fahrenheit. So powerful and beautiful a film can only increase one's awe of our small neighbors in the frozen regions.

In *The New York Times* recently, Jonathan Miller reported that some religious conservatives are invoking *March of the Penguins* as an inspiration for their various causes. Some praise the penguins for their monogamy. Opponents of abortion say it verifies "the beauty of life and the rightness of protecting it." A Christian magazine claims it makes "a strong case for intelligent design." For a while, on a conservative Web site you could find instructions to take a notebook, flashlight, and pen to the theater "to write down what God speaks to you" as you watch the film.

Fair enough. It would not be the first time human beings felt connected to a transcendental power through nature. But what you will not find in the film is any reference to global warming. Why is it relevant? Because to reproduce, the penguins must go to the thickest part of the ice where they can safely stand without fear it will break beneath their weight. Global warming obviously weakens the ice. If it becomes too thin, the penguins will lose the support necessary for reproduction. Yet the film is silent on this threat to these little creatures conservatives have taken as their mascots in the culture wars. The film's director explained that he wanted to reach as many people as possible and since "much of public opinion appears insensitive to the dangers of global warming," he didn't want to go there.

Again, fair enough. I can't fault him for the aspiration to tell the story for its own sake, in the simplest and most profound way. I can't fault him for wanting to avoid disturbing the comfort of viewers. I often wish that I were a filmmaker instead of a journalist and didn't have to give people a headache by reporting the news they'd rather not hear.

But what we don't know can kill us.

I know something about denial. Our oldest son is addicted to alcohol and drugs. I'm not spilling any family secrets here; my wife, Judith, and I produced a PBS series based on our family's experience, *Close to Home*, because we wanted to remind people that addiction hijacks the brain irrespective of race, creed, color, or street address. He's doing well, thank you—he's been in recovery for ten years now and has become one of the country's leading public advocates for treatment. But we almost lost him more than once because he was in denial and so were we. For a decade prior to his crash he would not admit to himself what was happening, and he was able to hide it from us; he was, after all, a rising star in journalism, married, a homeowner, and a faithful churchgoer. Naturally we believed the best about him. A drug addict, slowly poisoning himself to death? Not our son! The day before he crashed I was concerned about his behavior and asked him to lunch. "Are you in trouble?" I asked. "Are you using?" He looked me squarely in the eyes and said, "No, Dad, not at all. Just a few problems at home." "Well," I said, placing my hand on his, "I'm really glad to hear that." And I switched the subject. The next day he was gone. We searched for days before his mother and a friend tracked him down and coaxed him from a crack house to the hospital. Denial almost cost us our son.

They say denial is not a river in Egypt. It is, however, the governing philosophy in Washington. The president's contempt for evidence is mind-boggling. Here is a man who was quick to launch a "preventative war" against Iraq on faulty intelligence and premature judgment but who refuses to take preventive action against a truly global menace about which the scientific evidence is overwhelming.

Unfortunately, the people in his core constituency who could most effectively call on this president to lead have been largely silent. I mean the Christian conservatives who gave President Bush fifteen million votes in 2000 and maybe twenty million in 2004. Some of these Christian conservatives are implacable. They have given their proxies to the televangelists, pastors, and preachers who have signed on with the Republican Party and turned their faith into a political religion, a weapon of partisan conflict.

But millions of these people believe they are here on Earth to serve a higher moral power, not a partisan agenda. They overwhelmingly respond to natural disasters like last year's tsunami or the AIDS crisis in Africa by opening wide their hearts and wallets. Unfortunately, although many of them may believe Christians have a moral obligation to protect God's creation, most remain uninformed about the true scope of the environmental crisis. As a result, they typically vote their consciences on social issues rather than environmental ones.

Listen to this anguished moral missive from Joel Gillespie, a conservative Christian who recently wrote to *On Earth* magazine:

> I'll admit that when I pushed the button for President Bush, I did
> so with some sadness, given his dismal environmental record. But
> many of us who love the natural world . . . feel we face an almost
> impossible either-or predicament. Voting for pro-environmental
> candidates usually means voting for a package of other policies
> that we will never swallow. We're forced to choose unborn babies
> or endangered species, traditional marriage or habitat protection,
> cleaning up the smut that comes across the airwaves or the smut
> that fouls our air. And the fact that we are forced to make such
> choices has harmed the natural environment and the special
> places we love and cherish.

Many evangelical Christians share Gillespie's dilemma. They need to be challenged to look more closely at their moral choices—to consider whether it is possible to be pro-life while also being anti-Earth. If you believe uncompromisingly in the right of every baby to be born safely into this world, can you at the same time abandon the future of that child, allowing its health and safety to be compromised by a government that gives corporations license to poison our bodies and the environment?

During the Terri Schiavo right-to-die case last spring, President Bush said, "It is wise to always err on the side of life." He pleaded for a "culture of life." But by ignoring the counsel of thousands of environmental scientists, the president is not erring on the side of life. He is playing dice with our children's future—dice that we have likely loaded against our own species, and perhaps against all life on Earth.

There is a market here for journalists who are hungry for new readers. The conservative Christian audience is some fifty million readers strong. But to reach them, we have to understand something of their belief systems.

Reverend Jim Ball of the Evangelical Environmental Network, for example, tells us "creation-care is starting to resonate not just with evangelical progressives but with conservatives who are at the center of the evangelical spectrum." Last year, in a document entitled "For the Health of the Nation: An Evangelical Call to Civic Responsibility," the National Association of Evangelicals declared that our Bible "implies the principle of sustainability: our uses of the Earth must be designed to conserve and renew the Earth rather than to deplete or destroy it." In what might have come from the Sierra Club itself, the declaration urged "government to encourage fuel efficiency, reduce pollution, encourage sustainable use of natural resources, and provide for the proper care of wildlife and their natural habitats." Ball and a few evangelical leaders have also pushed for adding a climate change plank to their program, standing up to no-nothings like James Dobson, Jerry Falwell, and Pat Robertson.

But we can't expect to engage this vast conservative Christian audience with journalism's standard style of reporting. Environmental journalism has always spoken in the language of environmental science. But evangelicals and Pentecostals speak and think in a different language.

Theirs is poetic and metaphorical: a speech anchored in the truth of the Bible as they read it. Their moral actions are guided not by the newest Intergovernmental Panel on Climate Change report but by the books of Matthew, Mark, Luke, and John.

Here's an important statistic to ponder: 45 percent of Americans hold a creational view of the world, discounting Darwin's theory of evolution. I don't think it is a coincidence then that in a nation where nearly half our people believe in creationism, much of the populace also doubts the evidence of climate change science. Contrast that to other industrial nations where climate change science is overwhelmingly accepted as truth; in Britain, for example, where 81 percent of the populace wants the government to act boldly on the threat to Earth. It is simply that millions of Christians read the story of Genesis to dismiss or distrust a lot of science—not only evolution, but paleontology, archaeology, geology, genetics, even biology and botany. To those Christians who believe that our history began with Adam and Eve in the Garden of Eden and that it will end soon on the plains of Armageddon, environmental science with its urgent evidence of planetary peril must look at best irrelevant. At worst the environmental woes we report may be stoically viewed as the inevitable playing out of the end of time as presented in the book of Revelation. For Christian dominionists who believe the Lord will provide for all human needs and never leave us short of oil or other resources, no matter how we overpopulate the Earth, our reporting may be viewed as a direct attack on biblical teachings that urge humans "to be fruitful and multiply." It's even possible that among many of these religious conservatives, our environmental reporting—if they see it at all—could seem arrogant in its assumptions, mechanistic, cold, and godless in its worldview. That's a tough indictment, but one that must be faced if we want to understand how people get their news.

If I were a freelance journalist looking to offer a major piece on global warming to these people, how would I go about it? I wouldn't give up fact-based analysis, of course—the ethical obligation of journalists is to ground what we report in evidence. But I would tell some of my stories with an ear for spiritual language, the language of parable, for that is the language of faith.

Let's say I wanted to write a piece about the millions of species that might be put on the road to extinction by global warming. Reporting that story to a scientific audience, I would talk science: tell how a species decimated by climate change could reach a point of no return when its gene pool becomes too depleted to maintain its evolutionary adaptability. Such genetic impoverishment can eventually lead to extinction.

But how to reach Christians who doubt evolution? How would I get them to hear me? I might interview a scientist who is also a person of faith and ask how he or she would frame the subject in a way to engage the attention of other believers. I might interview a minister who would couch the work of today's climate and biodiversity scientists in a biblical metaphor: the story of Noah and the Flood, for one. The parallels of this parable are wonderful to behold. Both scientists and Noah possess knowledge of a potentially impending global catastrophe. They try to spread the word, to warn the world, but are laughed at, ridiculed. You can almost hear some Philistine telling old Noah he is nothing but a "gloom and doom" environmentalist, spreading his tale of abrupt climate change, of a great flood that will drown the world, of the impending extinction of humanity and animals if no one acts.

But no one does act, and Noah continues hearing the voice of God: "You are to bring into the ark two of all living creatures, male and female, to keep them alive with you." Noah does as God commands. He agrees to save not only his own family but to take on the daunting task of rescuing all the biodiversity of Earth. He builds the ark and is ridiculed as mad. He gathers two of every species, the climate does change, the deluge comes as predicted. Everyone not safely aboard drowns. But Noah and the ark's complete complement of Earth's animals live on. You've seen depictions of them disembarking beneath a rainbow, two by two, the giraffes and hippos, horses and zebras. Noah, then, can be seen as the first great preservationist, preventing the first great extinction. He did exactly what wildlife biologists and climatologists are trying to do today: to act on their moral convictions to conserve diversity, to protect God's creation in the face of a flood of consumerism and indifference by a materialistic world.

Some of you are no doubt uncomfortable with my parable. Now you know exactly how a Christian who believes devoutly in creationism feels when we journalists write about the genetics born of Darwin. If we don't understand how they see the world, if we can't empathize with each person's need to grasp a human problem in language of faith, then we will likely fail to reach many Christians who have a sense of morality and justice as strong as anyone else's. And we will have done little to head off the sixth great extinction.

There is something else we should also be doing. We are journalists first, and trying to reach one important audience doesn't mean we abandon other audiences. Nor does it relieve us of our responsibility for old-fashioned muckraking. As a reminder of strong fact-based reporting, let's go back to America's first Gilded Age just over a hundred years ago. That was a time like now. Gross materialism and political corruption engulfed the country. Big business bought the government right out from under the people. Outraged at the abuse of power, the publisher of *McClure's Magazine* cried out to his fellow journalists: "Capitalists . . . politicians . . . all breaking the law, or letting it be broken? There is no one left [to uphold it]: none but all of us."

Then something remarkable happened. The Gilded Age became the golden age of muckraking journalism.

Lincoln Steffens plunged into the shame of the cities—into a putrid urban cauldron of bribery, intimidation, and fraud, including voting roles padded with the names of dead dogs and dead people—and his reporting sparked an era of electoral reform.

Nellie Bly infiltrated a mental hospital, pretending to be insane, and wrote of the horrors she found there, arousing the public conscience.

John Spargo disappeared into the black bowels of coal mines and came back to crusade against child labor. As he wrote in his 1906 book, *The Bitter Cry of Children*, Spargo had found there little children

> alone in a dark mine passage hour after hour, with no human soul
> near; to see no living creature except . . . a rat or two seeking to
> share one's meal; to stand in water or mud that covers the ankles,
> chilled to the marrow . . . to work for fourteen hours . . . for sixty
> cents; to reach the surface when all is wrapped in the mantle of
> night, and to fall to the earth exhausted and have to be carried
> away to the nearest "shack" to be revived before it is possible to
> walk to the farther shack called "home."

Upton Sinclair waded through hell and with "tears and anguish" wrote what he found on that arm of the Chicago River known as "Bubbly Creek" on the southern boundary of the stockyards where

> all the drainage of the square mile of packing houses empties into
> it, so that it is really a great open sewer . . . and the filth stays
> there forever and a day. The grease and chemicals that are poured
> into it undergo all sorts of strange transformations . . . bubbles of
> carbonic acid gas will rise to the surface and burst, and make rings
> two or three feet wide. Here and there the grease and filth have
> caked solid, and the creek looks like a bed of lava . . . the packers
> used to leave the creek that way, till every now and then the sur-
> face would catch on fire and burn furiously, and the fire depart-
> ment would have to come and put it out.

The Gilded Age has returned with a vengeance. Washington is again a spectacle of corruption, crony capitalism, and an arrogance matched only by dogmatism that acts as if there is no tomorrow. But there is a tomorrow. I see it every time I work at my desk. There, beside my computer, are photographs of Henry, Thomas, Nancy, Jassie, and SaraJane—my grandchildren, ages fourteen and down. They have no vote. They have no party. They have no lobbyists in Washington. They have only you and me—our pens and keyboards and microphones—to seek and to speak and to publish what we can of how power works, how the world wags and who wags it. The powers that be would have us merely cover the news; our challenge is to uncover the news they would keep hidden.

Much is riding on your environmental journalism. You may be the last in our craft who try to inform the rest of us about the most complex of issues involving the survival of life on Earth.

Last year, on my weekly *NOW with Bill Moyers*, we produced a documentary episode called "Endangered Species," about a neighborhood in Washington, D.C., known as Anacostia, just a few blocks from Capitol Hill. It is one of the most violent and dangerous neighborhoods in the city, one of those places that give Washington the horrendous distinction of the highest murder rate of any major city in the country. It's horrendous in other ways, too. The Anacostia River that gives the neighborhood its name is one of the most polluted in America; more than a billion gallons of raw sewage end up in it every year.

We went there to report on the Earth Conservation Corps, a project to recruit neighborhood kids to help clean up the river and community. For their efforts, they earn minimum wage, get health insurance, and are offered a $5,000 scholarship if they go back to school.

The area where they work is practically a war zone. Since the project began an average of one corps member has been murdered almost every year. One was beaten to death. One was raped and killed. Another died when he was caught in the middle of a shooting while riding his bike. Three were shot execution-style.

One of the most charismatic of the kids who joined the corps was named Diamond Teague. He worked so hard the others called him "Choir Boy." His work became his passion. It gave purpose and meaning to his life to try and clean up his neighborhood and river. But one morning while he was sitting on his front porch an assailant walked up and shot him in the head.

It's that kind of place, not far from where the swells of Congress are hosted and toasted by lobbyists for America's most powerful and privileged interests.

After his death Diamond Teague got the only press of his short life—thirty-one words in *The Washington Post*.

> A teenager was found fatally shot about 2:05 Thursday in the
> 2200 block of Prout Place SW, police said. Diamond D. Teague,
> 19, who lived on the block, was pronounced dead.

That's all. That was Diamond Teague's obit. Not a word about his work for the Earth's Conservation Corps. Not a word.

It was left to his friends to tell the world about Diamond Teague. One of them explained to us that they wanted people to know that just because a black man gets killed in the southeast corner of the nation's capital, "he's not just a drug dealer or gangbanger . . . and not just discount him as nobody when he deserves for people to know him and to know his life."

His friends made a video about him. They turned out for his funeral in uniform. They wept and prayed for their fallen friend. And then they went back to work, on a dusty patch of land squeezed between two factories that they envisioned as a park. "We see the bigger picture," one of Diamond's friends told us. "All great things have to start in roughness. We're just at the beginning of something that's gonna be beautiful."

They want to call it the Diamond Teague Memorial Park, in honor of their friend who was trying to save an endangered river and neighborhood but couldn't save himself.

On that fleck of land, where anything beautiful must be born in roughness, they see "the bigger picture."

Just blocks away, at opposite ends of Pennsylvania Avenue, in the White House and the Capitol, the blind lead the blind on yet another march of folly.

Who is left to open the eyes of the country—to tell Americans what is happening?

"There is no one left; none but all of us."

23. | DEMOCRACY, SECRECY, AND IDEOLOGY

The Twentieth Anniversary of the National Security Archive

DECEMBER 9, 2005

Of the public interest organizations that keep an eye on Washington for all of us, none is more vital, in my book, than the National Security Archive. Don't confuse it with the National Archives, which is the government attic where Uncle Sam keeps millions upon millions of historical valuables for us, from the original Declaration of Independence to the most recent presidential memorabilia. The National Security Archive is something else altogether—a nongovernment research institute whose mission is to bring government secrets to light. The archive finds that hidden fruit through the Freedom of Information Act, the federal law that established—over fierce opposition—the public's right to obtain information from federal agencies. You can go to www.nsarchive.org—considered a "hot site" by many journalists—and see for yourself why the archive won the prestigious George Polk Award for "piercing the self-serving veils of government secrecy." Asked to speak at the archive's twentieth anniversary, I accepted even before I knew more details would be emerging from that attempted coup at the Corporation of Public Broadcasting that led to the resignation of its chairman Kenneth Tomlinson just a month before my speech. The time and venue could not have been more perfect for talking about democracy, secrecy, and ideology.

* * *

I was pleased to be invited to this anniversary celebration of the National Security Archive. Your organization has become indispensable to journalists, scholars, and citizens who believe the United States belongs to the people and not to the government, and that to claim that ownership we need to know what the government doesn't want us to know. No one in this town has done more to fight for open democracy than the archive.

I admire your long campaign to ensure that the Freedom of Information Act fulfills its promise. As Herbert Foerstel reminds us in *Freedom of Information and the Right to Know*, every eighteenth-century democratic constitution includes the public's right to information, with two exceptions: Sweden and the United States. Many powerful forces in America would have preferred to keep it that way.

But in 1955 the American Society of Newspaper Editors decided to battle government secrecy. *The Washington Post*'s James Russell Wiggins and Representative John Moss of California teamed up to spearhead that fight. President Kennedy resisted their efforts. When he asked reporters to censor themselves on the grounds that these were times of "clear and present danger," journalists were outraged. Moss refused to give up, and in 1966 Congress passed the Freedom of Information Act, although in a much compromised form.

I was there, as the White House press secretary, when President Lyndon Johnson signed the legislation into law on July 4, 1966—signed it with language that was almost lyrical: "With a deep sense of pride that the United States is an open society in which the people's right to know is cherished and guarded."

Well, yes, but LBJ had to be dragged kicking and screaming to the signing ceremony. He loathed the very idea of the Freedom of Information Act; loathed the thought of journalists rummaging in government closets and opening government files; loathed them challenging the official view of reality. He dug in his heels and even threatened to veto the bill after it reached the White House. He might have followed through if Moss and Wiggins and other editors hadn't barraged him with pleas and petitions. He relented and signed "the damned thing," as he called it (I'm paraphrasing what he actually said in case children are present). He signed it, and then went out to claim credit for it.

Because of the Freedom of Information Act and the relentless fight by the archive to defend and exercise it, some of us have learned more since leaving the White House about what happened on our watch than we knew when we were there.

Consider the recent disclosures about events in the Gulf of Tonkin in 1964. These documents, now four decades old, seem to confirm that there was no second attack on U.S. ships on August 4 and that President Johnson ordered retaliatory air strikes against North Vietnam on the basis of intelligence that either had been "mishandled" or "misinterpreted" or deliberately skewed by subordinates to provide him the excuse he was looking for to attack North Vietnam.

I was not then a player in foreign policy and had not yet become the president's press secretary; my portfolio was politics and domestic policy. But I was often beside him during those frenetic hours. I heard his side of the conversations, but not what was being told to him by the Situation Room or Pentagon.

It was never nailed down for certain that there was a second attack, but I believe that LBJ thought there had been. It is true that for months he had wanted to send a message to Ho Chi Minh that he meant business about standing behind America's commitment to South Vietnam. It is true that he was not about to allow the hawkish Barry Goldwater to outflank him on national security in the fall campaign. It is also true that he often wrestled with the real or imaginary fear that liberal Democrats, whose hearts still belonged to JFK, would be watching and sizing him up according to their speculation of how Kennedy would have decided the moment. Clearly the president was prepared to act if the North Vietnamese presented him a tit-for-tat opportunity. But he wasn't at this time looking for a wider war, only a show of resolve, a flexing of muscles, the chance to swat the fly if it landed.

Nonetheless, this state of mind plus cloudy intelligence proved a combustible and tragic mix. In his belief that a second attack revealed a more deliberate intent (one alone might have been accidental, an intuitive response by an adversary to an unexpected encounter), the president did order strikes against North Vietnam, in effect widening the war. He asked Congress to enact a resolution already drawn up by his national security adviser, and three days later Congress responded with the Gulf of Tonkin Resolution that he would use for future large-scale commitments of American forces. Haste is often the enemy of judgment, and the consequences of haste this time would prove costly.

But did the president order up fabricated evidence to suit his wish? No. Did subordinates rig the evidence to support what they thought he wanted to do? It's possible, but I swear I cannot imagine who they might have been. Did the president act prematurely? Yes. Was the response disproportionate to the events? Yes. Did he later agonize over so precipitous a decision? Yes. "For all I know," he said the next year, "our navy was shooting at whales out there." By then, however, he found other reasons to escalate the war. All these years later it's painful to wonder what could have been if we had waited until the fog lifted, or had made the public aware of what we did and didn't know, trusting the debate in the press, Congress, and the country to help us shape policies more aligned with facts on the ground (in this case, on the sea) and with the opinion of an informed public.

I had hoped others would learn from our experience. Prior to the invasion of Iraq, I said on the air that Vietnam didn't make me a dove; it made me read the Constitution. Government's first obligation is to defend its citizens; there is nothing in the Constitution that says it is permissible for our government to launch a preemptive attack on another nation. Common sense carries one to the same conclusion: it's hard to get the leash back on once you let the wild dogs of war out of the kennel. Our present secretary of defense has a plaque on his desk that reads: "Aggressive fighting for the right is the noblest sport the world affords." Perhaps, but while war is sometimes necessary, to treat it as sport is obscene. At best, war is a crude alternative to shrewd, disciplined diplomacy and the forging of a true alliance acting in the name of international law. Unprovoked, "the noblest sport" of war becomes the slaughter of the innocent.

I left the White House in early 1967 for journalism and put those years and events behind me, except to reflect on how they might inform my reporting and analysis of what's happening today. I was chastened by our mistakes back then, and I am chagrined now when others repeat them.

In my files is an article by Jeff Cohen and Norman Solomon ("30-Year Anniversary: Tonkin Gulf Lie Launched Vietnam War") written a decade ago and long before the recent disclosures. They might have written it over again during the buildup for the invasion of Iraq. On August 5, 1964, the headline in *The Washington Post* read: AMERICAN PLANES HIT NORTH VIETNAM AFTER SECOND ATTACK ON OUR DESTROYERS: MOVE TAKEN TO HALT AGGRESSION. That, of course, was the official line, spelled out verbatim and succinctly on the nation's front pages. *The New York Times* proclaimed in an editorial that the president "went to the people last night with the somber facts." The *Los Angeles Times* urged Americans "to face the fact that the communists, by their attack on American vessels in international waters, have escalated the hostilities." It was not only Lyndon Johnson whose mind was predisposed to judge on the spot, with half a loaf. It was also those reporters and editors who were willing to accept the official view of reality as the truth of the matter. In *The "Uncensored War,"* Daniel Hallin found that journalists at the time had a great deal of information available which contradicted the official account of what happened in the Gulf of Tonkin, but "it simply wasn't used."

Tom Wells, who wrote the compelling book *The War Within: America's Battle Over Vietnam*, told Cohen and Solomon it was yet another case of "the media's almost exclusive reliance on the U.S. government officials as sources of information," as well as "their reluctance to question official pronouncements on national security issues."

I am taking up your time with this hoping you will understand why I have become something of a fundamentalist on the First Amendment protection of an independent press, a press that will resist the seductions, persuasions, and intimidations of people who hold great power—over life and death, war and peace, taxes, the fate of the environment—and, if permitted, would exercise that power arbitrarily, in secrecy.

In a telling moment, the Bush administration opposed the declassification of these forty-year-old Gulf of Tonkin documents. Why? Because they fear uncomfortable comparisons with the flawed intelligence used to justify the war in Iraq. And well they might. Just as telling is their opposition to the release of two intelligence briefings given to President Johnson in 1965 and 1968. The CIA claims they should be kept secret on the grounds that their release could impair its mission by revealing its sources and methods of forty years ago. Bull. The actual methods used by the CIA back then have largely been declassified, which is why I signed a statement in your support when the National Security Archive went to court over this matter. I was as disappointed as you when the federal judge, in his ruling this past summer, preferred the government's penchant for secrecy to the people's right to know what goes on in their name and with their money.

It must be said: there has been nothing in our time like the Bush administration's obsession with secrecy. This may seem self-serving coming from someone who worked for John F. Kennedy and Lyndon B. Johnson, who were no paragons of openness. But I am only one of legions who have reached this conclusion. See the recent pair of articles by the independent journalist Michael Massing in *The New York Review of Books*. He concludes: "The Bush Administration has restricted access to public documents as no other before it." And he backs this up with evidence. A recent report on government secrecy by the watchdog group OpenTheGovernment.org says the government classified a record 15.6 million new documents in fiscal year 2004, an increase of 81 percent over the year before the terrorist attacks on September 11, 2001. What's more, 64 percent of Federal Advisory Committee meetings in 2004 were completely closed to the public. No wonder the public knows so little about how the Bush administration has deliberately ignored or distorted reputable scientific research to advance its political agenda and the wishes of its corporate patrons. I'm talking about the suppression of that Environmental Protection Agency report questioning aspects of the White House Clear Skies Act; research censorship at the departments of health and human services, interior, and agriculture; the elimination of qualified scientists from advisory committees on kids and lead poisoning, reproductive health, and drug abuse; the distortion of scientific knowledge on emergency contraception; the manipulation of the scientific process involving the Endangered Species Act; and the internal sabotage of government scientific reports on global warming.

It's an old story: the greater the secrecy, the deeper the corruption.

This is the administration that has illegally produced phony television news stories with fake reporters about Medicare and government antidrug programs, then distributed them to local TV stations around the country. In several markets, the fake stories aired on the six o'clock news with nary a mention that they were propaganda bought and paid for with your tax dollars.

This is the administration that paid almost a quarter of a million dollars for the obliging commentator Armstrong Williams to talk up its No Child Left Behind education program and bankrolled two other conservative columnists to shill for programs promoting the president's marriage initiative.

This is the administration that tacitly allowed inside the White House a phony journalist under the nom de plume of Jeff Gannon to file Republican press releases as legitimate news stories and to ask President Bush planted questions to which he could respond with preconceived answers.

And this is the administration that has paid more than $100 million to plant stories in Iraqi newspapers and disguise the source, while banning TV cameras at the return of caskets from Iraq as well as prohibiting the publication of photographs of those caskets—a restriction that was lifted only following a request through the Freedom of Information Act.

Ah, FOIA. Obsessed with secrecy, Bush and Cheney have made the Freedom of Information Act their number-one target, more fervently pursued for elimination than Osama bin Laden. No sooner had they come into office than they set out to eviscerate both FOIA and the Presidential Records Act. The president has been determined to protect his father's secrets when the first Bush was vice president and then president.

And now his own. Bush omerta.

This enmity toward FOIA springs from deep roots in their extended official family. Just read your own National Security Archive briefing book number 142, edited by Dan Lopez, Tom Blanton, Meredith Fuchs, and Barbara Elias. It is an account of how in 1974 President Gerald Ford's chief of staff, one Donald Rumsfeld, and his deputy chief of staff, one Dick Cheney, talked the president out of signing amendments that would have put stronger teeth in the Freedom of Information Act. As members of the House of Representatives, Rumsfeld actually co-sponsored the act and Ford voted for it. But then Richard Nixon was sent scuttling from the White House in disgrace after the secrets of Watergate came spilling out. Rumsfeld and Cheney wanted no more embarrassing revelations of their party's abuse of power. They were assisted in their arguments by yet another rising Republican star, Antonin Scalia, then a top lawyer at the Justice Department. Fast-forward to 2001, when in the early months of George W. Bush's administration, Vice President Cheney invited the tycoons of oil, gas, and coal to the White House to divide up the spoils of victory. They had, after all, contributed millions of dollars to the cause, and as Cheney would later say of tax cuts for the fraternity of elites who had financed the campaign, they deserved the payoff. But to keep the plunder from disgusting the public, the identities of the participants in the meetings were kept secret.

The Sierra Club and the conservative watchdog organization Judicial Watch filed suit to open this insider trading to public scrutiny. But after losing in the lower court, the White House asked the Supreme Court to intervene. Lo and behold, hardly had Justice Scalia returned from a duck-hunting trip with the vice president—the blind leading the blind to the blind—than the Supreme Court upheld the White House privilege to keep secret the names of those corporate predators who came to slice the pie. You have to wonder if sitting there in the marsh, shotguns in hand, Scalia and Cheney reminisced about their collaboration many years earlier when as young men in government they had tried to shoot down the dreaded Freedom of Information Act that kept them looking over their shoulders (Congress, by the way, overrode President Ford's veto).

This administration has much to fear from the Freedom of Information Act. Just a few days ago, FOIA was used to force the Department of Justice to make available legal documents related to the record of Samuel Alito, nominated by President Bush to the Supreme Court. The department reluctantly complied but under very restricted circumstances. The records were made available on one day, for three hours, from three to six p.m., for reporters only. No citizen or advocacy groups were permitted access. There were 470 pages to review. Michael Petrelis, on his blog spot (mpetrelis.blogspot.com), reckons this meant a reporter had about thirty-four seconds to quickly read each page and figure out if the information was newsworthy or worth pursuing further. "Not a lot of time to carefully examine documents from our next Supreme Court justice," he wrote.

And why wouldn't the White House want reporters roaming the halls of justice? According to *The Washington Post*, two years ago six Justice Department attorneys and two analysts wrote a memo stating unequivocally that the Texas congressional redistricting plan concocted by Tom DeLay violated the Voting Rights Act. Those career professional civil servants were overruled by senior officials, Bush's political appointees, who went ahead and approved the plan anyway.

We're only finding this out now because someone leaked the memo. According to *The Washington Post*, the document was kept under tight wraps and "lawyers who worked on the case were subjected to an unusual gag rule." Why? Because it is a devastating account of how DeLay helped launder corporate money to elect a Texas legislature that then shuffled congressional districts to add five new Republican members of the House, nailing down control of Congress for the radical and corporate Right.

They couldn't get away with all of this if we in the press were at the top of our game. Never has the need for an independent media been greater. People are frightened, their skepticism of power eclipsed by their desire for security. Writing in *The New York Times*, Michael Ignatieff has reminded us that democracy's dark secret is that the fight against terror has to be waged in secret, by men and women who defend us with a bodyguard of lies and armory of deadly weapons. Because this is democracy's dark secret, Ignatieff continues, it can also be democracy's dark nemesis.

Yet the press is hobbled today—hobbled by Wall Street investors who demand greater and greater profit margins at the expense of reporting. Layoffs are hitting papers all across the country. Just last week, *Newsday*, of which I was once publisher, cut seventy-two jobs and eliminated forty vacancies—that's in addition to fifty-nine newsroom jobs that had been eliminated the previous month. There are fewer editors and reporters with less time, resources, and freedom to burn shoe leather and midnight oil, make endless phone calls, and knock on doors in pursuit of the unreported story.

The press is also hobbled by intimidation from bullies in the propaganda wing of the Republican Party who hector, demonize, and lie about journalists who ask hard questions of this regime.

Hobbled, too, by what Ken Silverstein, a *Los Angeles Times* investigative reporter, calls "spurious balance," kowtowing to those with the loudest voice or the most august title who demand that when it comes to reporting, lies must be treated as the equivalent of truth; that covering the news, including the official press release, has greater priority than uncovering the news.

I want to share with you now a personal story of what can happen when a journalist reports what this administration doesn't want the public to know. I told this story earlier this year to the second national Media Reform Conference in St. Louis, but new details have emerged from the shadows that obscure much of what happens in this town.

Four years ago, PBS asked me to create a new weekly broadcast of news, analysis, and interviews. One mandate was to give viewers a choice, not an echo. So for inspiration we reached back to the words of Lord Byron that once graced the masthead of many small-town newspapers: "Without, or with, offence to friends or foes, I sketch your world exactly as it goes."

Over the months we reported how faraway decision-making affected the lives of regular people—how political influence led to mountaintop-removal mining and how the government colluded with industry to cover up the effect of mercury in fish on pregnant women. We described what life was like for homeless veterans and child migrants working in the fields. We exposed Wall Street shenanigans and tracked the Washington revolving door. We reported how Congress had rejected safeguards that would mitigate a scandal like Enron, and how those efforts were shot down by some of the same politicians who were then charged with investigating the scandal. We investigated Deputy Secretary of the Interior Steven Griles a full eighteen months before he had to resign over conflicts of interest involving the oil and mining industries for which he had been a lobbyist on the other side of that revolving door. We reported how ExxonMobil had influenced the White House to replace a scientist who believes global warming is real.

Such reporting angered the chairman of the Corporation for Public Broadcasting, Kenneth Tomlinson, a Republican who cast himself in the image of Karl Rove. Tomlinson set out, secretly, to discredit our broadcast—a campaign I have described elsewhere. But the story bears repeating because of details that have emerged only recently. Tomlinson, as these new disclosures reveal, was especially outraged by our documentary on the distress of people living in the small town of Tamaqua, Pennsylvania. A textile firm there had laid off more than a third of its work-force—the last gasp of an industry that had sustained the townspeople after the demise of the coal industry. With their jobs heading for Honduras and China, we put the plight of Tamaqua in the context of how the North American Free Trade Agreement—signed, by the way, by President Bill Clinton a dozen years ago—was contributing to growing inequality in America, with the widest gap between rich and poor since the Great Depression. By bringing the story of "free trade" down to scale in the little town of Tamaqua we put a human face on the consequences of globalization.

Our reporting contradicted the rosy scenarios of the Bush administration, and Tomlinson went on the warpath, describing what he saw as "liberal advocacy journalism"—the mantra hurled by right-wing polemicists for years against fact-based reporting that undermines their worldview. All I can say is that if reporting what happens to ordinary people because of events beyond their control, and the indifference of government to their fate, is "liberal," I plead guilty.

But Tomlinson did not content himself with public complaints. He began crudely to pressure PBS to counter my broadcast, and he reached out personally to an ideological soul mate, Paul Gigot, the right-wing editor of *The Wall Street Journal*'s editorial pages, to arrange for Gigot's recently cancelled CNBC broadcast (*The Journal Editorial Report*) to be resurrected by PBS. The story has been widely reported, but recently released e-mails between Gigot and Tomlinson reveal just how these two fierce defenders of the free market (and other Republican doctrine) secretly schemed to direct several million dollars of taxpayer funds to the prosperous *Wall Street Journal* so that "our side," as they called themselves, could get "an absolute duplication of what Moyers is doing." But Gigot's broadcast proved to be nowhere near what my colleague David Brancaccio and I were doing. We were digging, investigating, and reporting, as well as offering a wide range of voices—liberal and conservative among them; Gigot and his guests, all like-minded ideologues from his own staff, were merely opining. Indeed, in their private exchange of e-mails, Tomlinson informs Gigot that once he has received the public funds, he doesn't really need to do field reporting. Gigot is relieved, telling Tomlinson that not only is such reporting a waste of time and money, it is "boring." I'm not making this up: one of the most powerful editors in America admits that reporting—collecting the evidence, getting the facts, finding reality—is "boring."

Their secret e-mails irrefutably reveal that the right-wing chairman of the Corporation for Public Broadcasting and the right-wing editor of the editorial page of *The Wall Street Journal* colluded with public funds to subsidize that rich newspaper to create a broadcast on PBS that would be a vehicle exclusively for right-wing ideology. "Our side" turned out to be one more cog in the great Republican noise machine. It didn't last; Gigot's show failed to attract an audience and he soon took it to Fox News, where it found a compatible niche in Rupert Murdoch's empire (which now includes *The Wall Street Journal*). A couple of days after that announcement, *The Wall Street Journal* published a thoroughly disingenuous editorial, obviously written by Gigot, defending Kenneth Tomlinson's involvement in his scheme, while denigrating the inspector general of CPB who had investigated the mess at the request of members of Congress. The inspector found that Tomlinson had committed multiple transgressions: he broke the law, violated the corporation's guidelines for contracting, meddled in program decisions, injected politics into hiring procedures, and admonished CPB executive staff "not to interfere with his deal" with Gigot. The e-mails show Tomlinson bragging to Karl Rove about his success in "shaking things up" at CPB. They also confirm that he had consulted the White House about recruiting loyalist Republicans to serve as his confederates at the very organization that had been created in 1967 to prevent just such partisan meddling in public broadcasting.

As all this was becoming public, Tomlinson was forced to resign from the CPB board. He is now under investigation by the State Department for irregularities in his other job as chair of the Broadcasting Board of Governors, the agency that oversees Voice of America, Radio Free

Europe, and other international broadcasting sponsored by the United States.*

I have shared this sordid little story with you because it is a cautionary tale about the regime in power. If they were so determined to go with all guns blazing at a single broadcast on public television that is simply doing the job journalism is supposed to do, you can imagine the pressure that has been applied to mainstream media. And you can understand what's at stake when journalists and the state collude to further the party line, as Paul Gigot and Ken Tomlinson were doing.

In *The Gospel According to America*, David Dark reminds us of a lesson we always seem to be forgetting, that "as learners of freedom, we might come to understand that the price of liberty is eternal vigilance." He might well have been directly addressing the press when he wrote:

> Keeping one's head safe for democracy (or avoiding the worship of false gods) will require a diligent questioning of any and all tribal storytellers. In an age of information technology, we will have to look especially hard at the forces that shape discourse and the various high-powered attempts, new every morning, to invent public reality.

Look closely. They're still at it.

---

*Just as his improprieties had forced his retirement as Chairman of the Corporation for Public Broadcasting in 2005 (see page 283), Kenneth Tomlinson now came under investigation as Chairman of the Broadcasting Board of Governors, the federal board that oversees most United States government broadcasts to foreign countries, including VOA, Radio Free Europe, the Arab-language Alhurra, and Radio Marti. The State Department's Office of the Inspector General found that he had improperly used his office to promote his own business interests, including his horse racing operation, and had doled out a large consulting contract to a friend without the knowledge of other board members and without providing any of the required documentation. On January 9, 2007, Tomlinson asked that his name not be submitted for reconfirmation as chairman.

24. | LIFE ON THE PLANTATION

National Conference for Media Reform

JANUARY 12, 2007

Just as The Wall Street Journal was about to bid its vaunted independence farewell and sail into position as the flagship in Rupert Murdoch's armada, its editorial writers hoisted a "Welcome Aboard" signal to the Admiral of the Fleet in the form of an editorial praising the Federal Communications Commission for relaxing limits on media ownership—in other words, for allowing Big Media to swallow everything left in sight. Rupert greets no human act more warmly than the bowed knee of an editor who knows on which side his bread is buttered. You can imagine the smile on his face as his soon-to-be minions paid obeisance to his ravenous appetite. This particular Hail Caesar welcome on the eve of his annunciation reassured the conquering hero that "these columns have long favored letting the free market determine the size of a company." At that very moment the Republican majority on the FCC was about to change a rule that prevents "cross-ownership," freeing media conglomerates to increase their ownership of more news outlets in a single town—that is, to imprint a single thumb more indelibly on what local residents see, read, and hear. Rupert's smile must have widened to learn from an editorial page that would soon be his that we have "the free market" to thank for the beneficent conglomeration of media outlets that produced unblinking conformity of opinion in the buildup to the invasion of Iraq, ensuring George W. Bush that he could start a war without having to fear that some press baron would stab him in the back with a sharp dissenting opinion. Murdoch had said, just weeks before the invasion, "The greatest thing to come of this to the world economy, if you could put it that way, would be $20 a barrel for oil . . . The whole world will benefit from cheaper oil, which will be a bigger stimulus than anything else." Let us for the moment avoid glancing at the price of oil today and recall instead how CBS and ABC and NBC and Fox and, yes, the editorial page of The Wall Street Journal saluted and cheered the commander in chief as he announced "Mission Accomplished." Obviously we owe such courageous unanimity to the "free market." It has also delivered us Clear Channel with a thousand or more radio stations under a centralized control that could push the "mute" button when the Dixie Chicks approached a microphone. In its Orwellian world the right-wing editorial page of The Wall Street Journal, before and after Murdoch, says those of us who oppose greater conglomeration of media are actually opposing more vigorous media competition, for the result of all the consolidation—I am not making this up—is "a media landscape that is more diverse than ever." If Rupert believes that, he must believe oil is $20 a barrel. The national TV networks, the few cable news channels, and a small handful of semi-national newspapers set the national news agenda. These ten to twelve outlets disproportionately influence what most citizens will or will not learn, and Murdoch now controls three of them: the Fox Network, Fox News Channel, and The Wall Street Journal. Heading for Memphis and a gathering of more than three thousand people fighting for more diversity in media ownership, I flew over land that had once been huge estates cultivating cotton and tobacco. The plantation mentality is back—this time in the corporate boardrooms of media moguls.

* * *

On the door of my office is a quotation attributed to Benjamin Franklin: "Democracy is two wolves and a lamb voting on what to have for lunch. Liberty is a well-armed lamb contesting the vote."

My fellow lambs, it's good to be in Memphis and find you well armed with passion for democracy, readiness for action, and courage for the next round in the fight for a free and independent press.

I salute the conviction that brought you here. I cherish the spirit that fills this hall and the camaraderie we share today. All too often the greatest obstacle to reform is the reform movement itself. Factions rise, fences go up, jealousies mount—and the cause all believe in is lost in the shattered fragments of what was once a clear and compelling vision. By avoiding contentious factionalism, you have created a strong movement. I was skeptical when Robert McChesney and John Nichols first raised the issue of media consolidation a few years ago. I was sympathetic but skeptical. The challenge of actually doing something about this issue—beyond simply bemoaning its impact on democracy—was daunting. How could we hope to come up with an effective response to an inexorable force?

It seemed inexorable because for years a series of mega-media mergers had swept the country, each deal even bigger than the last. The lobby representing the broadcast, cable, and newspaper industry is extremely powerful, with an iron grip on lawmakers and regulators alike. Both parties bowed to their will when the Republican Congress passed, and President Clinton signed, the Telecommunications Act of 1996. That monstrous assault on democracy, with malignant consequences for journalism, was nothing but a welfare giveaway to the largest, richest, and most powerful media conglomerates in the world—Goliaths whose handful of owners controlled, commodified, and monetized everyone, and everything, in sight.

Call it the plantation mentality in its modern incarnation. Here in Memphis they know all about that mentality. As late as 1968 the civil rights movement was still battling the "plantation mentality" on race, gender, and power that permeated Southern culture long before and even after the groundbreaking legislation of the mid-1960s. When Martin Luther King Jr. came to Memphis to join the strike of garbage workers in 1968, the cry from every striker's heart—"I am a man"—voiced the long-suppressed outrage of a people whose rights were still being trampled by an ownership class that had arranged the world for its own benefit. The plantation mentality was a phenomenon deeply insinuated in the American experience early on, and it permeated and corrupted our course as a nation. The journalist of the American Revolution, Thomas Paine, had envisioned this new republic as "a community of occupations," prospering "by the aid which each receives from the other, and from the whole." But that vision was repeatedly betrayed, so that less than a century after Thomas Paine's death, Theodore Roosevelt, bolting a Republican Party whose bosses had stolen the nomination from him, declared: "Our democracy is now put to a vital test, for the conflict is between human rights on the one side and on the other special privilege asserted as a property right. The parting of the ways has come."

Today, a hundred years after Teddy Roosevelt's death, those words still ring true. America is socially divided and politically benighted. Inequality and poverty grow steadily along with risk and debt. Many working families cannot make ends meet with two people working, let alone if one stays home to care for children or aging parents. Young people without privilege and wealth struggle to get a footing. Seniors enjoy less and less security for a lifetime of work. We are racially segregated in every meaningful sense except the letter of the law. And survivors of segregation and immigration toil for pennies on the dollar compared to those they serve.

None of this is accidental. As Norton Garfinkle writes in *The American Dream vs. the Gospel of Wealth*, the historic vision is that continuing economic growth and political stability can be achieved by supporting income growth and the economic security of middle-class families without restricting the ability of successful businessmen to gain wealth. The counter-belief is that providing maximum financial rewards to the most successful is the way to maintain high economic growth. This belief has prevailed for a generation now. The upward distribution of wealth has been willed from the top, as corporate and political policy. Most of the wealth created over the past twenty-five years has been captured by the top 20 percent of households, and most of the gains went to the wealthiest. The top 1 percent of households captured more than 50 percent of all gains in financial wealth. These rich households hold more than twice the share their predecessors held on the eve of the American Revolution. The choice cannot be avoided: What kind of economy do we seek, and what kind of nation do we wish to be? Do we want to be a country in which the rich get richer and the poor get poorer? Or do we want an economy that strengthens the social contract embodied in the preamble to the Constitution, offers upward mobility, and supports a middle-class standard of living? In Garfinkle's words:

> When the richest nation in the world has to borrow hundreds of billions of dollars to pay its bill, when its middle-class citizens sit on a mountain of debt to maintain their living standards, when the nation's economy has difficulty producing secure jobs or enough jobs of any kind, something is amiss.

You bet something is amiss. And it goes to the core of why we are here in Memphis for this conference. We are talking about a force—media—that cuts deep to the foundation of democracy. When Teddy Roosevelt dissected the "real masters of the reactionary forces," he concluded that they "directly or indirectly control the majority of the great daily newspapers that are against us." Those newspapers "choked" (his word) the channels of information ordinary people needed to understand what was being done to them.

And today? Two basic pillars of American society—shared economic prosperity and a public sector capable of serving the social contract—are crumbling. The third pillar—an independent press—is under sustained attack, and the channels of information are choked.

A few huge corporations now dominate our media landscape. Almost all the networks carried by most cable systems are owned by one of the major media conglomerates. Two-thirds of today's newspaper markets are monopolies. As ownership gets more and more concentrated, fewer and fewer independent sources of information have survived in the marketplace. And those few significant alternatives that do survive, such as the Public Broadcasting Service and National Public Radio, are under growing financial and political pressure to reduce critical news content and pay more attention to the prevailing arrangements of power than to the bleak realities of powerlessness that shape the lives of ordinary people. Tell me now: When is the last time you saw or heard on public broadcasting what life is really like for working and poor Americans?

What does today's media system mean for the notion of the "informed public" cherished by democratic theory? Quite literally, it means that virtually everything the average person sees or hears outside of her own personal communications is determined by the interests of executives and investors whose singular goal is increasing profits and raising the company's share price. More insidiously, this relatively small group of elites determines what ordinary people do not see or hear. In-depth news coverage of anything, let alone of the problems people face day-to-day, is as scarce as sex, violence, and voyeurism are pervasive. Successful business model or not, by democratic standards this is censorship of knowledge by monopolization of the means of information. It has one clear consequence: there is more information and easier access to it, but it's more narrow in content and perspective, so that what is seen from the couch is overwhelmingly a view from the top.

Pioneering communications scholar Murray Edelman wrote that "Opinions about public policy do not spring immaculately or automatically into people's minds; they are always placed there by the interpretations of those who can most consistently get their claims and manufactured cues publicized widely." For years our media marketplace has been dominated by a highly disciplined, thoroughly networked "noise machine," to use David Brock's term, creating a public discourse that changed how American values are perceived. Day after day, the ideals of fairness, cooperation, and mutual responsibility have been stripped of their essential dignity and meaning in people's lives. Day after day, the egalitarian language of our Declaration of Independence is shredded by sloganeers who speak of the "death tax," the "ownership society," the "culture of life," "compassionate conservation," "weak on terrorism," the "end of history," the "clash of civilizations," "no child left behind." They have even managed to turn the escalation of a preemptive war into a "surge"—as if it were a current of electricity charging through a wire instead of blood spurting from a soldier's ruptured veins. We have all the Orwellian filigree of a public sphere in which words conceal reality and the pursuit of personal gain and partisan power is wrapped in rhetoric that turns truth to lies and lies to truth.

So it is that "limited government" has little to do anymore with the Constitution or local autonomy; now it means corporate domination and the shifting of risk from government and business to struggling families and workers. "Family values" now means imposing a sectarian definition on everyone else. "Religious freedom" means majoritarianism and public benefits for organized religion without any public burdens. And "patriotism" means blind support for failed leaders. It's what happens when an interlocking media system filters through commercial values and ideology the information and moral viewpoints that people consume in their daily lives.

By no stretch of the imagination can we say the dominant institutions of today's media are guardians of democracy. Despite the profusion of new information "platforms" on cable, on the Internet, on radio, blogs, podcasts, YouTube, and MySpace, among others, the resources for solid original journalistic work, both investigative and interpretive, are contracting rather than expanding. I'm old-fashioned in this, a hangover from my days as a cub reporter and later a publisher. I agree with Michael Schudson, one of our leading scholars of communication, who writes in the January/February 2007 Columbia Journalism Review that "while all media matter, some matter more than others, and for the sake of democracy, print still counts most, especially print that devotes resources to gathering news. Network TV matters, cable TV matters, but when it comes to original investigation and reporting, newspapers are overwhelmingly the most important media." But newspapers are purposely dumbing down, responding to Wall Street's insatiable appetite for rates of return far beyond reasonable. Meanwhile, despite some initial promise following the shock of 9/11, television has returned to its tabloid ways, chasing celebrities and murderers—preferably both at the same time—while its pundits wallow in a self-referential view of the world.

Worrying about the loss of real news is not a romantic cliché of journalism. It has been verified by history: from the days of royal absolutism to the present, the control of information and knowledge had been the first line of defense for failed regimes facing public unrest.

The suppression of parliamentary dissent during Charles I's "eleven years tyranny" in England (1629–40) rested largely on government censorship operating through strict licensing laws for the publication of books. The Federalists' infamous Sedition Act of 1798 sought to quell Republican insurgency by making it a crime to publish "false, scandalous, and malicious writing" about the government or its officials.

In those days, governing bodies attacked journalistic freedom with the blunt instruments of the law—padlocks for the presses and jail cells for outspoken editors and writers. Over time, with spectacular wartime exceptions, the courts and the Constitution have struck those weapons out of their hands. But now they've found new methods, in the name of "national security" and even broader claims of "executive privilege." The number of documents stamped "Top Secret," "Secret," or "Confidential" has accelerated dramatically since 2001, including many formerly accessible documents that have now been reclassified as secret.

Beyond what is officially labeled secret or privileged information, the plantation harbors a culture of official manipulation, working through favored media insiders, to advance political agendas by leak, innuendo, and spin. There are, for example, those misnamed public information offices that churn out blizzards of factually selective releases on a daily basis. As we saw in the run-up to the invasion of Iraq, the plantation mentality that governs Washington turned much of the press corps into sitting ducks for government and neoconservative propaganda. There were notable exceptions—Knight Ridder's bureau, for one—but on the whole all high-ranking officials had to do was say it, and the press repeated it until it became gospel. The height of myopia came with the admission by a prominent Beltway anchor that he felt it his responsibility to provide officials a forum to be heard. The watchdog group Fairness and Accuracy in Reporting found that during the three weeks leading up to the invasion, only 3 percent of U.S. sources on the evening news of ABC, CBS, NBC, CNN, FOX, and PBS expressed skeptical opinions of the impending war. Two years after 9/11, almost 70 percent of the public still thought it likely that Saddam Hussein was personally involved in the terrorist attacks of that day. An Indiana schoolteacher told *The Washington Post*, "From what we've heard from the media, it seems like what they feel is that Saddam and the whole Al Qaeda thing are connected." With a cuckolded media, the administration assured that a large majority of the public shared this erroneous view during the buildup to the war—a propaganda feat that Saddam himself would have envied. It is stunning—and frightening—how major media organizations were willing, even solicitous, hand puppets of a state propaganda campaign, cheered on by the partisan ideological press that was pumping for war.

There are other ways the plantation mentality keeps reality from Americans. Compared to the magnitude of the problem, the average person knows little about how money determines policy. Polls tell us that most people generally assume that money controls our political system. But people will rarely act on something they understand only in the abstract. It took a constant stream of images—water hoses, dogs, and churches ablaze—for the public at large finally to understand what was happening to black people in the South. It took repeated scenes of devastation in Vietnam before the majority of Americans saw how we were destroying the country to save it. And it took repeated crime-scene images to maintain public support for many policing and sentencing policies. Likewise, people have to see how money in politics actually works, and concretely grasp the consequences for their pocketbooks and their lives, before they will act. Our press supplies almost nothing that would reveal who really wags the world, and how. When I watch one of those faux debates on a Washington public affairs show, with one politician saying this is a bad bill and the other politician saying this is a good bill,

I yearn to see the smiling, nodding Beltway anchor suddenly interrupt and insist: "Good bill or bad bill, this is a *bought* bill. Whose financial interest are you serving here?"

Then there are the social costs of "free trade." For more than a decade, free trade has hovered over the political system like a biblical commandment, striking down anything that gets in the way of unbridled greed. Like dominoes they have fallen: trade unions, environmental protections, indigenous rights, even the constitutional standing of our own laws passed by our elected representatives. The broader negative consequence of this agenda—increasingly well documented by scholars—gets virtually no attention in the dominant media. Instead we get optimistic scenarios of coordinated global growth, and instead of substantive debate, we get a stark, formulaic choice between free trade to help the world and gloomy-sounding "protectionism" that will set everyone back.

The degree to which this has become a purely ideological debate, devoid of any factual basis that can help people weigh net gains and losses, is reflected in Thomas Friedman's astonishing claim, stated not long ago in a television interview, that he endorsed the Central American Free Trade Agreement without even reading it—that is, simply because it stood for "free trade." No questions asked.

It is not indifference or laziness or incompetence that plagues the press, but simply the fact that most journalists on the plantation have so internalized conventional wisdom they simply accept the system is working as it should.

Similarly, the question of whether our political and economic system is truly just or not is off the table for investigation and discussion by our dominant media elites. Alternative ideas, alternative critiques, alternative visions rarely get a hearing, and uncomfortable realities—growing inequality, the resegregation of our public schools, the devastating onward march of environmental deregulation—are obscured because independent sources of knowledge and analysis are so few and far between.

So if we need to know what is happening, and Big Media won't tell us; if we need to know why it matters, and Big Media won't tell us; if we need to know what to do about it, and Big Media won't tell us—it's clear what we have to do: we have to tell the story ourselves.

This is what the plantation owners have always feared. Over all those decades in the South when they used human beings as chattel and quoted scripture to justify it, they secretly lived in fear that one day, instead of saying, "Yes, Massa," those gaunt, weary, sweat-soaked field hands bending low over the cotton under the burning sun would suddenly stand up straight, look around at their stooped and sweltering kin, and announce: "This can't be the product of intelligent design. The boss man's been lying to me. Something is wrong with this system."

This is the moment freedom begins—the moment you realize someone else has been writing your story and it's time you took the pen from his hand and started writing it yourself. When the garbage workers struck here in 1968, and the walls of these buildings echoed with the cry "I am a man," they were writing their own story. Martin Luther King Jr. came here to help them tell it, only to die on the balcony of the Lorraine Motel. The bullet killed him, but it couldn't kill the story. You can't kill the story once the people start writing it.

I'm back now where I started—with you and with your movement. The greatest challenge to the plantation mentality of the media giants is the innovation and expression made possible by the digital revolution. I may still prefer the newspaper for its investigative journalism and in-depth analysis, but we now have in our hands the means to tell a different story than Big Media tells. I mean the *other* story of America that says free speech is not just corporate speech, that news is not just what officials say it is, that people are not just chattel in the field, living the boss man's story. This is the real gift of the digital revolution. The Internet, and cell phones and digital cameras that can transmit images over the Internet, make possible a nation of storytellers—every citizen a Tom Paine. Let the man in the big house on Pennsylvania Avenue think that over. And the woman of the House on Capitol Hill. And the media moguls in their chalets at Sun Valley, gathered to review the plantation's assets and multiply them. Nail it to the door—they no longer own the copyright to America's story; it's not a top-down story anymore. Other folks are going to write the story from the ground up and the truth will be out, that the media plantation, like the cotton plantation of old, is not divinely sanctioned, and it's not the product of natural forces.

Robert McChesney has eloquently reminded us how each medium—radio, television, and cable—was hailed as a technology that would give us greater diversity of voices, serious news, local programs, and lots of public service for the community. But in each the advertisers took over. More than one hundred times in the Communications Act of 1934 you will read the phrase "public interest, convenience and necessity." Educators, union officials, religious leaders, parents were galvanized by the promise of radio as "a classroom for the air," serving the life of the country and the life of the mind. Then the media lobby cut a deal with the government to make certain nothing would threaten the already vested interests of emerging radio networks and the advertising industry. What happened to radio then happened subsequently to television and to cable, and if we are not diligent, it will happen to the Internet. We will end up with a media plantation for the twenty-first century dominated by the same corporate and ideological forces that produced the system we have today.

Twice now you've shown us what can be done to confront the plantation owners. Four years ago when FCC chairman Michael Powell and his ideological sidekicks decided that it was OK if a single corporation owned a community's major newspaper, three of its TV stations, eight radio stations, its cable-TV system, and its major broadband Internet provider, you said, "Enough's enough." Free Press, Common Cause, Consumers Union, Media Access Project, the National Association for Hispanic Journalists, and others, working closely with commissioners Jonathan Adelstein and Michael Copps, began organizing public hearings across the country. People spoke up about how poorly the media was serving their communities. You flooded Congress with petitions. You never let up. When the court said Chairman Powell had to back off, the decision cited the importance of involving the public in these media decisions. Incidentally, Powell not only backed off, he backed out. He left the commission to become "senior adviser" at a "private investment firm specializing in equity investments in media companies around the world." That firm made a bid to take over both the Tribune and Clear Channel, two mega-media companies that just a short time ago were under the corporate friendly purview of . . . you guessed it . . . Michael Powell. That whishing sound you hear is Washington's perpetually revolving door, through which they come to serve the public and through which they leave to join the plantation.

You showed that the public cares about media and democracy. You turned a little-publicized vote on a seemingly arcane regulation into a big political fight and public debate. It's true, as Commissioner Copps has reminded us, that since that battle three years ago, more than 3,300 TV and radio stations have had their assignment and transfer grants approved. Even under the old rules, consolidation grows, localism suffers, and diversity dwindles. It's also true that even as we speak Michael Powell's successor, Kevin Martin, put there by President Bush, is ready to take up where Powell left off and give the green light to more conglomeration. So get ready to fight.

More recently you lit a fire under citizens to put Washington on notice that it had to guarantee the Internet's First Amendment protection in the telecom industry. Because of you, the so-called Internet neutrality—I prefer to call it the "equal access" provision of the Internet—became a public issue that once again reminded the powers that be that people want the media to foster democracy. This is crucial because in a few years virtually all media will be delivered by high-speed broadband, and without equality of access the Net could become just like cable television, where the provider decides what you see and what you pay.

Inside the Beltway plantation, the media thought the merger between Bell South and AT&T—the largest telecommunications merger in our history—was on a fast track for approval. After all, the Bush Department of Justice had blessed the deal last October without a single condition or statement of concern. But they hadn't reckoned with Michael Copps and Jonathan Adelstein and with this movement. Free Press and SavetheInternet.com orchestrated eight hundred organizations, 1.5 million petitions, countless local events, legions of homemade videos, smart collaboration with allies in industry, and a top-shelf communications campaign. Who would have imagined that sitting together in the same democratic broadband pew would be the Christian Coalition, Gun Owners of America, Common Cause, and MoveOn.org? Who would have imagined that these would link arms with some of the most powerful "new media" companies to fight for the Internet's First Amendment ground?

We owe a tip of the hat to Republican commissioner Robert McDowell. Despite what must have been a great deal of pressure from his side, he did the honorable thing and removed himself from the proceedings because of a conflict of interest. So AT&T had to cry "uncle" to Copps and Adelstein with a "voluntary commitment" to honor equal access for at least two years. The agreement marks the first time that the federal government has imposed true neutrality—equal access—requirements on an Internet access provider since the debate erupted almost two years ago. You changed the terms of the debate. It is no longer about whether equality of access will govern the future of the Internet; it's about when and how. It also signals a change from defense to offense for the backers of an open Net. Arguably the biggest, most effective online organizing campaign ever conducted on a media issue can now turn to passing good laws rather than always having to fight to block bad ones. Senator Byron Dorgan, a Democrat, and Senator Olympia Snowe, a Republican, introduced the Internet Freedom Preservation Act in January 2007 to require fair and equitable access to all content. And over in the House, those champions of the public interest—Edward Markey and Maurice Hinchley—will be leading the fight.

I bring this up for a reason. Big Media is ravenous. It never gets enough, it always wants more, and it will stop at nothing to get it. Last week on his Web site MediaChannel.org, Danny Schechter recalled how some years ago he marched with a band of media activists to the headquarters of all the Big Media companies concentrated in the Times Square area. Their formidable buildings, fronted with logos and limos and guarded by rent-a-cops, projected their power and prestige. Danny and his cohorts chanted and held up signs calling for honest news and an end to exploitative programming. They called for diversity and access for more perspectives. "It felt good," Danny said, but "seemed like a fool's errand. We were ignored, patronized, and marginalized. We couldn't shake their edifices or influence their holy 'business models'; we seemed to many like that lonely and forlorn nut in a *New Yorker* cartoon carrying an 'end of the world is near' placard."

Well, yes, that's exactly how they want us to feel—as if media and democracy are a fool's errand. To his credit, Danny didn't buy it. He's never given up. Neither have some of the earlier pioneers in this movement—Andy Schwartzman, Don Hazen, Jeff Chester. Let me confess that I came very close to not making this speech today, in favor of just getting up here and reading from this book—*Digital Destiny*, by Jeff Chester. Make this your bible. As Don Hazen writes in his review on Alternet this week, it's a "respectful, loving, fresh, intimate comprehensive history of the struggles for a 'democratic media'—the lost fights, the opportunities missed, and the small victories that have kept the corporate media system from having complete carte blanche over the communications channel."

It's also a scary book. Jeff describes how "we are being shadowed online by a slew of software digital gumshoes working for Madison Avenue. Our movements in cyberspace are closely tracked and analyzed. And interactive advertising infiltrates our unconsciousness to promote the 'brandwashing of America.' " Jeff asks the hard questions: Do we really want television sets that monitor what we watch? Or an Internet that knows what sites we visit and reports back to advertising companies? Do we really want a media system designed mainly for advertisers?

But this is also a hopeful book. Here's a man who practices what the Italian philosopher Gramsci called "the pessimism of the intellect and the optimism of the will." Jeff Chester sees the world as it is and tries to change it despite what he knows. So you'll find here the core of this movement's mission.

But as the Project in Excellence concluded in its State of the Media Report for 2006, "At many old-media companies, though not all, the decades-long battle at the top between idealists and accountants is now over. The idealists have lost." The commercial networks are lost, too—lost to trivia, farce, and ideology. Not much hope there. Can't raise the dead. So other ways must be secured if the public is to have access to diverse, independent, and credible sources of information. That means going to the market to find support for stronger independent media. (Michael Moore and others have proved progressivism doesn't have to equal penury.) It means helping to protect news gathering from predatory forces. It means fighting for more participatory media, hospitable to a full range of expression. It means building on Lawrence Lessig's notion of the creative common and Brewster Kahle's Internet archives with the philosophy of universal access to all knowledge. It means bringing broadband service to those many millions of Americans who are too poor to participate in the digital revolution. It means ownership for women and people of color. It means reclaiming public broadcasting and restoring it to its original robust and fearless mission as an alternative to the dominant media, offering journalism you can't ignore, public affairs of which you're a part, and a wide range of civic and cultural discourse that leaves no one out. We need to remind people that the federal commitment to public broadcasting in this country is about $1.50 per capita compared to $28 to $85 per capita in other democracies.

That's quite an agenda, and there's no assurance you will succeed. The armies of the Lord are up against mighty hosts. But as the spiritual leader Thomas Merton wrote to an activist grown weary and discouraged while protesting the Vietnam War: "Do not depend on the hope of results . . . concentrate on the value . . . and the truth of the work itself."

And in case you do get lonely, I'll leave you with this.

As my plane was circling Memphis the other day I looked out across those vast miles of fertile soil that once were plantations watered by the Mississippi River and the sweat from the brows of countless men and women who had been forced to live someone else's story. I thought about how in time they rose up—one here, then two, then many—forging a great movement that summoned America's conscience and brought us close to the elusive but beautiful promise of the Declaration of Independence. As we made our last approach to land, the words of a Marge Piercy poem began to form in my head, and I remembered all over again why we were coming here.

> What can they do
> to you? Whatever they want.
> They can set you up, they can
> bust you, they can break
> your fingers, they can
> burn your brain with electricity,
> blur you with drugs till you
> can't walk, can't remember, they can
> take your child, wall up
> your lover. They can do anything
> you can't stop them
> from doing. How can you stop
> them? Alone, you can fight,
> you can refuse, you can
> take what revenge you can
> but they roll over you.

> But two people fighting
> back to back can cut through
> a mob, a snake-dancing file
> can break a cordon, an army
> can meet an army.

> Two people can keep each other
> sane, can give support, conviction,
> love, massage, hope, sex.
> Three people are a delegation,
> a committee, a wedge. With four
> you can play bridge and start
> an organization. With six

you can rent a whole house,
eat pie for dinner with no
seconds, and hold a fund raising party.
A dozen make a demonstration.
A hundred fill a hall.
A thousand have solidarity and your own newsletter;
ten thousand, power and your own paper;
a hundred thousand, your own media;
ten million, your own country.

It goes on one at a time,
it starts when you care
to act, it starts when you do
it again after they said no,
it starts when you say We
and know who you mean, and each
day you mean one more.*

*Marge Piercy, "The Low Road," *The Moon Is Always Female* (New York: Alfred A. Knopf, 1980).

25. | JOURNALISM MATTERS

Annual Conference of the
Association for Education in Journalism
and Mass Communication

AUGUST 9, 2007

In the buildup to the invasion of Iraq we learned what the late, great reporter A. J. Liebling meant when he described the press as "the weak slat under the bed of democracy." The slat broke after the invasion and some strange bedfellows fell to the floor: establishment journalists, neocon polemicists, rightwing warmongers masquerading as fair and balanced, administration flaks leaking lies as classified secrets—all romping on the same mattress in the foreplay to disaster. Five years, thousands of casualties, and hundreds of billion dollars later, most of the media co-conspirators caught in flagrante delicto are still prominent, still celebrated, and still holding forth with no more contrition than a weathercaster who has made a wrong prediction as to the next day's temperature. "Go, and sin no more!" is the biblical injunction most frequently ignored by the press. Collectively, we never seem to learn. As the presidential nomination races began to roll out in 2007, the Pew Research

Center found that two-thirds of all political stories—in print, online, and on television and radio—concentrated on the horse race at the expense of examining the candidates' public records. The study concluded that the coverage had been sharply at odds with what the public says it wants, as voters are eager to know more about the candidates' positions on issues and their personal backgrounds, more about lesser-known candidates, and more about debates. "Only 12 percent of the stories seemed relevant to voters' decision making; the rest were more about tactics and strategy," The New York Times noted. There are always exceptions to whatever our latest dismal collective performance yields—America produces some world-class journalism, including coverage of the Iraq war by men and women as brave as Ernie Pyle—but I still wish we had some kind of professional oath, a Hippocratic vow of our own, that might haunt us in the night when we stray from our mission. My friend Michael Winship, president of the Writers Guild, recently reminded me of the prescience of the late Walter Lippmann, the ultimate Washington journalistic insider, who described journalism as "the last refuge of the vaguely talented" (ouch!). Nonetheless, Lippmann also acknowledged that while the press may be a weak reed on which to lean, it is the indispensable support for democracy:

> In an exact sense the present crisis of western democracy is a crisis of journalism . . . Everywhere today men are conscious that somehow they must deal with questions more intricate than any that church or school had prepared them to understand. Increasingly they know that they cannot understand them if the facts are not quickly and steadily available . . . All that the sharpest critics of democracy have alleged is true, if there is no steady supply of trustworthy and relevant news. Incompetence and aimlessness, corruption and disloyalty, panic and ultimate disaster, must come to any people which is denied an assured access to the facts.

So it is that for all the blunders for which we are culpable, for all the disillusionment that has set in among journalists with every fresh report of job cuts and disappearing news space, for all the desecration especially visited on broadcast journalism by the commercial networks, for all the nonsense to which so many aspiring young journalists are consigned, and for all the fears that corporate behavior is eroding the quality of the craft, I still answer em-

phatically when young people ask, "Should I go into journalism today?" Sometimes it is difficult to urge them on, especially when serious questions are being asked about how loyal our society is to the reality as well as the idea of an independent and free press. But I almost always answer, "Yes—if you have a fire in your belly, you can still make a difference." I try to explain my answer in this speech to the Association for Education in Journalism and Mass Communication—the teachers who often light that fire.

* * *

Half a century ago my own journalism teachers—Selma Brotze in high school, Cecil Shuford and Jim Rogers at North Texas State, and Dewitt Reddick and Paul Thompson at the University of Texas—stoked my passion for journalism, as you do for so many young people today.

That passion bloomed early. In 1950, on my sixteenth birthday, I went to work for the daily newspaper in the small East Texas town where I grew up—the *Marshall News Messenger*. It was a good place to be a cub reporter—small enough to navigate but big enough to keep me busy and learning something every day. I soon had a stroke of good luck. Some of the old-timers were on vacation or out sick, and I was assigned to cover what came to be known as the "Housewives' Rebellion." Fifteen women in my hometown decided not to pay the Social Security withholding tax for their domestic workers. They argued that Social Security was unconstitutional, that imposing it was taxation without representation, and that—here's my favorite part—"requiring us to collect [the tax] is no different from requiring us to collect the garbage." They hired themselves a lawyer but lost the case and wound up holding their noses and paying the tax.

I've thought over the years about those women and the impact their story had on my life and on my journalism. They were regulars at church, their children were my friends, many of them were active in community affairs, and their husbands were pillars of the business and professional class in town. They were respectable and upstanding citizens. So it took me a while to figure out what had brought on their spasm of reactionary rebellion. It came to me one day many years later. Fiercely loyal to their families, to their clubs, charities, and congregations—fiercely loyal, in other words, to their own kind—they narrowly defined democracy to include only people like themselves. The women who washed and ironed their laundry, wiped their children's bottoms, made their husband's beds, and cooked their families' meals, these women too would grow old and frail, sick and decrepit, lose their men and face the ravages of time alone, with nothing to show from their years of labor but the crease in their brow and the knots on their knuckles.

My life and work were marked by this experience. In time I came to realize that small revolt in Marshall, Texas, embodied the oldest story in America: the struggle to determine whether "We the People" is a political reality—one nation, indivisible—or merely an economic arrangement masquerading as piety and manipulated by the powerful and privileged to sustain their own way of life at the expense of others.

Some of the stories I wrote about the housewives were picked up by the Associated Press. One day the managing editor, Spencer Jones, called me over and pointed to the AP ticker beside his desk. Moving across the wire was a notice citing the *News Messenger* for our reporting. I was hooked. I went off to college two years later with enough experience to land a job working for the school's news office. The spring of my sophomore year I wrote a letter to Senator Lyndon B. Johnson, whom I'd never met, and said I wanted to become a political journalist; could he teach me something about politics? I spent the summer in Washington and then at his urging transferred to the University of Texas where I attended classes full-time and worked overtime at the Johnsons' radio and television station. We were the first in Texas to buy a station wagon, paint it red, and christen it—what else?—Red Rover. I wheeled around town in style, broadcasting from crime scenes and accidents and the state legislature, which some people said was the biggest crime scene in town.

My path led me on to graduate school, through seminary, and in 1960 back to Washington, where I helped organize the Peace Corps before the assassination of John Kennedy thrust Lyndon Johnson into the

White House and me with him. I left in 1967 to become publisher of *Newsday* until it was sold to the *Los Angeles Times*, and then made the leap from print to television, to PBS and CBS and back again to public television—one of those vagrant journalistic souls who, intoxicated with the moment, is always looking for the next high: the lede yet to be written, the photo yet to be taken, the interview yet to be conducted, the story yet to be told.

I mention all this not to review my CV with the intention of applying for an adjunct position—although don't count that out—but to put in perspective what I want to say about the changing landscape of journalism. Before he became a celebrated humorist Robert Benchley was a student at Harvard. He arrived at his final examination in international law to find the test consisted of one question: "Discuss the abstract of the international fisheries protocol and dragnet and procedure as it affects (A) the point of view of the United States and (B) the point of view of Great Britain." Benchley was desperate but he was also honest. He wrote: "I know nothing of the point of view of Great Britain in regard to the arbitration of the international fisheries problem and nothing of the point of view of the U. S. I will therefore discuss the issue from the point of view of the fish."

Here's the point of view of one small fish in the vast ocean of media.

Journalism's been a good life for me. A continuing course in adult education—my own. It enabled me to cover the summits of world leaders and the lives of poor people in Newark. I was paid richly as a CBS news analyst to put in my two cents' worth on just about anything that had happened that day. I produced documentaries on issues and subjects that fascinated me—from money in politics to the Chinese experience in America, the history of the Hudson River, the power of myth, and the making of a poem. With journalism came a passport into the world of ideas—my favorite beat. I've enjoyed the sometimes intimidating privilege of talking to some of the wisest and sanest people around—scientists, historians, scholars, philosophers, artists, and writers—and asking them important questions: Why is there something instead of nothing? What do we mean by a moral life? Can we learn to be creative?

One of my favorite questions of all—what does it mean to be a Texan?—I put to the sainted writer, raconteur, and radio personality John Henry Faulk shortly before his death in 1990. Faulk was the popular CBS radio host hounded by the right wing out of his job and into court where he won an important case. John Henry told me the story of how he and his friend Boots Cooper were playing in the chicken house behind their homes in central Texas when they were about twelve years old. They spied a chicken snake in the top tier of nests, so close it looked like a boa constrictor. John Henry said, "All our frontier courage drained out of our heels—actually, it trickled down our overall legs—and Boots and I made a new door through the henhouse wall." John Henry's momma came out and, learning what all the fuss was about, said to the boys, "Don't you know chicken snakes are harmless? They can't hurt you!" And Boots, rubbing his forehead and behind at the same time, said, "Yes, Mrs. Faulk, I know that, but they can scare you so bad, it'll cause you to hurt yourself."

That's an important lesson to teach your students. I had to work hard at times to remember it. After the early twists and turns that put me in the White House as LBJ's press secretary, it took me a while to get my footing back in journalism. I had to learn all over again that what's important for the journalist is not how close you are to power but how close you are to reality. I would touch that reality in assignment after assignment, from reporting on famine in Africa and guerrilla war in Central America to documentaries about working families in Wisconsin ravaged by global economics and corporate cruelty.

I also had to relearn another of journalism's basic lessons. The job of trying to tell the truth about people whose job it is to hide the truth is almost as complicated and difficult as trying to hide it in the first place. One of my mentors told me that "news is what people want to keep hidden; everything else is publicity." When you're digging for what's hidden, unless you're willing to fight and refight the same battles until you turn blue in the face, drive your colleagues nuts going over every last detail to make certain you've got it right, and then take hit after unfair hit accusing you of bias, there's no use even trying. You have to love it, and

I do. But I have had to keep telling myself to remember John Henry Faulk's counsel: Don't spook!

When the Washington producer Sherry Jones and I reported the first documentary ever about the purchase of influence by political action committees, we unfurled across the Capitol grounds yard after yard of computer printouts listing campaign contributions to every member of Congress. On that printout were names of politicians who had been allies just a few years earlier when I worked at the White House. Some of them were even supporters in Congress of public television, and they were outraged at our transgression. They made themselves heard to PBS.

The story told of the medieval knight who returns to the castle after a long absence. He rides back through the gate with his helmet battered, his shield dented and broken, and his horse limping. The master of the castle looks down from the parapet and shouts, "Sir Knight, what has happened to you?" And the knight answers, "Oh, Sire, I've been pillaging and plundering your enemies to the east and the west." The lord of the castle looks down at him puzzled and says, "But I have no enemies to the east and the west." And the knight answers, "Now you do." Well, I'm here to tell you we journalists have enemies, too.

Later, when Sherry and I went digging into the Iran-Contra scandal for our documentary *High Crimes and Misdemeanors*, Washington's right-wing vigilantes ran to their allies in Congress who accused PBS of committing in public the terrible sin—horrors!—of journalism. The Clinton White House also complained after we reported on the unbridled and illegal fund-raising by Democrats in the 1996 campaign.

But taking on political scandal is nothing compared to what can happen if you raise questions about corporate power in Washington. When the indomitable producer Marty Koughan and I started looking into the subject of pesticides and food for a *Frontline* documentary, Marty learned that the industry was attempting behind closed doors to dilute the findings of a National Academy of Sciences study on the effects of pesticide residues on children. The industry heard we were poking around and mounted a sophisticated and expensive campaign to discredit our broadcast before it aired. Television reviewers and the edito-

rial pages of key newspapers were flooded with allegations and innuen-
dos. It was a steady whispering campaign, difficult to discern and confront. A columnist for *The Washington Post* took a dig at the broadcast
without even seeing it and later admitted to me that the dirt had
been supplied by a top lobbyist for the chemical industry, who was his
neighbor. The industry even prepared letters, which some nervous public television station managers signed and sent to PBS in Washington
protesting a film they hadn't even seen. My colleagues at PBS stood
firm—even though some of those snakes were boa constrictors—and the
documentary aired, the journalism held up, and the National Academy
of Sciences was emboldened to release the study that the industry had
tried to stifle.

But win the battle, and war goes on. Sherry Jones and I spent more
than a year working on another documentary called *Trade Secrets*. This
one was a two-hour special based on revelations—found in the industry's
own archives—that big chemical companies had deliberately withheld
from workers and consumers damaging information about toxic chemi-
cals in their products. These internal documents were a fact. What they
contained was not a matter of opinion or point of view. You could read
right there in the industry's own records what the companies knew,
when they knew it, and what they did with what they knew—which was
to bury it.

The facts portrayed a deep and pervasive corruption in a major
American industry and raised profound implications for public policy.
When the companies got wind of what we were doing, they sharpened
their hatchets and went to work. They hired a public relations firm here
in town noted for using private detectives and former CIA, FBI, and
drug enforcement personnel to investigate competitors and critics. One
of the firm's founders is on record boasting of using "unconventional"
methods—including deceit—on behalf of his clients. To say they tried
to smear the messenger is an understatement. To complicate matters, the
single biggest congressional recipient of campaign contributions from
the chemical industry was the very member of Congress whose committee had jurisdiction over public broadcasting's appropriations. We didn't

use any public funds to produce the documentary, but that didn't spare PBS from another barrage of ferocious pressure. Nonetheless, *Trade Secrets* aired—every fact documented—and a year later the National Academy of Television named it the outstanding investigative documentary of the year.

Nowadays journalists who try to dig up what's hidden still bring down on themselves the opprobrium of government and corporations. But they must also face the wrath of right-wing media whose worldview is to see a liberal lurking behind every fact. Journalism is under withering fire these days from ideologues—those true believers who have closed their minds to all contrary evidence and hung a sign on the door with the words: DO NOT DISTURB. Any journalist whose reporting dares to challenge the party line becomes a candidate for Guantánamo. Rush Limbaugh, notably, railed against journalists for their reporting on the torture at Abu Ghraib, which he dismissed as a little sport for soldiers under stress. He told his audience: "This is no different from what happens at the Skull and Bones initiation . . . You ever heard of people [who] need to blow off some steam?" The Limbaugh line became a drumbeat in the right-wing echo chamber from which many millions of American now get their news. So I wasn't surprised to read that nationwide survey by the *Chicago Tribune* in which half of the respondents said there should have been some kind of press restraint on reporting about the prison abuse and just as many said they "would embrace government controls of some kind on free speech, especially if it is found unpatriotic."

Imagine: free speech as sedition.

Tell your students: silence is sedition.

Those of you who saw our documentary *Buying the War* know that journalists who tried to challenge the administration's fabricated evidence for invading Iraq found the patriot police on their tail. Whatever Kool-Aid he's brewing for *The Wall Street Journal,* Rupert Murdoch could make a singular contribution to journalism simply by uncoupling Fox News from the Republican fog machine and giving it the mandate to report reality instead of attacking those who do. For sure we'd get more real news—what Richard Reeves calls "the news you and I need to keep our freedoms."

I know you have some sleepless nights over what's happening to journalism. I do. A vigorous struggle for the survival of professional journalistic values is playing out with particular intensity inside the walls of your universities. The former *Washington Post* correspondent Neil Henry, now teaching at Berkeley, writes about this in his book *American Carnival: Journalism Under Siege in an Age of New Media*. He says that those of you in education "are in a constant state of flux, fighting to stay current with evolving industry demands and technological innovation while also seeking to protect the primacy of traditional standards in a world where such values are either misguided or threatened."

Because you are on the front lines of that struggle and know the issues well, I won't belabor the obvious. But no day passes without a reminder of it. Last Sunday I picked up my copy of *The New York Times* at the corner newsstand. The price had gone up to $4 from $3.50. There on the front page, below the fold, was a small box that read:

> Starting Monday, *The Times* is reducing the width of its pages by an inch and a half, to the national newspaper 12-inch standard. The move cuts newsprint expenses and, in some printing press locations, makes special configurations unnecessary. Slight modifications in design preserve the look and texture of *The Times*, with all existing features and sections and somewhat fewer words per page.

There you have the sign of the times: more money, less news. The rest is commentary—the loss of advertising, the consumer migration to digital media, changing viewer habits, shorter attention spans. With the rise of three-minute YouTube clips, I find myself thinking about the late Saul Bellow's prophesy during an interview I did with him two decades ago. He said the day would come when "no one will be heard who does not speak in short bursts of truth." Something will be lost. *Buying the*

War was a ninety-minute documentary that took almost fifteen months to produce. Our exposé *Trade Secrets* took a year. Knight Ridder's journalists Jonathan Landay and Warren Strobel needed weeks to gather, and then space to lay out, the evidence that challenged the official view of reality leading up to the Iraq war. For reporters time is the most valuable thing you invest; for Wall Street, the only measure is money.

You can read in the morning's paper of the latest casualties from Wall Street's assault on the newsroom. Starting last Thursday and continuing this week, managers at the *Orange County Register* have been tapping staffers on the shoulders and asking them to leave. The editor told them revenues are down 14 percent and profits 38 percent. Yet it was only three years ago that the owner, the privately held Freedom Communications, Inc., worked out a $1.3 billion buyout deal that saw more than half of the members of the founding family cash out their holdings. Two private equity firms—Blackstone Group and Providence Equity Partners—purchased nearly 40 percent of the shares. Now they are recouping their investment at the expense of employees. Many are longtime reporters, including fifty-year-old Michele Himmelberg, whose coverage of the National Football League helped women reporters gain access to locker rooms and won equal-access policies for all journalists. She had been working at the paper for nearly twenty-four years covering major news events and, in her words, "telling the stories of people who have shaped our community." Michele Himmelberg could be speaking for thousands of journalists when she was quoted by the *Los Angeles Times:* "News is a consumer product that will continue to be in demand. The question is, with the methods of delivery changing, how do the people who tell these stories earn a living?"

The question goes beyond newspapers. I heard this week from a talented freelance reporter in his thirties who made the media beat a specialty. He has been practicing this craft for fifteen years and loves it, but he has an offer from another field and will probably take it. He told me: "The problem in journalism isn't that there are no jobs; my students [he is an adjunct professor in a graduate journalism program] inevitably end up with great starter jobs. Most news organizations seem to prefer hiring freshly minted J-school grads and having them learn the beat anew. But that's where everything's stuck: at the starter level. As a freelancer in broadcasting, I don't have the profile in print to land big magazine assignments, the only kind that pay well. I'm at the top of NPR's freelance scales, but NPR pays freelancers dismally—I make less than $1,000 for a piece that takes four solid days to report and produce, which isn't nearly enough for a homeowner who's paying his own health premiums."

Talk to the Writers Guild about this. My colleague Michael Winship sent me the study the guild has just published describing how media conglomerates are destroying broadcast news with the same tactics other companies are using against their workers. They're cutting staff resources and replacing full-time news writers with part-timers and temps. CBS alone has cut the number of full-time news staff by about 60 percent since 1980; the budget for the CBS *Evening News,* where I succeeded Eric Sevareid as senior news analyst, was cut almost in half from 1991 to 2000. In 1989, CBS network television news employed twenty-eight researchers; ten years later, none. Half the guild members reported that at least several times a week, they use no more than a single Web site to check the accuracy of stories. Winship says that some writers are working "off the clock" to ensure that the facts are properly checked. When the guild asked its members "Do you think your news outlet spends enough time and energy making sure that your audience has enough information to make sound judgments on issues relevant to public life?" 72 percent said "Not enough" or "Not nearly enough."

Small wonder MSNBC anchor Mika Brzezinski recently tried to burn a script on the air in frustration over being asked to lead the day's news with a story about Paris Hilton rather than one about Bush's strategy in Iraq.

For an old-timer like me, this is all very sad. For young journalists it's all very confusing. That's exactly what twenty-five-year-old Steven Barrie-Anthony wrote in a recent blog on the *Huffington Post* (for which he wasn't paid). Barrie-Anthony had worked for a spell at the *Los Ange-*

les Times before winning a scholarship for further study, and now he's wrestling with a multimedia future.

Here's what he writes:

> It's a terribly confusing time to be a young journalist, but you won't hear many of us complaining out loud. Jobs are too precious, corporate owners too fickle . . .
>
> The subtext to any conversation about journalism, these days, is the effect of the Internet on newspapers and society in general. There's little question that the Web will prove deadly to major newspapers unless we figure out how to make real money from online content. Among journalists and media watchers, there's a tendency to either bemoan this development as the end of days, or to worship the ambiguous phoenix emerging from these ashes. The Net is either a democratizing force that will transcend fractious boundaries and borders and move us toward Buddhist-style interconnection, or a barrage of contagious subjectivity masquerading as objectivity and undermining the very concept of truth.
>
> As young journalists, we straddle an interesting divide: we understand well and often trumpet the virtues of traditional journalism, and yet we sheepishly get much of our news online or via *The Daily Show*. We have MySpace accounts, write blogs and read them, and have come to view Google as an extension of the brain. At this very moment I'm ignoring the advice of a Pulitzer Prize–winning journalist friend, who maintains that writing for the *Huffington Post* without getting paid is a bad use of time and energy. My inky side understands the problem with journalists working gratis—it devalues the trade—while another part of me thirsts for the immediacy, the intimacy that this venue provides . . .
>
> This is clearly the worst of times.
>
> On the other hand, I sometimes find myself delighted by all this chaos and ferment. This point could be argued that the in-

ventions of the quill and scroll, the printing press, the typewriter, the mimeograph, the ballpoint pen, the personal computer, and so forth, are in sum only half the equation in a large transformation to a written and shared conception of self and world. Now that the Internet has completed the circuit, given everybody access to an audience, the point could be argued that society has been so dramatically altered that traditional journalism . . . has been rendered largely moot.

Could this be—I dare say it—the best of times?

At almost three times his age I would no doubt strike that twenty-five-year-old as a codger, but in fact I understand the tug he's feeling. I'll make a confession to you. I start my day with Josh Marshall and end it with Jon Stewart—and both of them were on my first broadcast this year. Josh Marshall because his talkingpointsmemo.com drove the story of the firings of the federal prosecutors; without the muscle and money of the mainstream press Josh relies instead on a small underfunded network of journalists whose single-mindedness is a thing to behold and imitate. Jon Stewart because Mark Twain is alive and well on Comedy Central holding the powers that be accountable to intelligence and wit.

Whether it's the best of times or the worst, I can't say. But I remember from my seminary studies that as Adam and Eve were on their way out of the Garden he reportedly said to her: "My dear, we live in a time of transition."

So do we, and this association needs to lead the way in making sure journalists can do the best of things in the worst of times. We need to call on our field, our craft, our allies, sympathizers, and the public to address what is at stake in this new world order—because the market will not deliver to democracy the news we need to survive.

While I was at CBS News back in the 1980s, I saw firsthand the deleterious impact of Reagan-era deregulation. Television, according to the FCC chairman Mark Fowler, was just another appliance—a "toaster with pictures." Accompanying that first major wave of deregulation were changes in the ownership of the three major broadcast networks of that time. As a result of those takeovers, electronic journalism took a serious hit, with investigative reporting and serious long-form documentary programming eliminated and overseas bureaus closed. The commission today is besieged for favors on behalf of the corporations that largely control our media and telecommunications systems. These industries spend even more than the oil-and-gas lobby to influence the government. As a result we have fewer owners of the key media outlets—a trend now extending into new media as well. In addition to Murdoch's acquisition of MySpace, Google is buying the country's most important digital video distribution service, YouTube. Google is also in the process of further expanding its advertising power with the purchase of Double-Click, another leading online advertising battle. Viacom, Time Warner, Microsoft, Yahoo, and others have been collectively spending hundreds of millions to strengthen their position in the new world of broadband interactive media.

There has been breathtaking—and largely unreported—spending to acquire or merge with companies in the media and telecommunications field. In 2006, there were $72 billion worth of mergers and acquisitions in the entertainment and media sector alone, along with an array of corporate alliances involving media, technology, and distribution companies. In the first half of this year, $33.4 billion worth of mergers and acquisitions have taken place in the marketing and advertising field, according to Advertising Age.

The key to the media future, it seems, is controlling and utilizing consumer data for targeted audiences—interactive marketing to track us wherever we are and to create ever-evolving digital profiles of our interests so that "they" can send us personalized and powerful interactive messages designed to get us to behave in ways "they wish." Buy this car, vote for that candidate.

Take a look at what Advertising Age says about Murdoch's recent coup:

> A News Corp–owned Wall Street Journal begs a question: in a
> world where the attention of consumers and hence advertisers is

divided among video games, *American Idol,* and the like, can a business built solely to deliver news—especially long, serious articles about complicated topics—remain independent and successful? . . . The nation's leading purveyor of business information, still an agenda-setter for the planet's biggest economy, becomes a cog in a vertically integrated, multinational creator and distributor of entertainment, a machine engineered to pump out synergies such as *The Simpsons* movie or, more scarily, that aborted O. J. Simpson extravaganza, rather than Pulitzers . . . Sure, Mr. Murdoch will pump capital into the paper, allowing it to build out its international operation, but some are predicting that one effect of that bulking up could be to further his business goals, especially in China. And *Journal* reportage, now a means to the purist end of watch-dogging the business community, will be called upon also to add more grist to that massive multimedia content mill, in the form of the Fox business network—which is already being positioned as more pro-business than CNBC, absurd as that sounds.

You would hope that in a society where capitalism and corporations have more power than any other aggregation of human beings, the business press would bark as loud as the most vigilant watchdogs in Washington. Don't bet on it from Murdoch's empire. He flatters power to profit from it, and there's no reason to think he will change when he dominates business news.

Where, then, does journalism stand as the future of our media world is being determined by the likes of Murdoch and by business models that target us as consumers instead of citizens? Honest reporting is so essential to the food chain of democracy, we can't just throw up our hands and say that newspapers and professional journalism have to accept a fate where they become more marginalized—or made irrelevant from changes in attitudes and behaviors about media, especially from young people. But if journalism remains a vital profession, secure in its mission to report on reality without fear or favor, we need a serious, widespread, sustained public campaign for the press in democracy. You can be in the vanguard to engage the field in its mission—and to help educate and inform the public about the consequences and choices regarding the fate of journalism. We need a public debate to help light up this crossroad, one that will take us from the old media world even more fully into the new digital one.

We can't look to the conglomerates to tell us what's really going on. Except on the business page, the news media has been largely silent about the deregulation and media mergers that are happening at the expense of journalism. During the debate on the deregulatory Telecommunications Act of 1996, which included a massive giveaway of public property—the airwaves—to the TV networks and other broadcasters, television virtually ignored the story. It was newspapers without any broadcast interests that took a stand editorially against the giveaway—versus the many papers that were either silent or supported the Beltway deal to better promote their corporate agendas.

So we need to go to the public to affirm foursquare that journalism matters. Let's remind the country of the crucial role investigative reporting plays; how news bureaus abroad are a form of "national security" that can be relied on to tell us what our government won't; how as America grows more diverse, it's essential to have reporters, editors, producers, and writers who abundantly reflect those new voices and concerns; how the independent and truth-seeking journalist arms citizens with the information they need to hold the powerful accountable.

I know. I know. We're up against the odds. Ed Wasserman of Washington and Lee University writes of the "palpable sense of decline, of rot, of a loss of spine, determination, gutlessness" that pervades the field today. David Simon goes further. The former *Baltimore Sun* reporter covered urban life so brilliantly that his work inspired books and TV series such as *Homicide* and *The Wire*. Now he expresses increasing cynicism "about the ability of daily journalism to affect any kind of meaningful change." And he concludes: "One of the sad things about contemporary journalism is that it actually matters very little."

Maybe.

But Hrant Dink thought journalism matters. He edited the only Armenian newspaper in Turkey. "I want to write and ask how we can change this historical conflict into peace," he told the Committee to Protect Journalists. Dink was the target of death threats from nationalists who saw his work as an act of treachery. And on January 19 he was shot and killed outside his newspaper's offices. Hrant Dink died because journalism matters.

Sahar Hussein Ali al-Haydari thought journalism matters. Targeted twice for abduction last year, she had recovered after surgery following an assassin's attempt on her life. Later in the year a gunman killed her fiancé. Al-Haydari was investigating a suicide attack on a police station when she, too, was shot to death. Not knowing she was dead, a source called to give her more information for the story. One of the gunmen answered her phone and said to the caller: "She went to Hell." Sahar Hussein Ali al-Haydari died because journalism matters.

Luis Carlos Barbon Filho thought journalism matters. He was thirty-seven, a reporter for ten years, who drew attention in 2003 with an investigation into a child prostitution ring for his daily paper, *Realidade*. His work resulted in the arrests and conviction of four businessmen, five local politicians, and a waiter—only the waiter is still in jail. After he was forced to shut down his paper because of financial problems, two masked assailants shot him twice at close range. He died, leaving his wife a widow and his two children fatherless. Because journalism matters.

It mattered to Miguel Pérez Julca, the popular Peruvian radio commentator. His radio program, *El Informativo del Pueblo (Bulletin of the People)*, uncovered allegations of government corruption connected to local crime. For weeks he received death threats on his cell phone. Then, on March 17, two hooded gunmen shot and killed Miguel Pérez Julca in front of his wife and children. Because journalism matters.

Chauncey Bailey believed journalism matters. The editor of the *Oakland Post* was murdered a week ago on the streets of his city. The nineteen-year-old suspect told police he ambushed and killed Bailey for writing negative stories about suspicious activities at a local bakery. Fifteen hundred people turned out this week for his funeral because journalism matters.

Tell your students that journalism matters. Tell them over and again. So that no matter the medium or the technology or the odds, some of them will go out to make sure it does.

Part V

RELIGION

26. | GOD HELP US

The Charles E. Wilson Chalice Award from
Religion in American Life

JUNE 1, 2000

"Have you ever delved into the mysteries of Eastern religion?" one California weirdo asks another in the comic strip Shoe. "Yes," comes the reply. "I
was once a Methodist in Philadelphia." For a long time that was about the
extent of Americans' exposure to the varieties of religious experience. As the
scholar Diana Eck reminds us, for most of our history our religious discourse
was dominated by a culturally conservative European heritage—people like
me. Alternative visions of faith rarely reached the mainstream. That was
changing markedly as we turned the corner into the twenty-first century.
Eight of ten Americans still called themselves Christian, but the clout and
clamor of politically charged conservatives and fundamentalists masked the
reality that Christians are a far more motley lot than is represented by a media obsessed with the most vociferous voices of the Right. Other faiths were
making their presence felt, in no small part because of swelling immigration;
no itinerant journalist could fail to note the changes, especially one who finds

faith and practice as compelling a beat as politics and economics. Heading into the millennium, we were entering a new religious landscape. When the ecumenical organization Religion in American Life asked me to speak in the summer of 2000, I was urged to describe that landscape as I saw it and to raise some of the promises and perils for democracy of the emerging pluralism. I tried, but because I am a reporter, not a prophet, I did not anticipate the violent earthquake that was to shake the landscape one year after I delivered these remarks.

* * *

I take my text from Peter Shaffer's *Equus,* from the character Martin Dysart:

> I wish there was one person in my life I could show. One instinctive, absolutely unbrisk person I could take to Greece and stand in front of certain shrines and sacred streams and say, "Look! Life is only comprehensible through a thousand local gods. And not just the old dead ones with names like Zeus—no, but living Geniuses of Place and Person. And not just Greece, but modern England! Spirits of certain trees, certain curves of brick wall, certain chip shops, if you like, and slate roofs—just as of certain frowns in people and slouches" . . . I'd say to them:
>
> "Worship as many gods as you can see—and more will appear."

So it was in Greece, and now in America. We are destined to become a dynamically pluralistic society, and this is an exciting time to be a journalist interested in the life of the spirit.

Our nation is being re-created right before our eyes. Diana Eck vividly describes an America dotted with mosques—in places like Toledo, Phoenix, and Atlanta. We have huge Hindu temples—in Pittsburgh, Albany, and California's Silicon Valley. There are Sikh communities in Stockton and Queens, New York, and Buddhist retreat centers in the mountains of Vermont and West Virginia. A Buddhist American died on the *Challenger*. A Muslim American is mayor of a town in my native state of Texas. Hindu Americans are now managers of Boston, Edison, and Proctor & Gamble.

Because every religion conveys possible ways of expressing human experience and self-understanding, and because each can appear utterly incomprehensible to the other, we are facing what Gerald Burns describes as a "contest of narratives."

What is happening in America is a reflection of what is happening around the globe. In *The New York Times*, Gustav Niebuhr recently reported on how Christianity is no longer "a predominantly Western religion." The majority of Christians now live outside Europe and North America. To take one example, the *World Christian Encyclopedia* documents the fascinating migration of the Moravians, whose roots run to central Europe and to American communities that date to the eighteenth century. Of the 700,000 Moravians worldwide, half are in east Africa, in Tanzania, where the annual membership increase is more than the total Moravian membership of 50,000 in the United States. Furthermore, as Niebuhr reported, there are more missionaries at work today than ever before in history, of whom at least 100,000 are being sent out by Protestant churches in non-Western countries. Korea alone has some 8,000 Protestant missionaries serving outside the country. The religious landscape of our world is changing, too.

I would like to live long enough to cover the consequences of these transformations as the twenty-first century matures and the changes multiply. No one knows how the world's religions will co-exist as they take root in America. In my optimistic moments I imagine we might all take heed of that injunction in the Koran which says: "If we had wished we could have made you one people, but as it is, we have made you many. Therefore, vie among yourselves in good works." But I am not always optimistic. I recall that although we Americans pride ourselves on not only tolerating but also celebrating diversity, tolerance was always more the ideal than the reality. So we have to wonder whether we can avoid the intolerance, the chauvinism, the fanaticism, the bitter fruits that occur when different religions rub up against each other.

It's no rhetorical question. The religious scholar Elaine Pagels said recently that "there's practically no religion I know of that sees other people in a way that affirms the other's choice." More disturbing, we frequently have reason to remember that the first murder arose out of a religious act. Adam and Eve have two sons—the first parents to cope with what it means to raise Cain. Both brothers are rivals for God's favor so both bring God an offering. Cain, a farmer, offers the first fruits of the soil. Abel, a shepherd, offers the first lamb from the flock. Two generous gifts. But in the story God plays favorites, chooses Abel's offering over Cain's, and the elevation of the younger leads to the humiliation of the elder. Cain is so jealous that he strikes out at his brother and kills him. Their rivalry leads to violence and ends in death. Once this pattern is established, it's played out in the story of Isaac and Ishmael, Jacob and Esau, Joseph and his brothers, and down through the centuries in generation after generation of conflict between Muslims and Jews, Jews and Christians, Christians and Muslims, so that the red thread of religiously spilled blood runs directly from east of Eden to Beirut to Bosnia to Belfast—to every place in the world where brothers and believers, sisters and seekers turn from compassion to competition.

In his book *In Praise of Religious Diversity*, James Wiggins reminds us that virtually every armed conflict occurring on the planet today is explicitly driven by religious motives or by memory traces of persisting religious conflict. So we get Sunni Muslims in Afghanistan fighting a civil war with Shiite Muslims. We get fundamentalists in Algeria shooting teenage girls in the face for not wearing a veil and cutting professors' throats for teaching male and female students in the same classroom. We get Muslim suicide bombers killing busloads of Jews. And a fanatical Jewish doctor with a machine gun mowing down praying Muslims in a mosque. The young Orthodox Jew who assassinated Yitzhak Rabin declares on television: "Everything I did, I did for the glory of God." In India, Hindus and Muslims kill one another. Here in America, Muslims bomb New York's World Trade Center to smite the Great Satan. Timothy McVeigh blows up the federal building in Oklahoma City, killing 168 people, in part as revenge against the government for killing David Koresh and his followers. Groups calling themselves the Christian Identity Movement and the Christian Patriot League collect arsenals, and at a political convention in Dallas not long ago, at a so-called Christian booth in the exhibit hall, you could buy an apron with two pockets— one for the Bible and one for a gun.

Religion has a healing side; we know this. But we have been loath to admit that religion also has a killing side. In William Penn's words, "To be furious in religion is to be furiously irreligious."

So in the real world of democracy how do we cope with a thousand local gods? How do I hold my truth to be the truth when everyone else sees truth differently?

I put this question to the renowned scholar of comparative religion Huston Smith, who has spent his adult life trying to penetrate the essence of the world's great faiths. In his classic study he wrote that "religions are like rivers, dynamic and changing, bearing the heritage of the past to water the fields of the present. These rivers are converging and we need to build bridges." I asked him how we are to do this. If you saw our series *The Wisdom of Faith*, you saw Huston Smith actually thinking before he answered—one of those eloquent moments of silence that are rare on television—and then he said, "We listen. We listen as alertly to the other person's description of reality as we hope they listen to us."

This frightens some people. They fear that hearing what others have to say about faith will lead to the loss of their own distinctive tradition. They fear they may have to shed the uniqueness of their own beliefs to embrace a flimsy ecumenicism in which all religions are reduced to saying the same thing. They even imagine they will be dragged into accepting some vapid consensus of "one faith for one world."

It doesn't have to be. We saw the alternative in *Genesis*, our series produced for PBS. There were ten broadcasts over ten weeks, each devoted to one of the great stories from the first book of the Bible. A simple series, by television's standard—seven people facing one another in a circle of conversation. But none of our work on television until then had created more media response prior to broadcast than those ten discussions. All over the country people organized into groups so they could watch the programs together and then talk about them afterward. One organization alone signed up a million people just for that purpose.

Thomas Moore says conversation is "the interpretation of worlds." The people I interview provide me with a passport into an experience I would not likely enter without their invitation. Furthermore, talking with people who agree with you is like jogging in a cul-de-sac. When I was growing up in East Texas, Baptists talked about the Bible with Baptists, Presbyterians with Presbyterians, Episcopalians with Episcopalians, Methodists with Methodists, and Jews with Jews. But we never talked about the Bible across our faiths, much less across our race. It's why you could grow up even in a small town well churched, well taught, and well loved and still be ignorant of people just blocks away.

So we wanted to be sure our participants in *Genesis* didn't come from the same neighborhood. We sought out people from different backgrounds, different faiths, professional fields, age, and gender. We wanted to see if they could talk about their beliefs in public without politicizing religion or polarizing the community. We hoped to show that you can disagree passionately about things that matter without surrendering your own principled beliefs or without going for your neighbor's throat; that we can engage with others in serious conversation about the most deeply felt subjects—our religious beliefs, the nature of faith, our relationship with one another—and truly challenge one another, teach one another, and learn from one another. In a 2006 interview, Salman Rushdie told me that in a democracy all ideas—including religion—are arguable and that

> Citizens of a free society do not preserve their freedom by pussyfooting around their fellow citizens' opinions, even their most

cherished beliefs. In free societies you must have the free play of
ideas, there must be an argument, and it must be impassioned and
untrammeled. Free societies are dynamic, noisy, turbulent, and
full of radical disagreement. You can't cry foul when your ideas are
challenged, even when you assert your ideas of God.

We put that idea to the test, and it worked. Our Genesis conversations were notably enriched because we didn't all come from the same
neighborhood. Often we disagreed and sometimes the more we talked,
the more we disagreed. We were critical, even skeptical—no one was po-
litely dishonest enough to let a point pass that called for a challenge.
Talking about the issues exposed our differences, but it also brought
closer together people who had been strangers when they met. We were
constantly reminded that differences between faiths are real, not to be
papered over for reasons of protocol, but we discovered that people with
deep differences can teach and learn from one another. It's marvelous
how minds, hearts, and lives can be profoundly touched with genuine
understanding when you listen to the loves of others.

I believe that within the religious quest—in that deeper realm of
spirituality which may well be the primal origin of all religion—lies what
Gregg Easterbrook calls "an essential aspect of the human prospect."
Here we are confronted with questions of life and purpose, of meaning
and loss, of yearning and hope. We seek the answers to those questions
first in our own tradition. T. S. Eliot wrote that "no man has ever
climbed to the higher stages of the spiritual life who has not been a believer in a particular religion, or at least a particular philosophy." As I
have dug deeper into my own roots, I have come to see that all the great
religions grapple with things that matter, although each may come out
at a different place; that each arises from within and expresses a lived
human experience; and that each and every one of them deserves attention for the unique insight they offer into the human prospect. From
Buddhists I have learned about the delight of contemplation and "the
infinite within." Sufi Muslims have opened me to a deeper understanding of worship and prayer. The ancient prophets of Judaism will not al-

low me to forget the imperative of justice; from Hindus I have learned about "realms of gold hidden in the depth of our hearts"; from Confucianists about the empathy necessary to sustain the fragile web of civilization. Nothing I take from these traditions has come at the expense of my own story. Faith is not acquired in the same way you choose a meal in a cafeteria, but there is something liberating about no longer being quite so tone-deaf to what others have to report from their experience. This discovery leads us away from an ineffectual and condescending toleration of other faiths to an anticipation and engagement with them and to the understanding so beautifully expressed by Kathleen Norris when she writes: "We are all God's chosen now." In the next breath she prays, "God help us because we are."

postscript: Charles E. Wilson was the namesake of the award presented to me by Religion in American Life when I delivered this speech. The rich, successful, and powerful Charlie Wilson did not need my sympathy; he was never even aware of my existence, although my parents owned one of his Chevrolets and at the time I figured the president of General Motors kept a list in his desk drawer of every Chevrolet owner in America. Of course, we had bought ours second-hand, and I suppose even Charlie couldn't keep up with what happened to his cars once the used-car dealers took them over from the original owners. Still, I admired Wilson all the more when I joined the ROTC during my freshman year in college—the very year Eisenhower was elected president and made Wilson his secretary of defense. During confirmation hearings, the Senate Armed Services Committee pressured Wilson to sell his stock in General Motors, then worth about $2.5 million. Wilson said, sure, he would do that. Then someone asked if as secretary of defense Wilson thought he could make a decision adverse to GM, which had been one of the giants of our defense production effort during World War II and was now permanently fixed in the new solar system of what Eisenhower himself, leaving office eight years later, would call the military-industrial complex. Charlie Wilson could hardly walk through the corridors of the Pentagon without so much as a nod of his head failing to help or hurt GM, but again Charlie said, sure, he could make a decision even if it affected GM adversely. Then he made an altogether too-common mistake among confident people who appear before congressional hearings: he kept talking. He wanted the committee to know that he didn't think the problem would ever come up "because for years what was good for General Motors was good for the country and vice versa." As often happens in Washington, his remark was garbled in translation and passed into lore as the arrogant claim: "What's good for General Motors is good for the country." As someone who would later experience the chain-saw mentality of Washington, I felt sorry for Wilson as he watched his more nuanced and complex idea hurtle into history in a way he never intended. I confess to being all the more sympathetic because he was a Baptist layman. I admired his early leadership in the National Council of Churches and as a founder and chairman of Religion in American Life, whose mission was to foster church attendance, financial support, and ecumenical cooperation. Charlie would never have recognized the religious landscape at the turn of the century. And although I never met him, I suspect he would have been stunned by its transformation after 9/11.

27. | THE SPORT OF GOD

*Union Theological Seminary Presents Judith and Bill Moyers
the Union Medal*

SEPTEMBER 7, 2005

Pages of my notebook are filled with the militant language of Christian warriors "marching as to war" long before the Islamist terrorists struck on 9/11. Patrick Buchanan calls Republicans to a "holy war." Ralph Reed boasts of putting his opponents in "body bags." His surrogate announces that "only Christians can restore this nation . . . only Christian believers doing the work . . . in the thick of battle." Representative (now Senator) Charles Schumer, after a hearing on violence and harassment by militia groups, is warned: "You should make no mistake that you are a conceited, arrogant kike son of a bitch [who] will suffer physical pain and mental anguish before we transform you into something a bit more useful . . . a lampshade or wallets or perhaps soap." Right-wing terrorist Randall Terry cries, "Let a wave of hatred wash over you." Yes, yes, I know: speech is free and metaphors don't kill. Don't they? Holy war. Body bags. Thick of battle. These metaphors kill politics, culture, the soul. A little reading and you will hear in your head in the middle of the night forebears of this war-filled rhetoric echoing the crusades of Europe: feverish days when the spirit of religion was infused with toxic zeal aroused by persecuting priests and pious princes, and armed hosts, pausing just long enough to kill the Jews in Germany, rode forth to rout the "accursed race" of Turks and Arabs whose numbers stretched from Jerusalem to Constantinople. Summoned to war "against the infidels" for the cause of Christ, the crowds responded: "Deus lo vult! It is God's will." God rode at the head of their warrior columns and Jesus—the teacher Jesus who had talked of loving one's neighbor and forgiving one's enemy; who looked with compassion on the wounded and sick; who gathered to him the outcast and the stranger, the despised and forsaken; the healing Jesus, who welcomed into his embrace the frightened prostitute, forlorn leper, and hungry beggar; who invited even the loathsome tax collector to fellowship—this same Jesus was now yoked to the flashing shield and slashing sword! Yes, yes, pagans kill, and heathens and godless demagogues and dictators; and, after all, the terrorists on 9/11 weren't just shouting death, they were delivering it. But religion sanctifies, inflames, and exalts righteous murder. And in the days after 9/11 the chromosomes of fury deep in the bowels of half-grown faith cried: Deus lo vult! So coincidence or not, when Joseph Hough, the president of Union Seminary in New York City, called to say that Judith and I had been selected to receive Union's highest recognition—the President's Medal—and asked only in return that we speak what was on our minds, late that same night I opened my notebook where years ago on the flyleaf I had copied the words of Jonathan Swift:

> But mark me well; Religion is my name;
> An angel once: but now a fury grown,
> Too often talked of, but too little known.

* * *

At the Central Baptist Church in Marshall, Texas, where I was baptized in the faith, we believed in a free church in a free state. I still do.

My spiritual forebears did not take kindly to living under theocrats who embraced religious liberty for themselves but denied it to others. "Forced worship stinks in God's nostrils," thundered the dissenter Roger Williams as he was banished from Massachusetts for denying Puritan authority over his conscience. Baptists there were a "pitiful negligible minority" but they were agitators for freedom and therefore denounced as "incendiaries of the commonwealth" for holding to their belief in that great democracy of faith—the priesthood of all believers. For refusing to pay tribute to the state religion they were fined, flogged, and exiled. In 1651 the Baptist Obadiah Holmes was given thirty stripes with a three-corded whip after he violated the law and took forbidden communion with another Baptist. His friends offered to pay his fine for his release but he refused. They offered him strong drink to anesthetize the pain of the flogging. Again he refused. It is the love of liberty, he said, "that must free the soul."

Such revolutionary ideas held out the promise that America, with its Bill of Rights and Constitution that made no mention of God, would be "a haven for the cause of conscience." No longer could magistrates order citizens to support churches they did not attend and recite creeds that they did not believe. No longer would "the loathsome combination of church and state"—as Thomas Jefferson described it—be the settled order. Unlike the Old World that had been wracked with religious wars and persecution, the government of America would take no sides in the religious free-for-all that liberty would make possible and politics would make inevitable. The genius of the First Amendment is that it neither inculcates religion nor inoculates against it. Americans could be loyal to the Constitution without being hostile to God, or they could pay no heed to the Almighty without fear of being mugged by an official God Squad. It has been a remarkable arrangement honoring "soul freedom"—the inviolate right of each of us to believe and worship as our conscience determines, in a society that honors freedom over conformity.

That right is at risk.

Four years ago this week the poet's prophetic metaphor became real as "the great dark birds of history" plunged into our lives.

They came in the name of God. They came bent on murder and martyrdom. It was as if they rode to earth on the fierce breath of Allah himself, having been steeped in images of a violent and vengeful God who wills life for the faithful and horrific torment for unbelievers.

Yes, the Koran speaks of mercy and compassion and calls for ethical living. But these martyrs also found there a ferocity of instruction for waging war in God's name. The scholar Jack Nelson-Pallmeyer carefully traces this trail of holy violence in his book *Is Religion Killing Us?* He highlights many of the verses in the Koran that the Islamic terrorists could have had in their hearts and on their lips four years ago as they moved toward their gruesome rendezvous:

> Those who believe Fight in the cause of Allah, and Those who reject Faith Fight in the cause of Evil. (4:76)

> So We sent against them A furious Wind through days of disaster, that We might Give them a taste of a Penalty of humiliation In this Life; but The Penalty of the Hereafter will be More Humiliating still: And they Will find No help. (41:16)

> Then watch thou For the Day That the sky will Bring forth a kind Of smoke (or mist) Plainly visible, Enveloping the people: This will be a Penalty Grievous. (44:10-11)

> Did the people of the towns Feel Secure against the coming Of Our Wrath by night While they were asleep? Or else did they feel Secure against its coming in Broad daylight while they Played About (carefree)? Did they then feel secure Against the Plan of Allah?—But no one can feel Secure from the Plan of Allah, except those (Doomed) to ruin. (7:97-99)

So the holy warriors came—an airborne death cult, their sights on God's enemies and Paradise beyond.

In the aftermath of 9/11 I kept reminding myself not only of the horror of that day but of the humanity that was revealed when through the smoke and fire we glimpsed the heroism, compassion, and sacrifice of people who did the best of things in the worst of times. I keep telling myself that this beauty in us is real, that it makes life worthwhile and democracy work, and that no terrorist can take it from us.

But as a journalist I always look for the other side of the story. In his book *The Decline and Fall of the Roman Empire*, Edward Gibbon once wrote of historians what could be said of journalists:

> The theologians may indulge the pleasing task of describing religion as she descended from Heaven, arrayed in her native purity. A more melancholy duty is imposed on the historian [read: journalist]. He must discover the inevitable mixture of error and corruption which she contracted in a long residence upon earth, among a weak and degenerate race of beings.

The historian and the journalist, in other words, must look at religion without the halos.

Muslims have no monopoly on holy violence. As Nelson-Pallmeyer points out, God's violence in the sacred texts of both faiths reflects a deep and troubling pathology "so pervasive, vindictive, and destructive" that it contradicts and subverts the collective weight of other passages that exhort ethical behavior or testify to a loving God.

For days now we have watched those heartbreaking scenes on the Gulf Coast: the steaming, stinking, sweltering wreckage of cities and suburbs; the fleeing refugees; the floating corpses, hungry babies, and old people huddled together in death, the dogs gnawing at their feet; stranded children standing in water reeking of feces and garbage; families scattered; a mother holding her small child and an empty water jug, pleading for someone to fill it; a wife, pushing the body of her dead husband on a wooden plank down a flooded street; desperate people struggling to survive.

Now transport those current scenes from our newspapers and television back to the first book of the Bible, Genesis. The destruction wrought by Katrina brings to life what we rarely imagine so graphically when we read of the great Flood that devastated the known world in biblical times. If you read the Bible as literally true, as many do, this flood was ordered by God.

> And God said to Noah, "I have determined to make an end of all flesh . . . behold, I will destroy them with the earth." (6:5–13)

> "I will bring a flood of waters upon the earth, to destroy all flesh in which is the breath of life from under heaven; everything that is on the earth shall die." (6:17–19)

Noah and his family are the only humans spared; they were, after all, God's chosen. But for everyone else

> . . . the waters prevailed so mightily . . . that all the high mountains . . . were covered . . . And all flesh died that moved upon the earth, birds, cattle, beasts . . . and every man; everything on the dry land in whose nostrils was the breath of life, died . . . (7:17–23)

The Flood is merely Act I. Read on: this God first "hardens the heart of Pharaoh" to make sure the Egyptian ruler will not be moved by the plea of Moses to let his people go. Then because Pharaoh's heart is hardened, God turns the Nile into blood so people cannot drink its water and will suffer from thirst. Not satisfied with the results, God sends swarms of locusts and flies to torture them; rains hail and fire and thunder on them; destroys the trees and plants of the field until nothing green remains; orders every firstborn child to be slaughtered, from the firstborn of Pharaoh right on down to "the first-born of the maidservant behind the mill." The massacre continues until "there is not a house where one was not dead." While the Egyptian families mourn their dead, God or-

ders Moses to loot from their houses all their gold and silver and cloth-
ing. Finally, God's thirst for blood is satisfied, God pauses to rest—and
boasts: "I have made sport of the Egyptians."

Violence as the sport of God. God as the progenitor of shock
and awe.

And that's just Act II. As the story unfolds women and children are
hacked to death on orders from God, unborn infants are ripped from
their mother's wombs; cities are leveled—their women killed if they
have had sex, the virgins taken at God's command for the pleasure of his
holy warriors. When his holy warriors spare the lives of fifty thousand
captives God is furious and sends Moses back to rebuke them and tell
them to finish the job. One tribe after another falls to God-ordered
genocide: the Hittites, the Girgashites, the Amorites, the Canaanites,
the Perizzites, the Jebusites—names so ancient they have disappeared
into the mists. Yet they were fathers and mothers and brothers and sisters, grandparents and grandchildren, infants in arms, shepherds, thresh-
ers, carpenters, merchants, housewives—living human beings, flesh and
blood:

> And when the Lord your God gives them over to you, and you de-
> feat them; then you must utterly destroy them; you shall make no
> covenant with them, and show no mercy to them . . . (and) your
> eyes shall not pity them.

So it is written—in what to many is holy text.

Yes, I know: the early church fathers, trying to cover up the blood-
soaked trail of God's sport, decreed that anything that disagrees with
Christian dogma about the perfection of God is to be interpreted spiri-
tually.

Yes, Edward Gibbon himself acknowledged that the literal biblical
sense of God "is repugnant to every principle of faith as well as reason"
and that we must therefore read the scriptures through a veil of allegory.

Yes, we can go through the Bible and construct a God more pleas-
ing to the better angels of our nature.

Yes, Christians claim the Old Testament God of wrath was supplanted by the Gospel's God of love.

I know these things; all of us know these things. But we must also acknowledge that the "violence-of-God" tradition remains embedded deep in the tradition of monotheistic faith. There are people the world over who consider the texts to be literally God's word on all matters. Inside that logic are we to read part of the Bible allegorically and the rest of it literally? Can you believe in the virgin birth of Jesus, his crucifixion and resurrection, and the depiction of the Great Judgment at the end of times—all seen as biblically revealed—and dismiss the Bible's description of God as sadistic, brutal, vengeful, callow, cruel, and savage? Surely we must wrestle openly and honestly with the contradiction, all the more so after 9/11.

Let's go back to that day. The ruins were still smoldering when the reverends Pat Robertson and Jerry Falwell went on television to proclaim that the terrorist attacks were God's punishment of a corrupted America. They said the government had adopted the agenda "of the pagans, and the abortionists, and the feminists, and the gays and the lesbians"—not to mention the ACLU and People for the American Way. Just as God had sent the great Flood to wipe out a corrupted world, now God, disgusted with a decadent America, "is lifting his protection from us." Critics said such comments were deranged. But to their followers, Robertson and Falwell were being perfectly consistent with the logic of the Bible as they read it: God withdraws favor from sinful nations, and therefore the terrorists were meant to be God's wake-up call.

Not many people at the time seemed to notice that Osama bin Laden had also been reading his sacred book closely and literally, and had called on Muslims to resist what he described as a "fierce Judeo-Christian campaign" against Islam, praying to Allah for guidance "to exalt the people who obey Him and humiliate those who disobey Him."

Suddenly we were immersed in the pathology of a "holy war" as defined by literalists on both sides. We could see this pathology play out in General William Boykin. A professional soldier, General Boykin had taken up with a small group called the Faith Force Multiplier, whose members apply military principles to evangelism with a manifesto summoning warriors "to the spiritual warfare for souls." After Boykin had led Americans in a battle against a Somalian warlord, he announced, "I knew my God was bigger than his. I knew that my God was a real God, and his was an idol." Now Boykin was going about in fervent revivals preaching that America was in a holy war as "a Christian nation" battling Satan and that America's Muslim adversaries will be defeated "only if we come against them in the name of Jesus."

For such an hour, America surely needed a godly leader. So General Boykin explained how it was that the candidate who had lost the popular vote in 2000 nonetheless wound up in the White House. President Bush, he said, "was not elected by a majority of the voters—he was appointed by God." Instead of being reprimanded for evangelizing while in uniform, General Boykin is now the deputy undersecretary of defense for intelligence.

We can't wiggle out of this conundrum. We're talking about a powerful religious constituency that claims the right to tell us what's on God's mind and yearns to decide the laws of the land according to their interpretation of biblical revelation and to enforce those laws on the nation as a whole. For the Bible is not just the foundational text of their faith; it has become the foundational text for a political movement.

Yes, people of faith have always tried to bring their interpretation of the Bible to bear on American laws and morals. This very seminary is part of that tradition—it's the American way, encouraged and protected by the First Amendment. But what is unique today is that the religious Right has become the base of one of America's great political parties and is using God as a battering ram on almost every issue: crime and punishment, foreign policy, health care, taxation, energy regulation, and social services.

What's also unique is the intensity, organization, and anger these forces have brought to the public square. Listen to their preachers and evangelists: the loathing of other people's beliefs, of America's secular and democratic values, of an independent press and judiciary, of reason, science, and the search for objective knowledge—all have become the motivation for a sectarian crusade for state power. These people use the language of faith to demonize political opponents, mislead and misinform voters, censor writers and artists, ostracize dissenters, and marginalize the poor. They are the foot soldiers in a political holy war financed by wealthy economic interests and guided by savvy partisan operatives who know that couching political ambition in religious rhetoric can ignite the passion of followers as ferociously as when Constantine painted the sign of Christ (the "Christogram") on the shields of his soldiers and on the banners of his legions and routed his rivals in Rome. Never mind that the emperor himself was never baptized into the faith; it served him well enough to make the God said to be worshipped by Christians his most important ally and turn the sign of Christ into the one imperial symbol most widely recognized and feared from east to west.

Let's take a brief detour to Ohio and I'll show you what I am talking about. In recent weeks a movement called the Ohio Restoration Project has been launched to identify and train thousands of "Patriot Pastors" to get out the conservative religious vote in 2006. According to press reports, the leader of the movement—the senior pastor of a large church in suburban Columbus—casts the coming elections as an apocalyptic clash between "the forces of righteousness and the hordes of hell." The fear and loathing in Russell Johnson's message is palpable. He denounces public schools that won't teach creationism, require teachers to read the Bible in class, or allow children to pray. He rails against the "secular jihadists" who have "hijacked" America and prevent schoolkids from learning that Hitler was "an avid evolutionist." He links abortion to children who murder their parents. He blasts the "pagan left" for trying to redefine marriage. He declares that "homosexual rights" will bring "a flood of demonic oppression." On his church Web site you read: "Reclaiming the teaching of our Christian heritage among America's youth is paramount to a sense of national destiny that God has invested into this nation."

One of the prominent allies of the Ohio Restoration Project is a popular televangelist in Columbus named Rod Parsley who heads a $40 million-a-year ministry that is accessible worldwide via 1,400 TV stations and cable affiliates. Although he describes himself as neither Republican nor Democrat but a "Christocrat"—a gladiator for God marching against "the very hordes of hell in our society"—he nonetheless has been spotted with so many Republican politicians in Washington and elsewhere that he has been publicly described as a "spiritual adviser" to the party.

The journalist Marley Greiner has been following his ministry. She writes that because Rod Parsley considers the separation of church and state to be "a lie perpetrated on Americans—especially believers in Jesus Christ," he identifies himself as a "wall builder" and "wall buster." As a wall builder he will "restore Godly presence in government and culture; as a wall buster he will tear down the church-state wall." He sees the Christian church as a sleeping giant that has the ability and the anointing from God to transform America. The giant is stirring. At a rally in July he proclaimed to a packed house: "Let the Revolution begin!" And the congregation roared back: "Let the Revolution begin!"

The Revolution's first goal is to elect as governor next year the current God-fearing Republican secretary of state who oversaw the election process in 2004 when a surge in faith-based voters narrowly carried George W. Bush to victory. As General Boykin suggested of President Bush's anointment, this fellow has acknowledged that "God wanted him as secretary of state during 2004" because it was such a critical election. Now he is crisscrossing Ohio meeting with Patriot Pastors and their congregations proclaiming that "America is at its best when God is at its center."

The Ohio Restoration Project is spreading. In one month alone last year, in the president's home state of Texas, a single Baptist preacher added two thousand Patriot Pastors to the rolls. On his Web site he now encourages pastors to "speak out on the great moral issues of our day . . . to restore and reclaim America for Christ."

Alas, these "great moral issues" do not include building a moral economy. As the Christian Right trumpets charity (as in faith-based initiatives), the leaders of the movement are silent on justice. Inequality in America has reached scandalous proportions: a few weeks ago the government acknowledged that while incomes are growing smartly for the first time in years, the primary winners are the top earners—people who receive stocks, bonuses, and other income in addition to wages. The nearly 80 percent of Americans who rely mostly on hourly wages barely maintained their purchasing power. Even as Hurricane Katrina was hitting the Gulf Coast, giving us a stark reminder of how poverty can shove poor people into the abyss, the Census Bureau reported that one million people were added to the thirty-six million already living in poverty. And since 1999 the income of the poorest one-fifth of Americans has dropped almost 9 percent.

None of these harsh realities of ordinary life seem to bother the politically religious Right. On the contrary. In the pursuit of political power they have cut a deal with America's richest interests and their partisan allies in a law-of-the-jungle strategy to "starve" the government of resources needed for vital social services that benefit everyone while championing more and more public spending for rich corporations and larger tax cuts for the wealthy.

How else to explain the vacuum in their "great moral issues" of the plight of millions of Americans without adequate health care? Or of the gross corruption of politics by campaign contributions that skew government policies toward the wealthy at the expense of ordinary taxpayers? (On the very day that oil and gas prices reached a record high, the president signed off on huge taxpayer subsidies for energy conglomerates already gorging on windfall profits plucked from the pockets of average Americans filling up at gas stations across the country; yet the next Sunday you could pass one church signboard after another with no mention of a sermon on crony capitalism.)

This silence on economic and political morality is deafening but revealing. The religious Right has become the dominant force in America's governing party. Without them the government would not be in the hands of people who don't believe in government. They are culpable in upholding a system of class and race in which the rich thrive and the poor barely survive. And many of them are crusading not for a government of, by, and for the people but for one based on biblical authority.

This is the crux of the matter: to these believers there is only one legitimate religion and only one particular brand of that religion that is right; all others are immoral or wrong. They believe they alone know what the Bible means. Behind their attacks on the courts ("vermin in black robes," as one of their talk-show allies recently put it) is a fierce longing to hold judges accountable for interpreting the Constitution according to standards of biblical revelation as literalists define it. To get those judges they needed a party beholden to them. So the Grand Old Party—the GOP—has become God's Own Party, marching, in the words of the old hymn, "as to war."

At the Web site of an organization called America 21, on a red, white, and blue home page, there was a reminder that "There are 7,177 hours until our next National Election . . . ENLIST NOW." Click again and you could read a summons calling Christian pastors "to lead God's people in the turning that can save America from our enemies." Under the heading "Remember—Repent—Return" was language reminiscent of Pat Robertson and Jerry Falwell reminding us that "one of the unmistakable lessons [of 9/11] is that America has lost the full measure of God's pledge of protection." How is the country to be saved from the terrorists? We must "remember the legacy of our heritage under God and our covenant with Him and, in the words of II Chronicles 7:14: 'Turn from our wicked ways.' "

There, on the home page of that site, was praise for the president's political agenda, including his plans to phase out social security. The fine print on the bottom of the site read: "America 21 is a not-for-profit organization whose mission is to educate, engage, and mobilize Christians to influence national policy at every level. Founded in 1989 by a multi-denominational group of *Pastors and Businessmen*, it is dedicated to being a catalyst for revival and reform of the culture *and the government*" (emphasis added).

Reading those words, I remembered a book in my library by the late anthropologist Marvin Harris, who wrote in *America Now* that

> the attack against reason and objectivity is fast reaching the pro-
> portions of a crusade . . . We desperately need to reaffirm the prin-

ciple that it is possible to carry out an analysis of social life which rational human beings will recognize as being true, regardless of whether they happen to be women or men, whites or black, straights or gays, employers or employees, Jews or born-again Christians. The alternative is to stand by helplessly as special interest groups tear the United States apart in the name of their "separate realities" or to wait until one of them grows strong enough to force its irrational and subjective brand of reality on all the rest.

Those words were written twenty-five years ago, just as Jerry Falwell's Moral Majority was setting out on a long march for political supremacy. The forces Harris warned against have gained strength ever since and now control the executive and legislative branches of our government and intend to control the judiciary soon.

It has to be said that their success has come in no small part because of our acquiescence and timidity. Too many people of reason are willing to appease the pious on the grounds that sincere religious beliefs are beyond criticism. Democrats are afraid that if they take on the religious Right they will lose what little power they have. But they are compromising the strongest advantage in their favor—the case for a moral economy and for the checks and balances necessary to "a safe haven for the cause of conscience."

As I look back on the conflicts and clamor of our boisterous past, one lesson about democracy stands above all others: bullies—political bullies, economic bullies, and religious bullies—cannot be appeased; they have to be opposed with courage, clarity, and conviction. This is never easy. These true believers don't fight fair. *Robert's Rules of Order* is not one of their holy texts. But freedom on any front—and especially freedom of conscience—never comes to those who hesitate, hoping someone else will do the heavy lifting. Christian realism requires us to see the world as it is, without illusions, and to take it on, including the spurious claims of true believers that they speak for God.

Christian realism also requires love. I do not mean a vacuous and dreamy emotion. Reinhold Niebuhr, who taught so many years here at Union Theological Seminary where he wrestled constantly with applying Christian ethics to political life, put it this way: "When we talk about love we have to become mature or we will become sentimental. Basically love means . . . being responsible, responsibility to our family, toward our civilization, and now by the pressures of history, toward the universe of humankind."

We are called to practice that kind of love. But at the same time we must not fear taking up a robust and principled defense of secular politics against those forces that seek a monopoly over the public square. To do so would be to concede the emerging struggle between democracy and theocracy to the dogmatists who differ only in their understanding of the God who would rule when the dust settles.

Part VI

———|———

A COMMENCEMENT ADDRESS

28. | PASS THE BREAD

Hamilton College Baccalaureate Service

MAY 20, 2006

If there is a tougher audience for a journalist than a college commencement, I have yet to face it. Among the thousands of people in front of you are a variety of constituents: the graduates, whose relief at journey's end mingles with sadness at parting and anticipation at the unknown ahead of them; their parents, most of whom have sacrificed for this moment and want to celebrate its sweetness and symbolism; the faculty, who have sung the school anthem so many times on so many similar occasions that they simply mouth the indecipherable words; and the maintenance crews, eager to get it over, clean up, and go home. Your time as speaker is fixed, because the day is full, the acoustics questionable, and the attention spans waning. Yet this is a ritual with ceremonial, as well as personal, significance; it is meant for celebration. I never stand on the dais and look out across the audience without realizing that this is the only time these people will be in the same place together; they cherish the momentary closeness, are aware of its transience, and know that from here on out they will be on their own. The best thing the speaker can do is to let them know that he takes them seriously. They may pretend to be blasé about the occasion, but you know it matters to them, and you search to find that thread in their concerns that will connect the most cynical part of their being to the most idealistic. As a journalist I am honor bound to describe for them the world as I see it, without illusions; at the same time, I want them to know that even journalists celebrate joy, embrace hope, and recognize their capacity for both. Here at Hamilton College it is raining; for May—even in upstate New York—it is chilly. This "Little Ivy"—named for one of its first trustees, Alexander Hamilton—bristles with umbrellas and optimism. I had thought of keeping my speech as brief as the school motto: Know thyself. But as the procession moved down the aisle and a celebratory roar went up from friends and families of the graduates, I sensed this was no time to hurry. Soon enough they would be scattered to the four winds.

* * *

Fifty years ago I turned the same corner you are turning today and left college for the great beyond. Looking back across half a century I wish our speaker at the time had said something really useful—something that would have better prepared us for what lay ahead. Something like: "Don't go."

I'm not sure anyone from my generation should be saying anything to your generation except, "We're sorry. We're really sorry for the mess you're inheriting. We are sorry for the war in Iraq. For the huge debts you will have to pay for without getting a new social infrastructure in return. We're sorry for the polarized country. The corporate scandals. The corrupt politics. Our imperiled democracy. We're sorry for the sprawl and our addiction to oil and for all those toxins in the environment. Sorry about all this, class of 2006. Good luck cleaning it up."

You're going to have your hands full. I don't need to tell you of the gloomy scenarios being written for your time. Three books on my desk right now question whether human beings will even survive the twenty-first century. Just listen to their titles: *The Long Emergency: Surviving the Converging Catastrophes of the Twenty-First Century; Collapse: How Soci-*

eties Choose to Fail or Succeed; The Winds of Change: Climate, Weather, and the Destruction of Civilizations.

These are just three of the many recent books that make the apocalypse prophesied in the Bible look like child's play. I won't summarize them for you except to say that they spell out doomsday scenarios for global catastrophe. There's another recent book called *The Revenge of Gaia* that could well have been subtitled "The Earth Strikes Back" because the author, James Lovelock, says human consumption, our obsession with technology, and our habit of "playing God" are stripping bare nature's assets until Earth's only consolation will be to take us down with her. Before this century is over, he writes, "Billions of us will die and the few breeding pairs of people that survive will be kept in the Arctic where the climate remains tolerable." So there you have it: the future of the race, to be joined in a final and fatal march of the penguins.

Fortunately, that's not the only scenario. You can Google your way to more optimistic possibilities. For one, the digital revolution that will transform how we do business and live our lives, including active intelligent wireless devices that in just a short time could link every aspect of our physical world and even human brains, creating hundreds of thousands of small-scale business opportunities. There are medical breakthroughs that will conquer many ills and extend longevity. Economic changes will lift hundreds of millions of people out of absolute poverty in the next twenty-five years, dwarfing anything that's come along in the previous one hundred years. These are the many possible scenarios. But I'm a journalist, not a prophet. All I can say is that you won't be bored. I just wish I were going to be around to see what you do with the peril and the promise.

Since I won't be around, I want to take this opportunity to say a thing or two that has nothing to do with my professional life as a journalist. What I have to say today is very personal.

If the world confuses you a little, it confuses me a lot. When I graduated fifty years ago I thought I had the answers. But life is where you get your answers questioned, and the odds are that you can look forward to being even more perplexed fifty years from now than you are at this very moment. If your parents level with you, truly speak their hearts, I suspect they would tell you that life confuses them, too, and that it rarely turns out the way you think it will.

I am alternatively afraid, cantankerous, bewildered, often hostile, sometimes gracious, and battered by a hundred new sensations every day. I can be filled with pessimism as gloomy as the depth of the Middle Ages, yet deep within me I'm possessed of a hope that simply won't quit. A friend on Wall Street told me that he was optimistic about the market. I asked him, "Then why do you look so worried?" He replied, "Because I'm not sure my optimism is justified." Neither am I. So I vacillate between the determination to act, to change things, and the desire to retreat into the snuggeries of self, family, and friends.

I wonder if any of us in this great, disputatious, over-analyzed, over-televised, and under-tenderized country know what the deuce we're talking about, myself included. All my illusions are up for grabs, and I find myself reassessing many of the assumptions that served me comfortably much of my life.

Earlier this week I listened to a discussion on the radio about the new Disney Broadway production of *Tarzan*, the jungle hero who was so popular when I was growing up. As a kid I almost dislocated my tonsils trying to re-create his unearthly sound, swinging on a great vine in a graceful arc toward the rescue of his distressed mate, Jane, hollering bloody murder all the time. So what have we learned since? That Buster Crabbe and Johnny Weissmuller, who played Tarzan in the movies, never made that noise. It was a recording of three men, one a baritone, one a tenor, and one a hog caller from Arkansas—all yelling at the top of their lungs.

This world is hard on believers.

As a young man I was drawn to politics. I took part in two national campaigns, served in the Kennedy and Johnson administrations, and have covered politics ever since. But I understand now what Thomas Jefferson meant back in 1789 when he wrote: "I am not a Federalist because I never submitted the whole system of my opinions to the creed of any party of men, whether in religion, in philosophy, in politics, or anything else. If I could not go to Heaven but with a party, I would not go there at all." (Of course we know there'll be no parties in Heaven. No Democrats, no Republicans, no liberals, no conservatives, no libertarians or socialists. Just us Baptists.)

The hardest struggle of all is to reconcile life's polar realities. I love books, Beethoven, and chocolate brownies. Yet how do I justify my pleasure in these in a world where millions are illiterate and children go hungry? How do I live sanely in a world so unsafe for so many?

I don't know what they taught you here at Hamilton about all this, but I trust you are not leaving without thinking about how you will respond to the dissonance in our culture, the rivalry between beauty and bestiality in the world, and the conflicts in your own soul. All of us have to choose sides on this journey. But the question is not so much who we are going to fight against as it is which side of our own nature will we nurture: the side that can grow weary and even cynical and believe that everything is futile, or the side that for all the vulgarity, brutality, and cruelty yearns to affirm, connect, and signify.

Albert Camus saw beauty in the world as well as humiliation, and he said, "We have to strive, hard as it is, not to be unfaithful . . . in the presence of one or the other."

As I prepared to come here today, I put myself in your place. I asked what I'd want a stranger from another generation to tell me if I had to sit through his speech. Well, I'd want to hear the truth. The truth is, life's a tough act, the world's a hard place, and along the way you will meet a fair share of fools, knaves, and clowns. You'll even act the fool yourself from time to time when your guard is down or you've had too much to drink. Don't try to disguise or deny your lapse in judgment; get up and do better.

I'd like to be told that I will experience separation, loss, and betrayal, that I'll wonder at times where have all the flowers gone.

I'd want to be told that while life includes a lot of luck, life is more than luck. It is sacrifice, study, and work: appointments kept, deadlines met, promises honored.

I'd like to be told that it's okay to love your country right or wrong,

384 | BILL MOYERS

but it's not right to be silent when your country is wrong. And I would like to be encouraged not to give up on the American experience. To re-member that the same culture which produced the Ku Klux Klan, Lee Harvey Oswald, and Abu Ghraib also brought forth the Peace Corps, Martin Luther King, and Hamilton College.

And I would like to be told that there is more to this life than I can see, earn, or learn in my time. That beyond the day-to-day spectacle are cosmic mysteries we don't understand. That in the meantime—and the meantime is where we live—we infinitesimal particles of creation carry on the miracle of loving, by giving and sharing.

One of my favorite stories is by I. L. Peretz, a founder of modern Yid-dish literature and a man who struggled with the conflict between the transcendent and the mundane in everyday life. In one of his stories the protagonist, Bontshe Shvayg, is one of Earth's losers. Every possible mis-fortune befell him: he lost his wife, his children neglected him, his house burned down, his job disappeared—everything turned to ashes. Yet through all this Bontshe never complained, and he did everything he could to return good for evil. When he died the angels heard he was ar-riving at Heaven's gate and hurried to greet him. Even the Lord was there, so great was the regard for this man's character. It was the custom in Heaven that every newcomer was interrogated by the prosecuting an-gel, to ensure that all trespasses on Earth had been atoned. But when Bontshe reached those gates, the prosecuting angel arose and for the first time in the memory of Heaven, said, "There are no charges against this man." Bontshe is then invited to ask for his heart's desire—anything he wants. "Ask," says the Lord, "and it shall be given to you."

The old man raised his eyes slowly and said, "What I'd like most of all is a warm roll with fresh butter every morning." At this the Lord and all the angels wept at the beautiful simplicity of his request. The joy of life he found in that bread.

So I brought with me today this ordinary breakfast roll. Perhaps it is one like Bontshe Shvayg asked for in Heaven. I brought it to illustrate the last thing I want to say to you.

Bread is the great reenforcer of the reality principle. Bread is life.

But if you're like me you have a thousand and more times repeated the ordinary experience of eating bread without a thought for the process that brings it to your table. The reality is physical: I need this bread to live. But the reality is also social: I need others to provide the bread. I depend for bread on hundreds of people I don't know and will never meet. If they fail me, I go hungry. If I offer them nothing of value in exchange for their loaf, I betray them. The people who grow the wheat, process and store the grain, and transport it from farm to city; who bake it, package it, and market it—these people and I are bound together in an intricate reciprocal bargain. We exchange value.

This reciprocity sustains us. If you doubt it, look around you. Hamilton College was raised by people before your time, people you'll never know, who were nonetheless thinking of you before you were born. You have received what they built and bequeathed to you and in your time you will give something back. That's the deal. On it goes, generation to generation.

Civilization sustains and supports us. Bread is its great metaphor. All my life I've prayed the Lord's Prayer, but I've never prayed, "Give *me* this day *my* daily bread." It is always, "Give *us* this day *our* daily bread." Bread and life are shared realities. They do not happen in isolation. Civilization is an unnatural act. We have to make it happen, you and I, together with all the other strangers. My generation hasn't done the best job at honoring this ethical imperative, and our failure explains the mess we're handing over to you. You may be our last chance to get it right.

So good luck, Godspeed, enjoy these last few hours together, and don't forget to pass the bread.

Acknowledgments

Gerry Howard bears the blame for this book. It was his idea. He read several of my speeches as they circulated on the Internet and said they should be published as a book. I said speeches should be heard, not read. Gerry wouldn't give up, which explains, no doubt, why he is Doubleday's executive editor at large and I am not. As I continued to resist, he called in his heaviest artillery—our mutual friend and oppressor, Steve Rubin (who had earlier insisted on publishing Joseph Campbell's *The Power of Myth* and other books based on my television work). Intimidated and harassed, I yielded. Some of these speeches—or excerpts and versions of them—had appeared in publications such as *Army Times*, *The Nation*, *Sojourners*, *Christian Century*, the online journal *Grist*, and in an earlier book, *Moyers on America*. Frankly, however, I am today grateful to both Gerry and Steve for seeing something in these speeches worth putting between hard covers. They had a faithful and diligent co-conspirator in

Doubleday's Katie Halleron. My own executive assistant, Karen Kimball, did an extraordinary job of tracking down the original speeches, organizing them, and poring over them with her own fine-tooth comb; her judgment is as admirable as her ability to juggle twelve balls and swallow fire in the center ring of a circus as we also put a weekly broadcast on the air. My speeches, like those broadcasts, are the result of intense collaboration. Many people through the years have contributed immeasurably as researchers. Elizabeth Karnes, now assistant dean of the Middlebury Language School; Andie Tucher, now on the faculty of the Columbia Graduate School of Journalism; and Rebecca Wharton, one of my ablest producers, served long stints as my editorial associates during which they drafted or shaped ideas important to my television work and speeches. I have benefited enormously from the efforts of two colleagues, Julie Leininger Pycior, professor of history at Manhattan College, and Lew Daly, Senior Fellow at Demos. I owe an incalculable debt to the historian Bernard Weisberger, the author of many fine books on the American experience. Bernie and I collaborated closely on two PBS series, *A Walk Through the Twentieth Century* and *Report from Philadelphia*; we share a common passion for the progressive tradition in America and I consider it an honor to give voice to many of his ideas. Judith Davidson Moyers is my business and creative partner, the executive editor of everything I do, and my wife of fifty-four years. A man is fortunate who marries his muse.

INDEX

Printed in the United States
by Baker & Taylor Publisher Services